Housing and Housing Benefit Law

Housing and Housing Benefit Law

Third Edition

by

Alan Robinson
Kirsty Jenkins

Tottel
publishing

Tottel Publishing
Maxwelton House,
41–43 Boltro Road
Haywards Heath
West Sussex
RH16 1BJ

A CIP Catalogue record for this book is available from the British Library.

ISBN 1 84592 003 1

Typeset in Great Britain by Columns Design Ltd, Reading, UK
Printed by Thomson Litho Ltd, East Kilbride, Scotland

Preface

The third edition of this book has been fully updated to take into account some significant changes brought about by the *Homelessness Act 2002*, the *Housing Act 2004* and the *State Pension Credit Act 2002*.

The book is aimed at both landlords and tenants, and organisations and agencies engaged in advising or working with people who come into contact with housing and housing benefit authorities. It has been specifically written to be understood clearly by both practitioner and lay person.

Chapters 1 and 2 have been revised to take into account the changes resulting from local authorities implementing the *Homelessness Act 2002*. In particular, there are additions relating to the legal duty on local authorities to conduct a review of homelessness and publish a homelessness strategy. The section on choice based lettings has been updated as this agenda continues to move forward.

The book now includes a complete section on tackling anti-social behaviour as there have been significant changes in policy and practice since the previous edition. In addition, the imminent changes that will be brought in by the *Housing Act 2004* have been included throughout all the sections of the book, where relevant.

The calculation of housing benefit for those over pension age has been changed significantly by the *State Pension Credit Act 2002*. The policy of encouraging people back into work (especially lone parents) is reflected in the more generous amounts for child care which may be disregarded from income. The biggest change is yet to come, but is foreshadowed by a pilot scheme; the introduction of standard rent allowances, instead of the individual calculations which have been used up to now.

Chapter 11 includes examples of common problems we have encountered in our professional experience, together with some of the solutions that might be employed in addressing them. Appendix A contains sample letters which may be useful when contacting, questioning or challenging a housing provider or housing benefit section.

This book provides a comprehensive overview of housing and housing benefit law. Of course, each chapter could be a book in its own right and so readers are therefore directed to seek specialist advice where they require answers to complex legal issues. Readers will find that this book is full of guidance, practical information, and ideas on solving everyday housing and housing benefit issues.

We are grateful to Irena Sabic, who took on the chapter on Human Rights at short notice and produced a valuable guide to a rapidly changing area of law which is so fundamental to the rest of the book.

Kirsty Jenkins
Alan Robinson
February 2005

About the Authors

Kirsty Jenkins is a freelance housing consultant who has worked in social housing for the last 17 years. During this time she has worked in a range of fields including housing management, homelessness, lettings and allocations and rent recovery.

In recent years, Kirsty has specialised in supporting social landlords in implementing the many changes to legislation in homelessness and allocations. Kirsty has a BA Hons in Housing Management and Development and a Masters in Business Administration.

Alan Robinson is a solicitor with 30 years experience of advising, training, writing and researching about welfare law. He is the principal of Legal & Welfare Rights Training, which provides specialist welfare benefit training to the legal profession, and also runs his own legal practice specialising in work with the voluntary sector as well as welfare benefits.

Alan writes regularly on benefits for *Elderly Client Adviser*, and has written numerous articles and pamphlets about social security. For six years he contributed to Tolley's *Social Security and State Benefits Handbook*, and is the author of Tolley's *Social Security and Family Benefit Law: A Practical Guide*, and of Tolley's *Practical Guide to State Benefits and Personal Injury Awards*. He has lectured for both Shelter and Age Concern, and is a former Mental Health Act Commissioner. He is an associate lecturer with the Open University.
Alan has carried out research into aspects of the social security system at both Sheffield and York Universities, and holds an MA degree from both.

Contents

Chapter 9   Recent and Future Changes to Housing Benefit

Chapter 10   Human Rights in Housing

CONTENTS

Chapter 11   Common Problems

Appendix A   Standard Letters

Appendix B   Court Forms

Appendix C   Appeal Tribunal Documents

Appendix D   Housing Benefit Rates 2004/2005

Table of Statutes

Table of Statutory Instruments

References in the right-hand column are to para numbers.

Table of Cases

References in the right-hand column are to para numbers.

B

C

TABLE OF CASES

D

F

G

H

I

J

K

L

M

O

P

Q

R

S

TABLE OF CASES

T

W

CHAPTER 1

Applications for Housing

Introduction: what is social housing?

1.1 Social housing is one of the terms given to housing provided with the assistance of a government subsidy. The difference between social rented housing and private rented housing is that the former should be 'affordable'. This means that the government subsidy is used by local authorities and housing associations to keep rents significantly lower than those charged on the open market.

There is a real shortage of affordable housing in Britain and so there are mechanisms by which such housing is rationed. Social housing organisations keep waiting lists of individuals and households demanding affordable housing, and an allocations policy serves to allocate available housing to those most in need.

Social housing providers

1.2 In the main, two types of organisations provide social housing: local housing authorities and registered social landlords (RSLs). RSLs are landlords that are registered with the housing corporation: housing associations, housing action trusts (HATS), housing co-operatives, self-build groups and local housing companies.

The most common RSLs are housing associations. These are independent organisations that provide accommodation for those in housing need. They do this by building new homes and by rehabilitating old property. They may operate nationally or on a relatively small scale within a locality or provide accommodation for a specialised client group. The vast majority of housing

1

associations are non-profit-making bodies that are registeredeither as charities or as friendly societies. Housing associations must be registered with the housing corporation (or with Tai Cymru in Wales) in order to benefit from public funding. The housing corporation is also responsible for their management and control, setting performance standards and measuring outcomes.

Like local authorities, housing associations are required to demonstrate that they offer 'best value'. Since April 2003, both types of housing organisations are subject to inspection by the Audit Commission's Housing Inspectorate. After inspection, a formal report, that grades the quality of services provided and indicates the chances of improvement, is published and available to the public.

The impact of the Homelessness Act 2002

1.3 The *Homelessness Act 2002* made a number of changes to the legislation governing lettings and the allocation of local authority housing (*Housing Act 1996 (HA 1996), Part VI*). The main changes that were seen are:

- the facilitation of choice-based lettings schemes (see **1.15** below), and encouraging local authorities to think about the degree of choice that is currently offered to housing applicants;

- a new right to apply for social housing, thus removing the ability of local authorities to use blanket exclusion schemes as part of their allocations policy;

- giving authorities the ability to exclude or give lower priority to applicants who have been guilty of 'serious unacceptable behaviour'; and

- a right to assistance for those who have difficulty in applying for housing.

These issues are covered in this section of the book.

Access to social housing

1.4 The best place to start in order to apply for social housing is the local authority housing department. Until the introduction of the *Homelessness Act 2002* in January 2003, all authorities were required to establish and maintain a housing register – this is no longer the case. However, a local authority is required to publish an allocations scheme governing both priorities and procedures relating to how its affordable homes are let in the district.

All local authorities must make available advice and information to customers wishing to make a housing application (*HA 1996, s 166(1)*). This must be available free of charge. In addition, they must provide assistance to anybody who may have difficulty in applying for housing.

If the local authority has been through the process of large-scale voluntary stock transfer, it may have contracted out its housing function to a housing association (or other contractor) or other body as permitted by *HA 1996*. If this is the case, the applicant should make contact directly with the housing association to obtain details of the allocations scheme. The local authority will be able to direct applicants to the appropriate housing association if they do not know their contact details.

Joint housing registers

1.5 It is entirely up to the local authority to decide how it wishes to keep information on housing needs in its area. There is no requirement to maintain a housing register, although there is a requirement to publish a lettings policy. The reality is that most authorities still hold housing registers, even where a choice-based lettings scheme has been implemented (see **1.15** below). In the majority of local authority areas, a joint housing register is held. This means that the majority of social housing providers in the district allocate their homes using the local housing authority's housing register, rather than each organisation holding its own housing waiting list.

There are different types of joint housing registers – the most extreme kind is where there is a common housing allocations scheme. In this scenario, the local housing authority will carry out all the allocations to social housing in the area, with RSLs giving the housing authority full nomination rights, or all of their housing stock in that district to allocate. In situations such as this, RSLs agree that the housing authority has designed such a good housing register, which assesses housing need accurately and prioritises the applicants well, that it would be a duplication of work for them to hold their own waiting lists. This saves the RSL time and money in terms of administration. It also means that the housing authority can provide a fully integrated service to customers and make the best use of all the social housing stock in the district – many see it as part of the strategic role of the housing authority.

From the point of view of the applicant, the advantage of having a common housing allocations scheme is that it is much more streamlined and he will probably only need to complete one application form which will provide access to all of the social housing in the district – this saves a lot of time and energy in requesting and completing housing application forms.

Some local authorities hold a joint housing register but the RSLs maintain some degree of autonomy and choice over the applicants they house. For example, when a property becomes available, the RSL may ask the local authority to 'top-slice' the waiting list by sending them the top-ten households – these applicants will then be prioritised according to the RSL's own allocations scheme.

In other local authority areas, the council may claim that they have a joint housing register but in reality the partner RSLs still hold their own lists. These RSLs probably hold back a percentage of their lettings for applicants who appear on their own lists. In these circumstances, an applicant should register with both the council and as many RSLs as possible to maximise his chances of rehousing.

There are many different ways in which a joint housing register can work; local authorities have worked in partnership with RSLs to develop joint registers which suit the particular circumstances and needs of the local area and the organisations working within it.

If a local authority does not operate a joint housing register with the RSLs in the area, the applicant must ask the housing authority for details of other organisations that provide housing and he should contact each organisation direct. Most local authorities have a standard list of RSLs operating in their area with details of the type of housing provision available.

Applying for social housing

1.6 The first step in making an application for housing is to contact the local authority to whom you wish to apply. Since the implementation of the *Homelessness Act 2002*, all authorities must have an open housing allocations policy. This means that even if you do not have a connection with that area, you should be able to apply for housing. However, be aware that in areas of high demand, many authorities will give extra priority to local people, so even if you are admitted onto the list, it could be unlikely that you will be rehoused. Make sure that you check the type of allocations policy carefully. There are no limits to the number of applications a person can submit to various authorities.

Applicants should contact the council to ask for an application pack. This should include an application form, details on how to apply and information on how the scheme works. Once an applicant is in receipt of an application form for housing, it should be completed and returned as quickly as possible as often the date of application becomes important in relation to the applicant's turn on the list for rehousing. The form will ask for a wide variety of information about the applicant for the housing register must contain certain prescribed information about the people who appear on it.

Housing association waiting lists

1.7 Housing associations may hold their own waiting lists for accommodation. Most work across local authority boundaries, and if there is not a joint housing register operating within an authority the housing association will need to hold their own waiting list for accommodation. There is no legislation requiring housing associations to frame their allocations scheme in a particular way, although they must be designed in accordance with the Housing Corporation Performance Standards. The waiting list will be subject to regulation by the Housing Corporation, and to inspection under the best value regime by the Audit Commission.

Allocations schemes

1.8 Local authorities are required to have a published allocations scheme that explains how they will allocate homes and what choice they offer to applicants. The scheme must include a specific statement on the choice an applicant can expect (*HA 1996, s 167(1A)*).

Authorities are free to establish their own priorities within their allocations scheme, but it must be framed around the reasonable preference groups (*HA 1996, s 167(2)*, as amended by *Homelessness Act 2002, s 16*). They are:

- those who are homeless (within the meaning of *Part VII* of *HA 1996* – see **CHAPTER 2 HOMELESSNESS**);

- people occupying unsanitary or overcrowded housing, or otherwise living in unsatisfactory housing;

- people who need to move on medical or welfare grounds; and

- people who need to move to a particular locality in the district of the authority to avoid hardship to themselves or others.

Additional preference may be given to other categories of people, as long as they have an urgent housing need (*HA 1996, s 167(2)*).

Local authorities are therefore required to frame their allocations policies around these groups of people. In addition, under *section 167(2A)* of *HA 1996*, there is a discretion to take into account the following factors:

- the financial resources available to the applicant to meet housing costs;

- any behaviour which affects the applicant's suitability as a tenant (eg previous history of rent arrears or anti-social behaviour); and

- local connection with the local authority.

Qualifying persons

1.9 Local authorities are required by the *Homelessness Act 2002* to consider all applications for housing. With limited exceptions, everyone has the right to apply for council housing. This includes existing tenants wishing to transfer.

People who are subject to immigration control under the *Asylum and Immigration Act 1996* will be ineligible to apply for housing unless specifically permitted to do so under regulations published by the Secretary of State. Certain other categories of people from abroad are also ineligible. To keep up to date with the categories of people included within this exemption, reference should be made to these regulations.

In addition, the *Homelessness Act 2002* allows a local authority to deem an applicant ineligible for accommodation if he has been found guilty of 'unacceptable behaviour serious enough to make him unsuitable to be a tenant' (*HA 1996, s 160A*). Unacceptable behaviour is defined as behaviour which would, if the applicant was already a secure tenant, entitle the housing authority to possession under *Part 1* of *Schedule 2* to the *Housing Act 1985* (*HA 1985*) (see **CHAPTER 3 TENANCIES**). These grounds are based on the tenant being at fault.

Where an applicant is deemed to be ineligible because of his unsuitable behaviour, the authority must notify him in writing of this decision and the reason for it (*HA 1996, s 160A(9)*). The applicant is entitled to request a review of this decision, and applicants who believe that they are no longer ineligible can reapply at any time, for example if their rent arrears have been cleared.

Prioritising housing applicants

1.10 Currently, probably the majority of local authorities hold a points-based waiting list, whereby points are awarded for certain attributes of an applicant's circumstances. When a vacancy occurs, the applicant with the highest number of points for that particular property size, type and location is allocated the home. Such pointing schemes have come under criticism recently because they are usually complicated and as such are both difficult to administer and difficult for customers to understand.

Consequentially, many authorities (and RSLs) are moving towards using banding schemes to prioritise applicants for rehousing. In such schemes, the organisation holds any number of bands of housing applicants. Each band will represent a broadly similar level of need for accommodation, and within that band the applicants are prioritised by date order of application. The bands might be, for example, urgent rehousing need, some housing need, and no particular urgency for rehousing. These schemes are generally considered to be fairer as waiting time for rehousing plays a major part. This is much easier for applicants to understand.

A number of housing organisations now operate choice-based lettings schemes. These are considered in more detail in 1.15 below.

Even where an applicant is placed in the category of urgent rehousing need, there may be a long wait for housing to be allocated. This is particularly true in the south of the country where demand far outstrips supply; some authorities in this position are now working with authorities in areas of low demand to try to encourage applicants for housing to consider relocating to obtain accommodation more quickly. It is therefore important that applicants discuss the availability of housing in their preferred area at the time of making an application. This will enable them to expand their options at the earliest possible date and to improve their prospects of being housed as soon as possible.

Requesting a review

1.11 Applicants for social housing have the right to request an internal review of any decision taken under the governing legislation. The review process should be fair and the authority must notify the applicant of the outcome of the review and the reasons for it. There is no appeal right to the county court; if the applicant still believes the review decision should be challenged he can apply for judicial review.

Offers of accommodation

1.12 Different local authorities have different policies on how offers of accommodation are made, whether they invite applicants for accompanied viewings, how many offers of accommodation they make to an applicant, penalties for refusal and so on. There is no legislation governing this. The authority should make its policies perfectly clear and applicants should ask to see a copy of the published allocations policy when they receive an offer of accommodation.

Normally an offer will be made to an applicant in writing. If he accepts that offer of accommodation a tenancy agreement will be issued. It may be that the applicant does not want to live in the home that has been offered and wishes to refuse the offer. Again, authorities have different policies on this and this is quite within the law. Some authorities operate a 'one offer only' policy, and if an applicant refuses an offer he is penalised in some way, usually by having his application deferred. Where an applicant wishes to refuse a property he is entitled to seek a review of the housing authority's decision that the property was suitable. (See **APPENDIX A** (Letter 1) for an example letter of review.)

Managing the housing register

1.13   In some local authority areas there is a significant wait for accommodation, whilst in others the wait is very short. It is simply a question of supply and demand. When the housing authority writes to advise an applicant that he is on the housing register it is required by *section 167* of *HA 1996* to give an indication of how long the wait for accommodation will be and whether the applicant falls into a group that will be given preference. Some authorities are still not good at doing this and it is advisable to speak with the section that has responsibility for dealing with the housing register. This is often called the housing needs team or the housing options team. Staff working within this section will be able to advise on the likely waiting time. The applicant will then be aware if he needs to explore other housing options at the same time. A person on the housing register is entitled to see his entry and receive a copy of it free of charge, and to be informed in general terms about the state of the register.

Most local authorities write to housing register applicants once a year to find out whether their circumstances have changed, and whether they wish to remain on the register. This is part of their role in keeping the housing register up to date. However, if an applicant's circumstances change at any time, he should advise the housing needs team of this as it may have a substantial influence on the speed at which the authority is able to assist him.

All data held on the register about a particular applicant is strictly confidential and will not be disclosed to any member of the public. However, information may occasionally need to be disclosed to other agencies, for example housing officers, doctors, social workers, or RSL staff.

False statements and withholding information

1.14   Under *section 171* of *HA 1996* an applicant commits an offence if he provides false information in his housing register application. Upon summary conviction the applicant is liable to a fine not exceeding level five on the standard scale. A false statement is where a person either:

- knowingly or recklessly makes a statement which is false; or

- knowingly withholds information that the authority has reasonably required him to give.

The offence can be committed by anyone, not merely the applicant – it could be a family member or a former landlord. Furthermore, if housing is allocated on the basis of a false statement then the landlord will have grounds for possession of the property.

Choice-based lettings

1.15 In April 2001, the Office of the Deputy Prime Minister (ODPM) selected 27 local authorities to be 'choice-based lettings' (CBL) pilots. The idea to test choice-based approaches to lettings with pilot schemes was originally proposed in the Housing Green Paper *Quality and Choice: A Decent Home For All*, published in April 2000. Choice-based lettings systems stem from Delft in the Netherlands, where applicants for social housing put themselves forward for homes rather than be allocated to them. In the Netherlands, choice-based letting accounts for 85% of all social housing lettings. The pilot schemes in this country received funding until March 2003. Following this, the ODPM published a formal evaluation of the pilots (*Piloting Choice Based Lettings – An Evaluation*, ODPM, May 2004). The results of the pilot scheme are very positive and the government has set a target that, by 2005, 25% of local authorities should be using CBL, with all local authorities using choice-based schemes by 2010. The *Homelessness Act 2002* facilitates choice-based lettings by repealing the requirement in *HA 1996* for local authorities to hold a housing register.

CBL schemes are designed to replace the traditional points-based allocations schemes found in most local authorities and housing associations. CBL gives applicants a greater role in deciding where they wish to live and when they want to move. There are a number of key principles at play in framing choice-based lettings schemes, including the following.

- *Putting the initiative on the customer* – rather than the housing officer allocating the property, the applicant puts himself forward for a property of his choice.

- *Providing information to enable applicants to make informed decisions* – information about the popularity of some housing helps applicants to be realistic about their housing options. Chances of rehousing may be improved if an applicant puts himself forward for less popular homes.

- *Better information about the homes on offer* – providing much more information to applicants to inform their decision, much in the same way as estate agents do. Often information on local amenities and schools is included in property details as well as information on the property itself.

- *Transparency* – feeding back to applicants who were successful in bidding for a particular property. This helps to keep applicants' expectations realistic.

Home ownership initiatives

1.16 The government has, since the introduction of the right to buy in the *Housing Act 1980* (*HA 1980*) (see **1.17** below), encouraged home ownership as the preferred tenure in the UK.

There have been a number of schemes and initiatives over the last two decades aimed at assisting low income households into home ownership. Most local authorities offer access to low cost home ownership schemes, and this is often done through the housing register; applicants will often be asked to indicate on their application form whether they are interested in home ownership. There are essentially two initiatives available currently. These are set out in **1.17** and **1.21** below.

The right to buy scheme

1.17 Under *Part 5* of *HA 1985*, secure tenants of local authorities and housing associations have a legal right to buy their home. If a tenant was a secure tenant with a local authority which then transferred its properties to a housing association under the LSVT regime, the tenant became an assured tenant but retains the right to buy. This is known as the preserved right to buy. There are two main rights:

- the right to buy the home outright; and

- the right to buy the home on a rent to mortgage scheme.

DISCOUNTED RATE

1.18 The right to buy scheme allows tenants to buy the home they occupy at a discounted rate. There are varying rates of discount according to how long the tenant has occupied the home (or occupied other homes as a secure tenant), and whether it is a house or a flat. For the tenant of a house, the discount is between 32% and 60%; for the tenant of a flat, the discount is between 50% and 70%. If a buyer resells the property within three years of exercising their right to buy, they must repay some or all of the discount they received.

NEW OR RECENTLY IMPROVED HOMES

1.19 There is a cost floor in terms of discount if the house is new or has recently been improved. If £5,000 or more has been spent on building, buying or improving the home in the 10 to 11 years preceding the submission of a right to buy request, then the discount must not reduce the price the tenant pays below what has been spent on the property. Additionally, there is a discount ceiling. *Section 131 of HA 1985* gives the Secretary of State power to limit the amount of discount, which he exercises by making an order to that effect. The following limits currently apply.

London or the South East:	£38,000
East:	£34,000
South West:	£30,000
North West and West Midlands:	£26,000
Wales, the East Midlands, Yorkshire and the Humber:	£24,000
North East:	£22,000

If, after purchase, the tenant decides to sell the property, the council is able to claw back some of the discount within a three-year period.

FORTHCOMING CHANGES TO THE RIGHT TO BUY SCHEME

1.20 The right to buy scheme is under the spotlight at the current time because of the impact it is having on reducing local authority housing stock, and therefore on the use of temporary accommodation and bed and breakfasts for homeless households. There is also a concern that the scheme is being exploited by finance companies. In January 2003, the Deputy Prime Minister announced that maximum right to buy discounts would be lowered in certain areas to tackle severe housing pressures and to discourage exploitation of the rules. It has since been revealed that 41 local authority areas in London and the south east will have their maximum discounts lowered – the maximum discount available to tenants in these areas has been reduced to £16,000. These areas were selected on the basis of being under the greatest housing market pressure (as evidenced by high prices and a high level of homelessness). This was done by a Parliamentary Order which came into effect on 27 March 2003.

The *Housing Act 2004* is bringing in further changes to the right to buy scheme. The Act contains provisions to modernise the right to buy scheme further. The main features of the Housing Bill in relation to the right to buy are:

- extending the initial qualification period from two to five years;

- extending from three to five years the period during which the discount must be repaid when the property is resold;

- changing the repayment due to a percentage of the resale value of the property rather than the current flat-rate basis;

- providing for the right to buy not to apply where there is a clear intention that the property in question will be demolished; and

- requiring landlords to give their tenants information on the costs and responsibilities of home ownership, to help tenants to decide whether to excuse the RTB.

The main focus of the provisions is to help to retain the supply of affordable housing and tackle profiteering. The government has been clear that it wishes to limit the financial returns available to incentives companies that seek to exploit the rules.

The *Housing Act 2004* also brought to an end the rent to mortgage scheme in place within local housing authorities.

Homebuy

1.21 The government introduced the Homebuy scheme in April 1999. Applicants need to be able to fund 75% of the purchase price of a home through a mortgage and/or personal savings. A housing association will then lend the remaining 25% interest-free. When the applicant decides to sell, the 25% is repayable. If the applicant wishes at any time to buy the housing association out, he may purchase the property outright. The 25% is always repaid on the market value at the time.

CHAPTER 2

Homelessness

The Homelessness Act 2002

2.1 The law relating to homelessness is contained in *Part VII* of the *Housing Act 1996 (HA 1996) (ss 175–218)*. As with allocations and lettings, the legislation has been changed by the *Homelessness Act 2002*. The two pieces of legislation now have to be read together. The Homelessness Code of Guidance, published in July 2002, is also important as it has statutory force. The major changes are as follows.

- A return to the full rehousing duty, ie homeless applicants will be offered permanent tenancies (as opposed to the restricted two year duty that was introduced in 1996).

- There is a requirement to take a strategic approach to homelessness. Local authorities are required to carry out a review of homelessness in the district and to publish a strategy for tackling it.

- A new ability for local authorities to offer housing to non-priority homeless households accommodation (aimed at low demand areas).

- *Section 197* of *HA 1996* is repealed – this was the provision that allowed local authorities to point applicants towards accommodation available in the private sector as a discharge of duty.

- Changes to offers relating to suitability issues.

Additionally, the groups of people which local authorities have a duty to rehouse have been extended by the *Homelessness (Priority Need for Accommodation) (England) Order 2002 (SI 2002 No 2051)*. This Order extends priority need to:

- homeless 16 and 17 year olds;

- care leavers aged 18 to 20;

- people who are vulnerable because of time spent in care, the Armed Forces, prison or custody; and

- people who are vulnerable because of violence.

In Wales, the priority groups were extended from 1 March 2001 by the *Homeless Persons* (*Priority Need*) (*Wales*) *Order 2001* (*SI 2001 No 607*) to include:

- a person aged 18 to 21 who is a care leaver, or who is at particular risk of sexual or financial exploitation;

- anybody aged 16 or 17;

- a person fleeing actual or threatened domestic violence;

- a person who has been homeless since leaving prison or the Armed Forces.

The categories are wider than those in England, in that there is not always a need to prove vulnerability.

Making a homelessness application

2.2   When an applicant approaches a local authority to make a homelessness application, the authority is required to make a number of enquiries to establish some key facts (*HA 1996, s 184*). The authority will make enquiries to establish whether the applicant is eligible for assistance and if so, whether any duty is owed to him or her. This can take time; the Code of Guidance states that enquiries should be completed within 30 working days, and communicated to the applicant within three days of making the decision. The Code also says that enquiries should be initiated on the day of the application, or the following day, with a view to reaching a decision as to whether there is a duty to provide interim accommodation where enquiries are likely to be protracted. There is a duty under *HA 1996, s 188* to provide interim accommodation where the applicant appears to be homeless, eligible for assistance and in priority need.

The authority will make decisions by considering the homelessness legislation, the Code of Guidance and any relevant case law. Once the enquiries are complete, the authority must notify the applicant, in writing, of its decision and the reasons for it, and inform the applicant of his right to request a review of the decision and the timescales for doing this.

In a similar way to the contracting-out of the housing register (see **1.4** above), some local authorities may have contracted out their statutory homelessness duties, and so an applicant may need to approach a housing association to make a homelessness presentation. The local authority will advise the applicant if this is the case.

In making its enquiries, the local authority must ask a number of questions regarding the applicant's case. These are:

- Is the applicant eligible for assistance?

- Is the applicant homeless or threatened with homelessness?

- Is the applicant in a priority need group?

- Is the applicant intentionally homeless?

- Does the applicant have a local connection with the district?

Each of these is explored in more detail at **2.3–2.12** below.

Is the applicant eligible for assistance?

2.3 [*HA 1996, s 185*]

There are two categories of people who are not eligible for assistance under the legislation:

- persons subject to immigration control within the meaning of the *Asylum and Immigration Act 1996*, unless they fall within a class prescribed by the Secretary of State; and

- asylum seekers and their dependants who are not otherwise disqualified as persons from abroad.

One of the classes prescribed by regulations for the purposes of the first of the above categories is those who are habitually resident, lawfully present, and a national of a state which has ratified the European Convention on Social and Medical Assistance. However, a person who has temporary permission to enter the country is not 'lawfully present'; *Szoma v Secretary of State for Work and Pensions* [2003] EWCA Civ 1131.

People who are not eligible for assistance are still entitled to receive advice and information about homelessness (see **2.17** below on housing advice).

Is the applicant homeless or threatened with homelessness?

2.4   [HA 1996, s 175]

Having established whether the applicant is eligible for assistance, the homelessness officer will need to ascertain whether the applicant is either homeless or will be threatened with homelessness. A person is homeless if:

- he or she has no accommodation available for occupation either in the UK or elsewhere (see **2.5** below);

- he or she has accommodation but cannot secure entry to it;

- he or she has accommodation but it is a movable structure, and there is nowhere available to put it; or

- accommodation is available but it is unreasonable to expect him or her to occupy it (see **2.6** below).

A person is deemed to be threatened with homelessness if it is likely that he or she will become homeless within 28 days.

ACCOMMODATION AVAILABLE TO OCCUPY

2.5   *Section 176 of HA 1996* states that accommodation shall be regarded as available for a person's occupation only if it is also available to someone who might reasonably be expected to live with the person.

REASONABLE TO CONTINUE TO OCCUPY

2.6   It is not reasonable for a person to continue to occupy if it is probable that this will lead to domestic violence or other violence against him or her, or against somebody living in the family.

Additionally, the Code of Guidance outlines other situations where it may not be reasonable to continue to occupy, including:

- where the physical conditions of the property make it unsuitable – this might include a house in substantial disrepair, a house with no bathroom facilities, a property which a disabled applicant cannot access in consequence of physical disability, etc;

- where the property is overcrowded; and

- where the type of property makes it unsuitable for long-term occupation (eg night shelter, hostel) or where there is no security of tenure.

In assessing reasonableness to occupy, the local authority may have regard to the current local housing situation in the district.

Affordability

2.7 One factor that must be considered by a housing authority under the 'reasonable to occupy' premise is the issue of affordability. The *Homelessness (Suitability of Accommodation) Order 1996 (SI 1996 No 3204)* states that affordability must be taken into account, in particular:

● the financial resources available to the applicant;

● the cost of the accommodation;

● maintenance payments; and

● other reasonable living expenses.

This particular issue is an important consideration when addressing applications from those on low income, those reliant on Housing Benefit for help with their rent where rent restrictions have been applied and those who are owner/occupiers unable to accommodate mortgage liabilities, etc.

Is the applicant in a priority need group?

2.8 The homelessness legislation defines a number of categories of people who should be assisted with rehousing. *Section 189 of HA 1996* states that the following applicants have a priority need for accommodation:

● an applicant who is pregnant or resides with a person who is pregnant;

● a person with whom dependent children might reasonably be expected to reside (this might include applicants whose children are not living with him or her because of inadequate housing);

● a person who is vulnerable as a result of old age, mental illness or mental impairment or physical disability or other special reason, or someone with whom such a person resides; and

● a person who is homeless or threatened with homelessness as a result of an emergency such as flood, fire or other disaster.

The *Homelessness (Priority Need for Accommodation) (England) Order 2002 (SI 2002 No 2051)* adds to this list. The additional categories of applicants with a priority need are:

● 16 and 17 year olds who are not being looked after by Social Services;

● care leavers;

- people who are vulnerable as a result of having been in the Armed Forces;

- people who are vulnerable because of having been in prison; and

- people who are vulnerable because of violence or threats of violence from another person.

As noted above (see **2.1**), the categories of priority need are slightly extended in Wales.

If an applicant is homeless and eligible for assistance, but not in one of the priority need groups identified above, the local authority has a duty to provide the applicant with advice and assistance to help him secure accommodation. However, this duty does not extend to actually providing the accommodation.

Provision of interim accommodation

2.9 If the local authority has reason to believe that the applicant is homeless, eligible for assistance and has a priority need, it has a duty to provide interim accommodation pending a decision. This duty is irrespective of the possibility of referring the case to another local authority under the local connection regime (see **2.12** below). The interim accommodation must be suitable although the applicant does not have the right to request a review of this.

The duty to provide interim accommodation ceases when the applicant is notified of the local authority's decision, even if the applicant requests a review of the decision. The authority does, however, have a discretion to continue to provide interim accommodation pending the outcome of the review. In all cases, the authority must be seen to act reasonably otherwise it could be challenged by the applicant in the county court.

Where an applicant is eligible for assistance, unintentionally homeless and has a priority need for accommodation, the local authority must ensure that accommodation is available for the applicant (*HA 1986, s 193(2)*). This duty only ceases when one of the following occurs.

- The applicant refuses an offer of accommodation to discharge the duty (ie temporary accommodation) which the local authority deems suitable. However, this duty not only ends when the applicant has been informed by the local authority of the consequences of refusal and of his right to request a review of the suitability of accommodation offered. Under *section 202(1a)* of *HA 1986*, applicants can still request a review of suitability even if they have already accepted the offer.

- The applicant accepts a permanent allocation from the housing register (under *Part VI* of *HA 1996*).

- The applicant refuses a final offer of accommodation under *Part VI* of *HA 1986*. There are a number of conditions attached to this:
  - the applicant must have been informed of the outcome of his refusal and his right to request a review on suitability;
  - the offer was made in writing and it stated that it was a final offer;
  - the local authority is satisfied that it is a suitable offer and it would have been reasonable for the applicant to accept it.

- The applicant accepts an offer of an assured tenancy from a private landlord (not a shorthold).

- The applicant accepts a qualifying offer of an assured shorthold tenancy. Such an offer is qualifying if:
  - it has the approval of the local authority in joint working with the landlord;
  - it is for a fixed term;
  - it is accompanied by a written statement making clear that the applicant does not have to accept it, but if he or she does the local authority's duty to him or her will cease.

UNREASONABLE OFFER OF ACCOMMODATION

2.10 An applicant may refuse an offer of accommodation if the accommodation is not suitable. What is or is not suitable accommodation is dependent upon the circumstances of each individual applicant. For instance, an offer of accommodation which is not within reasonable travelling distance for a child who is due to take exams, or who attends a special school, may be considered unsuitable. Likewise an offer of accommodation in an area where the applicant may be considered 'at risk', and this risk is real and not fanciful, may not be a suitable offer of accommodation.

Such unsuitable offers of accommodation may well also constitute a breach of *Article 8* of the *Human Rights Act 1998* (HRA 1998), which accommodates the right to respect for family life (see **CHAPTER 10 HUMAN RIGHTS IN HOUSING**).

In such cases the applicant should exercise his right to request a review of the decision stating his or her reasons. (See **APPENDIX A** for an example letter of review (Letter 1).)

Is the applicant intentionally homeless?

2.11 Having established that the applicant is eligible for assistance, homeless or threatened with homelessness and in a priority need group, the next test is to establish whether the applicant is homeless intentionally. There are a few points to note on intentionality.

- A person becomes homeless intentionally if he or she deliberately does or fails to do something and consequentially loses the accommodation. For example, if the applicant simply stops paying the rent or mortgage without good cause he or she may be deemed to be intentionally homeless. Likewise if the applicant is the subject of an anti-social behaviour order, and breaches that order, he or she may be deemed to be intentionally homeless.

- An act or omission in good faith cannot be treated as deliberate.

- If a person enters into an arrangement to leave property in order to obtain rehousing under *Part VII* of *HA 1996* he or she is deemed to be intentionally homeless.

If an authority is satisfied that an applicant is homeless, is eligible for assistance, has a priority need and is not homeless intentionally, accommodation must be secured for the applicant, unless the applicant is to be referred to another local authority (see **2.12** below).

Does the applicant have a local connection with the district?

2.12 *Section 199* of *HA 1996* sets out the local connection provisions relating to homelessness. An authority must establish whether the applicant has a connection with its district. A person has a local connection with the district of a housing authority if he or she has a connection with it for any of the following reasons:

- he or she is, or was in the past, normally resident there through choice (service in a particular place in the Armed Forces, being there in prison, or being detained there under the mental health legislation, or being dispersed by the National Asylum Support Service to a particular place, is not residence of choice);

- he or she is employed there;

- he or she has family associations; or

- there are special circumstances.

After completing its enquiries and establishing that a duty is owed to the applicant under *section 193* of *HA 1996*, the local authority may choose to refer the case to another authority in the following circumstances:

- neither the applicant nor any member of their family has a local connection with the district that has received the homelessness application;

- the applicant or member of the family does have a local connection with the district of the other authority; and

- there is no risk of domestic violence if the applicant (and their family, if appropriate) is referred to the district with the connection.

All three of these factors must be present before a referral is made to another authority. The decision to refer to another authority is discretionary. If an applicant has a local connection with more than one authority, the wishes of the applicant should be taken into account when determining which authority to make the referral to.

Once an applicant has been notified that he or she is going to be referred to another authority, the original authority must provide accommodation until the other authority has made a decision as to whether they intend to accept the referral.

Right to review and appeal on homelessness decisions

2.13 Applicants have a right to request a review of a number of decisions made following a homelessness application. These include:

- any decision on eligibility for assistance, ie whether he is a person from abroad who is not eligible for assistance;

- a decision on intentionality;

- a decision on priority need;

- a decision that the applicant is not threatened with homelessness;

- any decision made to notify another authority under referral of cases; and

- any decision as to the suitability of accommodation offered.

A request for review must be made within 21 days of the applicant being notified of the decision, or longer if the authority considers it reasonable to allow it. There is no right to request a review of a decision made on an earlier review, ie no second right of appeal.

The authority is under no obligation to provide accommodation pending the outcome of the review. However, if the authority refuses to do so, the applicant may appeal to the county court and the court may order that accommodation must be provided. In considering this matter, the county court must proceed by way of principles of judicial review, ie the merits of the decision are not considered unless the decision was totally unreasonable.

The local authority must notify the applicant of the outcome of the review and, if it is an adverse decision, the reasons for it.

An applicant also has the right to appeal to the county court on a point of law. The authority is required to inform the applicant of the right of appeal, and that this must be done within 21 days. The court may allow an appeal outside of 21 days if there is good reason. The right to appeal to the county court ensures that the process of review and appeal complies with the requirements of *Article 6* of *HRA 1998* (the right to a fair hearing), which an internal review alone would not.

Procedures for the review process

2.14   Different local authorities organise their review processes in different ways. The Secretary of State has the power to make regulations on the procedures that local authorities should follow. The current regulations are found in the *Allocation of Housing and Homelessness (Review Procedures) Regulations 1999 (SI 1999 No 71)*. *HA 1996* and the Regulations state that an officer carrying out a homelessness review must be senior in rank to the person making the original decision, and must not have been involved in making the original decision. The review must be completed within eight weeks, unless the parties agree longer. An oral hearing does not have to be offered, except where there has been a procedural irregularity.

Applicants with children who are intentionally homeless or ineligible for assistance

2.15   *Section 12* of the *Homelessness Act 2002* inserts a new *section 213A* into *HA 1996*. This applies where an applicant has children under 18 years old and it is likely that the council will have no rehousing duty towards them. This could give rise to a duty to Social Services because the child may become a 'child in need'. The purpose of this section is to alert Social Services as soon as possible to the case. This will give Social Services the opportunity to consider the case and plan any action. This new section therefore requires housing authorities to have arrangements in place to ensure that all such applicants are notified to Social Services. Under the *Children Act 1989, s 17(6)*, the Social Services department has the power to provide accommodation for children in need. The power arises, however, only in limited circumstances.

Protection of property

2.16 This is an area where local authorities have very different policies. If an authority is under a duty to rehouse a homeless applicant, it may well be under a duty to take reasonable steps to prevent the loss of an applicant's property, or prevent damage to it (*HA 1996, s 211(2)*). The duty arises when two conditions are met:

● there is a danger of loss or damage because of the applicant's inability to deal with the property; and

● no other suitable arrangements have been made.

The duty is to protect the property, not necessarily to store it, although the authority can store the property and levy a reasonable charge, the request for assistance must be reasonable.

Provision of advisory services

2.17 Local authorities have a duty to provide housing advisory services. This duty was designed to ensure that people everywhere have access to a good quality housing advice service. The introduction of the *Homelessness Act 2002* strengthened this duty, and now housing advice services are becoming the focus in the drive to reduce homelessness and to provide alternative solutions to bed and breakfast accommodation. The Homelessness Directorate has set all local authorities the target of having no families living in bed and breakfast after March 2004, except in emergencies, and then for a maximum of six weeks.

The Code of Guidance (page 15) sets out issues where advice may help to prevent homelessness. This includes advice on housing options in the area, details of RSLs, tenants' rights, welfare rights, deposit schemes, dealing with debt, the availability of housing grants and so on.

There is a clear distinction between the two duties of advice and information, and the service provided by the local authority must cover both. The table below outlines what a comprehensive advisory service should cover.

Advice	**Information**
Setting out a person's housing options.	Providing information leaflets.
Actively obtaining information from other sources.	Explaining what happens.
Providing help with letters or form-filling.	Signposting to other services.
Active referral to another more specialist agency, eg money advice service.	

The precise issues to be covered by the advice service can be developed locally to suit the needs of the area, but they must focus on homelessness and the prevention of homelessness. They must be available free of charge.

A local authority is likely to be able to meet this advice duty in a range of ways:

- by providing the service themselves, either as part of an integrated service or through an 'arm's length' housing aid centre (which has the benefit of being able to offer independent advice);

- by securing the service from some other organisation; and

- by working in partnership with another organisation.

Local authorities interpret the legislation in different ways and a spectrum in terms of housing advice services can be seen. On the one hand, there is basic provision, which is attached to the role of the homelessness officer within a local authority, and on the other hand, there are full housing aid centres financed and staffed by local authorities. Some authorities provide more independent services, by contracting out the provision of housing advice. It is up to each authority to decide how the service should be provided and the precise issues addressed by the service. Most local authorities are looking to develop their housing advice services as a way of meeting the government's targets on prevention and eliminating the use of bed and breakfast accommodation and to help deliver the Homelessness Strategy.

Homelessness reviews and strategies

2.18 The *Homelessness Act 2002* imposed a new duty on local authorities to carry out a review of homelessness in their area and to publish a homelessness strategy. The first strategy had to be published by July 2003, and thereafter authorities must publish a new homelessness strategy based on the results of a further review at least every five years. The legislation itself is quite prescriptive about what a review needs to cover and what the resultant strategy must contain. In addition to the Act itself, authorities should refer to the Code of Guidance and to the publication *Homelessness Strategies – A Good Practice Handbook* (DTLR, February 2002).

Section 2(1) of the *Homelessness Act 2002* specifies that a homelessness review must be a review of:

- the levels and likely future levels of homelessness in the district;

- the activities which are carried out for the following purposes:
    - preventing homelessness,
    - securing accommodation for homeless people, and
    - providing support for people who are, or who may become homeless; and

- the resources available to the housing authority, Social Services and other agencies in the district for these activities.

The results of the review itself need to be published and made available at the council offices. A copy must be made available to members of the public if requested, although a reasonable charge can be made for this.

Under *section 3(1)* of the *Homelessness Act 2002*, the resultant homelessness strategy must be a strategy for:

- preventing homelessness in the district;

- securing sufficient accommodation for homeless people; and

- securing satisfactory support levels for those who are homeless or who need resettling following homelessness.

In carrying out both the review and the work on the strategy, local authorities are required to consult with a range of stakeholders. Annex 8 of the Code of Guidance sets out an indicative list of the organisations that local authorities may wish to consult, including RSLs, private landlords, letting agents, Connexions, probation, benefits agency, police, drug action teams and homeless people.

CHAPTER 3

Tenancies

Introduction

3.1 This chapter explores the complex issue of tenancies – it identifies the types of tenancies that exist, and the rights that tenants have. It focuses particularly on the secure tenancy and the assured shorthold tenancies on offer in the public sector. If a tenant is to be offered a unit of social housing, depending on who the landlord is, he could be offered a range of different types of tenancy or licence.

Secure tenancies

3.2 *HA 1980* created secure tenancies for public sector tenants; this was subsequently amended by *HA 1985, 1988* and *1996*. The definition of a secure tenancy and the rights of secure tenants are still contained in *HA 1985*.

A secure tenancy can be defined as a tenancy, whether fixed-term or periodic, of a dwelling house which is let as a separate dwelling to an individual, where that individual occupies the accommodation as his only or principal home. The landlord must be a prescribed public body, therefore this is the tenancy given by local housing authorities, ie for council tenants.

Exemptions

3.3 However, a tenancy may fulfil the criteria for being a secure tenancy but will not actually be secure if it falls within one of the exemption categories identified in *Schedule 1* to *HA 1985*. These are as follows.

- *Long leases* – a tenancy granted for a period of 21 years or more is a long lease.

- *Introductory tenancies* – in the first year of their tenancies, tenants of some local authorities may be granted an introductory tenancy (see **3.18** below).

- *Premises relating to employment* – a tenancy will not be secure if granted to an employee who must live there to enable him to fulfil employment duties.

- *Tenancies of land acquired for development* – a tenancy of a dwelling which is on land initially acquired for development and which is being used as temporary accommodation by the landlord.

- *Temporary accommodation for homeless people* – a tenancy granted to a homeless person as part of the council's duty under *Part VII* of *HA 1996* will not be secure. It can only be secure in this scenario if the council has notified the tenant that it is to be regarded as secure and was offered to him from the housing register, ie under *Part VI* of *HA 1996*.

- *Temporary accommodation for people taking up employment* – a tenancy granted to a person for the purpose of enabling him to take up employment in the district (who is not normally resident there) is not secure. This exemption only applies if the council has given prior notification to the prospective tenant.

- *Private sector leasing* – a tenancy of a property that has been leased from a private landlord to a local authority for use as temporary accommodation for homeless households. The private landlord in this situation must not be a body capable of granting secure tenancies and must be able to obtain vacant possession at the end of a specified period or when required. The landlord authority must not have any other interest in the property other than under the current lease.

- *Temporary accommodation during works* – tenancies granted on a temporary basis whilst works are carried out to the occupier's previous property, unless he was a secure tenant at his previous home.

- *Licensed premises* – a tenancy of a property that is part of premises licensed to sell alcohol for consumption on the premises.

- *Lettings to students* – a tenancy granted to a student to enable him to attend a designated course, provided that the landlord gave notice of this before the start of the tenancy, specifying that this exception applies and identifying the educational establishment.

- *Business tenancies* – a tenancy to which *Part II* of the *Landlord and Tenant Act 1954* applies.

- *Almshouses* – a licence to occupy an almshouse if the licence was granted by a charity which is authorised under its trusts to maintain the dwelling as an almshouse and has no power to grant tenancies.

Length of tenancy

3.4   A secure tenancy can be for a fixed term, periodic or statutory periods. A periodic tenancy is the most common type: this is where the tenancy is granted for an indefinite period with the rent being paid on a periodic basis, for example, weekly, monthly, or yearly. Where a tenancy is granted for a fixed (ie set) period of time this is known as a fixed-term tenancy.

If the tenancy carries on after the duration of the fixed term, without a further fixed term being granted, the tenancy becomes statutory periodic. A fixed-term tenancy can also become a statutory periodic tenancy if a court order is made ending the fixed term. This may happen in cases where the tenant has breached a condition of the tenancy. Once a fixed-term tenancy becomes statutory periodic, it can be ended in the same way as a periodic tenancy (see **3.6–3.9** below). However, no secure tenancy can be brought to an end without either:

- a court order (see **CHAPTER 6 POSSESSION PROCEEDINGS**); or

- the tenant giving required notice in writing to his landlord (see **APPENDIX A** (Letter 2)).

The rights of secure tenants

3.5   *HA 1980* gives secure tenants a package of rights with their tenancy. These are set out below.

- *Right to sublet the home* – secure tenants have the right to take in lodgers and, with the landlord's written consent, to sublet part of the home. If the tenant sublets all or part of his home without the written consent of the landlord, this will constitute a breach of tenancy and the tenancy will no longer be secure.

- *Right to exchange* – secure tenants may exchange their homes with other secure tenants or with housing association tenants (see **3.45** below).

- *Right to repair the home and receive compensation* – the local authority will be responsible for carrying out repairs to the property (as is the case with all other tenancies). These include repairs to the structure and exterior of the property and keeping facilities of the house in good working order. However, if the local authority does not carry out the repairs for which it is responsible in reasonable time, the tenant can do the repairs himself and receive compensation, but the tenant must give the council prior notice of his intention to do the repairs before going ahead (*Secure Tenants of Local Housing Authorities (Right to Repair) Regulations 1994 (SI 1994 No 133)*).

- *Right to improve the home* – the tenant, under the terms of his tenancy agreement, will not be able to carry out any improvement to his property unless he has prior written consent from the landlord.

- *Right to information* – a local authority must publish information for tenants about their tenancies, eg the right to buy, the right to repair, information about how to transfer and so on. They are also required to provide written tenancy agreements.

- *Right to be consulted* – local authorities must consult and take into account tenants' views on housing management issues (see **CHAPTER 5 TENANCY MANAGEMENT ISSUES**).

- *Right to buy* – tenants have a right to buy their property. However, the tenant or spouse must have resided in public sector property for at least two years, but not necessarily in the property which he wants to purchase.

Bringing tenancies to an end

3.6 There are only three ways in which a secure tenancy can be brought to an end:

- the tenant gives up the tenancy;

- one of the tenancy conditions is not being met – the most common example is that the property ceases to be occupied as the tenant's only or principal home; or

- a court order for possession takes effect under one of the grounds specified in *HA 1985*.

These are explained in detail at **3.7–3.14** below.

THE TENANT GIVES UP THE TENANCY

3.7 If a tenant wishes to terminate his secure tenancy then a notice to quit must be given to the landlord. Four weeks' notice or notice equivalent to the period of the tenancy is required, whichever is the greater. Where it is a joint tenancy, then only one of the tenants needs to sign the notice to quit; this will normally be binding on both tenants even if the other one does not agree. This can sometimes be problematic in situations of relationship breakdown.

A secure tenant may also surrender a tenancy where a landlord accepts the surrender. The surrender of a joint tenancy will only be effective where all the parties to the tenancy are in agreement.

30

THE TENANT CEASES TO OCCUPY AS PRINCIPAL HOME

3.8 One of the key conditions of a secure tenancy is that the tenant lives in it as his main home. It follows then, that if a tenant no longer occupies the property as his main or principal home, or if the tenant sublets the whole premises, then one of the key conditions for maintaining a secure tenancy is no longer satisfied.

In this scenario, the secure tenancy ends and a contractual tenancy is created which can be brought to an end by the landlord serving notice to quit and then obtaining a court order. Clearly, the difficulty for local authorities is that they need to distinguish between a property actually being abandoned and a temporary absence. If a tenant can show that he intends to return to the property, then the secure tenancy remains. Where it is a joint tenancy, so long as there is one tenant in occupation, the tenancy continues.

COURT ORDER FOR POSSESSION

3.9 The third way in which a secure tenancy can be brought to an end is where the court has ordered possession of the property. In order to get possession of a secure tenancy, the landlord must prove that there are grounds for possession. A notice seeking possession must be served on the tenant advising him of the action which is going to be taken, and upon its expiry the landlord can apply to the county court for a possession order (see also **CHAPTER 6 POSSESSION PROCEEDINGS**).

Notice seeking possession

3.10 The notice seeking possession (NSP) must be in a prescribed format, as set out in regulations, and must state in full the grounds under which possession is sought. The NSP has a date after which court proceedings can start and this date must be at least four weeks after the service of the notice; it must be a rent due date or the last day of the period of the tenancy.

There is one exception to this – a claim under Ground 2 (see **3.11** below – nuisance or annoyance to neighbours); possession proceedings for claims under Ground 2 can start immediately. The NSP is valid for 12 months, after which a new one must be served if possession is still sought. Quite often, in rent arrears cases for example, a tenant will make an arrangement to pay arrears at an agreed amount each week, so further proceedings are not necessary after the service of the NSP (see **CHAPTER 4 ENFORCEMENT OF RENT ARREARS**).

Grounds for possession

3.11 In a secure tenancy, the court can only make an order for possession on specified grounds which are set out in *HA 1985*, as amended by *Part V* of *HA 1996*. The grounds for possession fall into three main groups:

- grounds on which the court can make a possession order only if it is reasonable to do so (Grounds 1–8);

- grounds on which the court must make a possession order where suitable accommodation is available (Grounds 9–11); and

- grounds on which the court can make a possession order only if it is reasonable to do so and suitable accommodation is available (Grounds 12–16).

In order for a court to grant an order for possession, one or more of the grounds set out below must be proven. (For further details see **CHAPTER 6 POSSESSION PROCEEDINGS**.)

Note: The following grounds are grounds on which the court *may* order possession if it considers it reasonable.

(a) *Ground 1 – Rent arrears or breach of tenancy agreement* – Rent arrears must be of rent due at the time when court proceedings were started. However, there is no minimum rent arrears required.

(b) *Ground 2 – Nuisance or annoyance, or conviction for use of premises for immoral or illegal purposes* – A tenant or the person residing in the property, or a visitor to the property has been guilty of conduct causing a nuisance or likely to cause a nuisance to people engaged in lawful activities in the locality. Possession may also be sought if the same person is convicted of using the property for unlawful purposes or has committed an arrestable offence in the locality of the property.

(c) *Ground 2A – Domestic violence* – A married or cohabiting couple occupied the property, and one or both of the partners is a tenant. One partner left the property because of violence or threats of violence by the other, either towards the partner or a member of the family. The court must be satisfied that the partner who has left is unlikely to return. (This ground was introduced in 1996 and allows for possession from one tenant to leave the tenancy free for the remaining party of the relationship to safely reside.)

(d) *Ground 3 – Deterioration of premises or common parts* –The condition of the property has deteriorated owing to the neglect or the default of the tenant or a person living in the property. If the neglect is by a lodger or sub-tenant and the tenant has not taken such steps as he ought reasonably have taken to remove him or her from the property this ground still applies.

(e) *Ground 4 – Deterioration in the condition of the furniture provided by the landlord –* The condition of the furniture provided by the landlord has deteriorated owing to ill treatment by the tenant or person residing in the property. Again, if the ill treatment is by a lodger the tenant should have taken reasonable steps to remove him from the property, as any lodgers are wholly the responsibility of the tenant.

(f) *Ground 5 – Grant of tenancy induced by false statement to the landlord –* The landlord was induced to grant the tenancy either by the tenant or by a person acting on the tenant's behalf on the basis of false or misleading information which influenced the granting of the tenancy.

(g) *Ground 6 – Premium paid in connection with assignment –* This relates to assignment by way of mutual exchange (see **3.45** below) where a premium was paid in connection with it.

(h) *Ground 7 – Premises let in connection with employment, related to non-housing purposes and conduct inconsistent with these purposes –* This ground applies where the property forms part of another premises and is held mainly for purposes other than housing, and the property was let in connection with the person's employment. The tenant or person residing in the property has been guilty of conduct that means it would not be right for him to continue to occupy the property.

(j) *Ground 8 – Temporary rehousing during works and former premises are now available –* The property was made available for occupation by the tenant whilst works were carried out to the property previously occupied by the tenant as his main or principal home, and it was agreed that occupation of the new property would be given up when the previous tenancy was again available. This ground can be used when the works have been completed and the other property is available to occupy.

Note: The following grounds are grounds on which the court *may* order possession if suitable alternative accommodation is available.

(k) *Ground 9 – The property is overcrowded to the extent that the occupier is guilty of an offence –* The property is statutorily overcrowded.

(l) *Ground 10 – The landlord intends either to demolish or reconstruct or to do works to the property and needs possession in order to do so –* The landlord intends, within a reasonable time of gaining possession, to demolish or reconstruct the building, and cannot reasonably do so without gaining possession of the property.

(m) *Ground 10A – The property is to be sold by the landlord to allow redevelopment to take place* – The property is within a redevelopment area approved by the DETR or housing corporation, and the landlord intends to dispose of the property within a reasonable time of gaining possession.

(n) *Ground 11 – The landlord is a charity and it would conflict with the charitable objectives of the charity for the tenant to remain in occupation* – Where the property is required because the person in occupation is causing the charity to be in conflict with its objectives.

Note: The following grounds are ones where the court *may* order possession if it considers it reasonable and suitable alternative accommodation is available.

(p) *Ground 12 – Premises let in connection with employment, related to non-housing purposes, and required for new employee* – The property forms part of a building which is held mainly for non-housing purposes and consists of accommodation other than housing accommodation, or is situated in a cemetery, and the tenancy was made as a consequence of employment and that employment has now ceased. The landlord now requires the property for another employee, where it is conditional that a property has been provided.

(q) *Ground 13 – The property has been adapted or specifically designed to accommodate a physically disabled person and there is no one living in the property who is disabled* – The property has been adapted and is now required for someone else who needs that particular type of accommodation.

(r) *Ground 14 – Conflict of purposes of specialist housing association or trust* – The landlord is a housing association or housing trust, which lets properties to people with special circumstances (other than merely financial circumstances), and either there is no longer someone living in the property who meets that criteria, or the tenant has received an offer of secure move-on accommodation from a local authority. The landlord requires the property for someone who does meet the special circumstances criteria.

(s) *Ground 15 – The property is normally let as special needs housing and there is no one living in the property with special needs and the landlord requires the accommodation for someone with special needs* – This applies where the property is one of a group of properties, which the landlord lets to people with special needs; a social service or special facility is provided close by in order to assist the people with special needs. The property is no longer occupied by someone with special needs, and the landlord requires it for someone who has such needs.

(t)   *Ground 16 – The current tenant succeeded to the property as a member of the previous tenant's family and the property is now under-occupied* – The accommodation is larger than is reasonably required by the tenant and it is occupied by virtue of a succession by somebody other than the spouse of the deceased. A notice for proceedings of possession was served under *section 83* of *HA 1996* (or where it was not, the proceedings for possession were begun more than six months but less than 12 months after the date of the previous tenant's death).

APPLYING TO THE COURT FOR POSSESSION

3.12 Upon expiry of the NSP, the local authority needs to apply to the county court for a possession order if it still wants occupation of the property. A particulars of claim must be completed, stating the property to be recovered, the rent and the grounds under which possession is sought (and from October 2001 identifying any human rights issues – see **CHAPTER 10 HUMAN RIGHTS IN HOUSING**). The court will issue a summons giving a date for the hearing, which will be at least 21 days from the date the summons was issued.

The hearing will be attended by the housing officer as a witness, and is usually led by a legal representative from the landlord, although this is not always the case as experienced housing officers can confidently present their own case in straightforward proceedings. It is not unusual for the tenant not to attend the court hearing, particularly in rent arrears cases where the tenant is a persistent offender.

Also see **CHAPTER 6 POSSESSION PROCEEDINGS** on this topic.

COURT ORDER FOR POSSESSION

3.13 At the hearing, the court may make an order for possession. There are various ways in which this order can take effect:

- it may have immediate effect (known as possession forthwith);

- it may be suspended for a while (eg 28 or 14 days, usually to allow the tenant to vacate); or

- it may be suspended pending payment of arrears, either by lump sum or by instalments (this is the most usual type of suspended order).

The judge has fairly wide discretion as to how a possession order will be put into effect. In housing possession actions, the most common form of order is the suspended order. A suspended order does not end the tenancy unless the tenant breaches the terms; once this happens the tenancy has ended and the landlord can apply for a bailiff's warrant. The former tenancy can actually be revived by an application to the court to vary the possession order, which would be made by a well-advised tenant. If a breach has occurred but the landlord does not act to evict the tenant, the tenancy is not revived but rather the occupant is treated in law as a 'tolerated trespasser'. A new tenancy is not created unless it is the intention of both parties to do so.

Succession and secure tenancies

3.14   A person is able to succeed to a secure tenancy if he occupies the property as his only or principal home at the time of the tenant's death, and he is either the tenant's spouse or another member of the tenant's family who has lived with the tenant for the 12 months preceding the tenant's death. There is only one right of succession with a tenancy, so if the tenant was already a successor there is no further right of succession. A minor can be a successor (*Kingston-upon-Thames RLBC v Prince, The Times, 7 December 1998*).

It is important to point out that there is only one 'right' of succession, so if the case was that a husband and wife were joint tenants and one dies, the remaining spouse will use the right to succession by becoming the sole tenant. If then, for example, 15 years later the remaining spouse dies, his remaining child/ren (who may have lived in the property all of their lives) will not have the 'right' of succession.

Any succession following the expiry of the 'right' is a discretionary function carried out by the housing authority. (See **CHAPTER 10 HUMAN RIGHTS IN HOUSING** for the human rights implications.)

Licences

3.15   As outlined earlier in this chapter, most occupiers of council property have a secure tenancy. However, in some circumstances, a local authority will grant a licence rather than a secure tenancy.

Secure licence

3.16   A secure licence arises where someone is renting accommodation which is let as a separate dwelling. There are very few situations where a secure licence will be granted. The courts have held that a licence can only have secure tenancy status if the occupier has exclusive possession. Additionally, a licence cannot become secure if living accommodation (which can include a kitchen) is shared with anyone who is not a member of the tenant's household or his lodger. A secure licence confers all the same rights as a secure tenancy, except that the right to buy does not apply. It is ended in the same way as a secure tenancy.

Non-secure licence

3.17 Where a licence is excluded from secure status it is known as a non-secure licence. The rights of a non-secure licensee are those conferred on him by the contract he has signed. Non-secure licences are either fixed-term or periodic; if they are fixed-term they end at the expiry of the term; if they are periodic they must be terminated by a written notice to quit (NTQ). This NTQ must contain prescribed information and give four weeks' notice. If the licensee does not vacate, a court order for possession is required. There is no defence against possession for the licensee except if he can prove that a secure licence exists (or an incorrect NTQ has been served).

Introductory tenancies

3.18 Introductory licences, or introductory tenancies as they have become known, were created by *Part V* of *HA 1996*. They are intended to give local authorities and HATs more power to deal with anti-social behaviour amongst tenants. Introductory tenancies, in effect, operate as probationary tenancies, which will be converted, upon successful completion, into secure tenancies. In order to be able to give an introductory tenancy, the council must formally adopt an introductory tenancy scheme which must apply to all new tenancies of its housing stock and must not be selective.

Where a landlord has agreed an introductory tenancy scheme, this does not cover some lettings. If a tenant was previously a tenant of another local authority or of a housing association, he cannot be given an introductory tenancy. If, however, he held an assured shorthold tenancy, this does not count.

How introductory tenancies work

3.19 An introductory tenancy runs for 12 months, known as the trial period (*HA 1996, s 125*). If a tenant has spent time as an introductory tenant or as an assured shorthold tenant prior to the start of the introductory tenancy being granted, this will count towards the 12 month trial period. During the trial period, the introductory tenancy can cease to be an introductory tenancy if:

- a condition of a secure tenancy is not met (eg the occupier ceases to occupy the property as his main or principal home);

- the property is transferred to another landlord who cannot grant introductory tenancies (eg upon local authority sector housing voluntary transfer (LSVT));

- the local authority revokes the scheme; or

- the tenant dies without a successor.

Once the trial period is up, the tenancy automatically becomes secure unless the landlord has taken court action under the terms of the introductory tenancy.

Notice of proceedings for possession for introductory tenancies

3.20   If a landlord wishes to bring the tenancy to an end it must still do so with a court order (*HA 1996, s 128*). There is no requirement on the landlord to prove any grounds for possession, but it must prove that it has followed the correct procedure. As with secure tenancies, a NSP must be served on the tenant. However, the information contained in this NSP is different; it must:

- inform the tenant of the council's intentions;

- give reasons for the landlord's decision to apply for a court order;

- give the earliest date for proceedings to begin;

- inform the tenant of the right to request a review; and

- inform the tenant that he can get advice about the notice from a Citizens Advice Bureau, a housing aid centre, a law centre or solicitor.

Review of decision to seek possession

3.21   The tenant has 14 days (or longer if directed by the landlord) after the service of the NSP to request a review of the landlord's decision (*HA 1996, s 129*). The landlord must carry out the review; it should be carried out by a senior officer and by someone who was not involved in the original decision. The authority must inform the tenant of the outcome before the date for commencement of court proceedings given in the notice. If the decision confirms the original decision, the landlord must notify the tenant of the reasons for this. (See also **CHAPTER 6 POSSESSION PROCEEDINGS**.)

Guidance

3.22   There is Office of the Deputy Prime Minister (OPDM) guidance on introductory tenancies contained within the Department of the Environment Circular 2/97. The Local Authority Associations have also produced comprehensive good practice guidance on the running of an introductory tenancy regime. Since the introduction of *HRA 1998*, there has been a debate about how introductory tenancies would fare if challenged under this new piece of legislation.

Case law

3.23   In February 2001, a decision was made in a High Court judicial review case (*Johns and Mclellan v Bracknell Forest District Council, CO/ 3380/2000, 21 December 2000*), which raised important questions about the compatibility of the introductory tenancies regime with the European Convention on Human Rights. (See also **CHAPTER 10 HUMAN RIGHTS IN HOUSING**.)

The case was brought against Bracknell Forest District Council by two of its tenants; the DETR was joined as an interested party. The claimant's application that the introductory tenancy regime was incompatible with several of the Articles of the European Convention was dismissed in its entirety, with the judge ruling that there was no case for making a declaration of incompatibility under *section 4* of *HRA 1998*.

Changes introduced by the Housing Act 2004 to the law on introductory tenancies

The *Housing Act 2004* contains a number of provisions that will change the way in which some introductory tenancies will work. The government, in its drive to tackle anti-social behaviour (see **CHAPTER 5**), is using the Bill to ensure that the law on introductory tenancies compliments and works with the law contained within the *Anti-Social Behaviour Act 2004*.

The Housing Act contains provisions whereby a local authority can extend an introductory tenancy beyond the 12-month period. In particular, an LHA can extend the introductory tenancy by a further six months subject to serving a notice of extension on the tenant at least eight weeks before the original expiry date. The notice of extension must set out the reasons for the landlord's decision, inform the tenant of his right to request a review of the decision to do so, and the time by which this review must be requested.

Housing association tenancies

3.24 Most housing association tenancies are either secure tenancies or assured or assured shorthold tenancies, depending on whether they were granted prior to or after 15 January 1989. Housing association tenancies created before 15 January 1989 will be secure tenancies if the association is registered with the housing corporation. As such they are essentially the same as local authority secure tenancies (see **3.2** above), except that the regime for rent setting will be different (see **CHAPTER 5 TENANCY MANAGEMENT ISSUES**).

The majority of housing association tenancies are periodic tenancies, which can only be terminated by the landlord serving an NSP, followed by obtaining a court order. Housing association secure tenants enjoy the same rights as local authority secure tenants, except for the right to buy their homes.

Tenancies created after 15 January 1989 are likely to be assured tenancies as the housing corporation requires that, unless there are exceptional circumstances, this should be the case.

The Tenants' Charter

3.25 The requirement for tenancies created after 15 January 1989 to be assured tenancies (see **3.24** above) forms part of the Tenants' Charter, which, although not statutory, is a requirement of registration with the housing corporation. The rights conferred on tenants by the Tenants' Charter are:

- the right to succeed after the death of a tenant;

- the right to take in lodgers;

- the right to sublet part of the property, with written permission;

- the right to make improvements, with written permission;

- the right to compensation for improvements;

- the right to repair if the association defaults;

- the right to exchange; and

- the right to consultation and information.

Assured and assured shorthold tenancies

3.26 These were introduced by *HA 1988*, but important changes were made by *HA 1996* which took effect from 28 February 1997. An assured tenancy is the usual form of letting for a housing association or private landlord if:

- the tenancy began on or after 15 January 1989; and

- the property is let as separate accommodation and is the tenant's main or principal home.

Essentially, a tenancy will not be an assured tenancy if:

- the tenancy began before 15 January 1989;

- it is a business or holiday let;

- no rent is charged; or

- there is a resident landlord.

An assured shorthold tenancy is a type of assured tenancy, with all of the security of tenure of an assured tenancy. The main difference is that a landlord will find it much easier to evict an assured shorthold tenant as there is an extra ground for possession which can be used without having to prove a reason.

Assured and assured shorthold tenancies were introduced to stimulate the private rented sector, by allowing landlords to charge a full market rent. Shorthold tenancies allow landlords to let their property for a short period of time and obtain possession easily after six months.

HA 1996 made a change to the setting-up procedure for assured shortholds; for tenancies given after 28 February 1998, landlords no longer need to serve a *section 20* notice on the tenant prior to the start of the tenancy to advise that it is a shorthold. All tenancies are automatically shorthold tenancies, unless the procedure for setting up an assured tenancy is followed.

There is one situation where a housing association tenancy must be an assured shorthold and that is where the accommodation is provided under a local authority's duty under *Part VII* of *HA 1996*, ie to a homeless household. In the first year, the tenancy will automatically only have basic protection but the landlord can, if it wishes, notify the tenant that it is an assured shorthold. After a year of running, the tenancy will become assured shorthold, and this will continue until (and if) the tenancy is allocated under *Part VI* of *HA 1996* through the housing register.

Court orders for possession

3.27 A landlord wishing to repossess a property let on an assured tenancy must first serve a notice under *section 8* of *HA 1988*; this must be in the prescribed format. The NSP must state the grounds on which possession is being sought (the circumstances surrounding the use of this ground must be fully set out) and the earliest date on which court proceedings can start.

To regain possession of an assured shorthold tenancy, the process is much easier. Provided that two months' notice is given, the landlord has the right to regain possession without proving any grounds. This must be at least six months since the start of the original tenancy. If the tenant does not vacate at the end of the notice period, the landlord still needs to apply to the county court to start possession proceedings. (See also **CHAPTER 6 POSSESSION PROCEEDINGS**.)

Grounds for possession

3.28 The grounds for possession of an assured tenancy are set out in *Schedule 2* to *HA 1988*. They are divided into eight mandatory and ten discretionary grounds. If possession is sought on a mandatory ground, the court must order possession if the ground is proved. If possession is sought under a discretionary ground, the landlord must prove to the court that it is reasonable for the court to grant possession.

MANDATORY GROUNDS

3.29 The first five mandatory grounds are prior notice grounds. This means that the landlord must have informed the tenant in writing prior to the commencement of the tenancy that possession could be sought in the future on that ground. However, the judge does have discretion to waive this requirement if it is equitable for him to do so.

(a) *Ground 1 – Owner occupation* – Two months' notice of proceedings is required. There are two different situations where this ground could apply:
- the landlord at some time before the start of the tenancy lived in the property as his main or principal home; and
- the landlord requires the property for himself as a main and principal home, provided he did not purchase the house during the tenancy.

(b) *Ground 2 – Repossession by lender* – Two months' notice is required. The property is subject to a mortgage or charge, which was granted before the start of the tenancy and the lender is entitled to exercise a power of sale requiring vacant possession.

(c) *Ground 3 – Out of season holiday let* – Two weeks' notice is required. The tenancy is for a fixed term of not more than eight months, and at some time during the 12 months prior to the start of the tenancy it was occupied for a holiday.

(d)   *Ground 4 – Vacation lets of student accommodation* – Two weeks' notice is required. The tenancy is for a fixed term of not more than 12 months, and during the 12 months prior to the start of the tenancy, the accommodation was used as a student letting.

(e)   *Ground 5 – Minister of religion* – Two months' notice is required. The property is held for the purpose of being available for occupation by a minister of religion as a residence from which to perform his duties of office. The landlord must have given notice at the beginning of the tenancy that the property may be required for this purpose; and the property must actually be required for this purpose.

(f)   *Ground 6 – Redevelopment* – Two months' notice is required. The landlord intends to demolish, reconstruct or carry out substantial works to the whole or majority of the property and cannot do this with the tenant in residence. Landlords who purchased the property during the tenancy cannot use this ground.

(g)   *Ground 7 – Death of periodic assured tenant* – Two months' notice is required. The tenancy is a periodic or statutory periodic tenancy which has been passed on in the will of the former tenant. Possession proceedings must have started not later than 12 months after the death of the former tenant, or of the landlord first becoming aware of the death.

(h)   *Ground 8 – Serious rent arrears* – Two weeks' notice is required. At the time of the notice and at the time of the hearing, there must be at least:
- eight weeks' rent owing if it is paid weekly or fortnightly;
- two months' rent owing if it is paid monthly;
- one quarter's rent is three months in arrears if it is paid quarterly; or
- three months' rent is owing if it is paid annually.

DISCRETIONARY GROUNDS

3.30

(a)   *Ground 9 – Suitable alternative accommodation* – Two months' notice is required. Suitable alternative accommodation is available for the tenant or will be when the court order takes effect.

(b)   *Ground 10 – Rent arrears* – Two weeks' notice is required. Some rent is in arrears at the time of serving the notice and at the start of court proceedings.

(c)   *Ground 11 – Persistent delay in rent payments* – Two weeks' notice is required. There need not be any rent arrears at the time of the court hearing but the landlord must prove a history of late payment.

(d)   Ground 12 – Breach of tenancy obligation – Two weeks' notice is required. A breach of any term has occurred, other than rent.

(e)   Ground 13 – Deterioration in the condition of the property or common parts – Two weeks' notice is required. The tenant or member of his family or lodger must be guilty of an action or inaction which has caused the condition of the property or common parts to deteriorate. If the lodger has caused the condition, then the tenant must have failed to take reasonable action against him.

(f)   Ground 14 – Nuisance, annoyance, illegal or immoral use of property – Two weeks' notice is required but the landlord can specify in the notice a date for the commencement of proceedings which is less than two weeks. The tenant, or anyone living in the property or visiting it, has been guilty of behaviour likely to cause a nuisance or annoyance or has been convicted for using the property for an illegal or immoral purpose or has been convicted of an arrestable offence in or around the property.

(g)   Ground 14A – Domestic violence – Two weeks' notice is required. This ground only applies to assured tenancies granted by RSLs or charitable housing trusts. It can be used where a married or cohabiting couple has occupied the property and one partner has left and is unlikely to return because of violence or threats of violence.

(h)   Ground 15 – Deterioration of furniture – Two weeks' notice is required. Similar to Ground 13 above except that it applies to furniture.

(j)   Ground 16 – Employee of landlord – Two months' notice is required. The property was let because of the employment, but that has now ceased.

(k)   Ground 17 – Recovery of possession where grant is induced by false statement – Two weeks' notice is required. The tenant or a person acting on his behalf made a false statement knowingly or recklessly, which led to the offer of accommodation.

Accelerated possession procedure

3.31   From 1 November 1993, a landlord may use the accelerated possession procedure to obtain possession of an assured tenancy (see **CHAPTER 6 POSSESSION PROCEEDINGS**). This is available where Grounds 1, 3, 4 and 5 (see **3.29** above) are being used. These are mandatory grounds, and there is a requirement that the landlord gives notice prior to the start of the tenancy that possession may be sought on that ground.

The aim of the accelerated possession procedure is to create a simple paper procedure for possession in uncontested cases. They are to be used simply for possession, and no other claim can be made, for example, a money order for rent arrears, etc.

Development in creating unified tenancies

3.32 There has been a debate raging for many years now about the complexity of tenancy law in England and Wales, and there have been, in particular, calls for a unified tenancy to be used for both council and housing association tenants. This work is now progressing and the Law Commission has unveiled plans to create one long-term tenancy, primarily for use by councils and housing associations. Private landlords would mainly use a short-term tenancy, similar to the present assured shorthold tenancy. There is no indication at the current time of the likely timescales for this reform.

Assignment and relinquishment of tenancies

3.33 Some tenants have a right to pass on their public and private sector tenancies. This is known as assigning the tenancy to someone else. Assignment must be done using the correct procedure otherwise the tenancy may be lost. There are several ways this can be done, depending on a number of factors:

● the type of tenancy;

● what the tenancy agreement says;

● the reason for the assignment; and

● whether the landlord is in agreement.

The main methods of transferring a tenancy to someone else are:

● assignment;

● relinquishment;

● court transfer.

These are looked at in some detail below.

Assignment

3.34 This is the transfer of a property from one person to another. This can be done by the sole tenant or by the joint tenants acting together. This is the most common way of passing on a tenancy. After an assignment has taken place, the landlord and assignee have a direct landlord and tenant relationship and all the terms of the original tenancy apply, for example, the same rent should be paid, etc.

The assignment of a tenancy is by deed. The deed of assignment must give the names and addresses of the original tenants and the new tenants; it must also give details of the landlord. Signatures must be witnessed by an independent person.

The right to assign can be limited or prohibited by the tenancy agreement; it is also subject to statutory limits. The following types of tenancy are affected in this way:

- secure and introductory tenancies;

- protected and statutory tenancies;

- protected shorthold tenancies; and

- assured and assured shorthold tenancies.

SECURE TENANCIES

3.35 *HA 1985* prohibits the assignment of a secure tenancy except in certain circumstances where:

- the assignment is under the right to exchange (see **3.45** below);

- the court orders the assignment under family law or under the *Children Act 1989*;

- the assignment is to a potential successor (the tenancy may be assigned to a person who would be qualified under the right to succeed to the tenancy if the tenant died immediately before the assignment).

INTRODUCTORY TENANCIES

3.36 Introductory tenancies can only be assigned in two certain circumstances: by a court order under family law; or by the tenant to someone who would have been entitled to the right to succeed had the tenant died.

REGULATED TENANCIES

3.37 A regulated tenancy will either be in its contractual or its statutory period, and this will affect whether the tenancy can be assigned. If it is in its contractual period, the tenancy may be assigned with the consent of the landlord; a statutory tenancy cannot be assigned, technically speaking.

However, a transfer is permissible, whereby one tenant is substituted for another. Again the landlord must give his consent, and there must be a signed agreement.

PROTECTED SHORTHOLD TENANCIES

3.38 It is not possible to assign a protected shorthold tenancy unless there is a court order to do so under family law.

ASSURED AND ASSURED SHORTHOLD TENANCIES

3.39 The position depends on what it says in the tenancy agreement.

- If the tenancy agreement says nothing about assignment, it is not possible to assign unless the landlord consents. A landlord in this situation may withhold his consent if he chooses to do so.

- If the tenancy agreement permits assignment freely and without consent, then it is allowed.

- If the tenancy agreement makes provision for assignment with consent, the tenant will be able to assign with consent, and such consent cannot be unreasonably withheld.

- If the tenancy agreement forbids assignment, to do so would be in breach of the tenancy agreement, and could lead to possession action.

If it is a fixed-term assured or assured shorthold tenancy, rights to assignment are entirely governed by the tenancy agreement.

ARREARS AND ASSIGNMENT

3.40 An assignee is not liable for rent arrears which accrued prior to him taking on the tenancy, and arrears must be pursued with the original tenant. *Section 5* of the *Landlord and Tenant (Covenants) Act 1995* removed the original tenant's liability for any future tenancy obligations, including rent due after the assignment took place. So, if a tenancy arose before 1 January 1996, the landlord can take action for arrears against either the assignor or the assignee. If the landlord wishes to take action against the assignor, he must notify the assignor of the arrears on a prescribed form within six months of the rent falling due.

The assignor will be able to sue the assignee if he has to pay the rent arrears, as there is an implied term in all deeds of assignment that indemnifies the assignor. In the case of tenancies arising after 1 January, only the assignee can be held liable for rent due unless there is a prohibition against assignment, the landlord's consent should have been obtained and was not, or the original tenant agreed to act as a guarantor of the new assignee.

Relinquishment

3.41 This is the method by which a joint tenant can give up his rights to a property, leaving the rest of the tenancy intact, i e leaving it to the remaining joint tenant. It is commonly used where assignment is not possible.

Mobility in social housing

3.42 The government is concerned to promote mobility amongst social housing tenants in order to make the best use of the national social housing stock. The lettings and choice elements in the *Homelessness Act 2002* are partly aimed at increasing housing options for those in housing need, and opening up access to low demand housing is one arm of this. A number of the government-funded lettings and choice pilot schemes were running large cross-boundary schemes that offer the opportunity for tenants to move across local authority boundaries.

There are a number of government-initiated schemes that offer mobility to social housing tenants and applicants. HOMES (Housing Mobility and Exchange Services) is funded by the government to work with councils and housing associations, offering a range of services to help people move home.

New mobility services will be launched in Spring 2005 under the name of HEMS. The new scheme will provide a range of mobility services.

Homeswap

3.43 The Homeswap scheme is open to council, housing association and housing co-operative tenants who have permanent self-contained accommodation. The scheme can be used to facilitate tenants moving outside of their current local authority area. It is a self-help scheme designed to assist tenants in finding someone to swap homes with. Tenants need to register by completing a form which is held at most local authority and housing association offices. Once the form is received by Homeswap, the tenant is registered on the computer system, and the tenant can be assisted to move in two ways.

- Homeswap will do a regular computer search and send out details of anyone whose property details match the requirement of the applicant.

- Every month, Homeswap lists are produced and sent out to the local authority or housing association main office. These lists include any person wanting to move into that local authority area. The tenant will need to look through these lists regularly to see if there are any potential households with which to swap.

HOMES mobility scheme

3.44 Separate to the Homeswap scheme is a scheme called the HOMES mobility scheme. This is open to people wishing to move for a specific reason:

- to take up employment which is too far away to travel;

- to move closer to relatives either to give or receive support; or

- for a special pressing reason, for example, domestic violence, harassment.

There is no automatic right to move through this scheme, and landlords have no duty to rehouse. Most landlords agree to rehouse a certain number of HOMES mobility scheme movers each year. Applications to move should be directed towards the tenant's landlord, either the local housing authority or the local housing association office.

Right to exchange

3.45 Most secure tenants have a legal right to exchange. Assured tenants have the right to exchange if it is written into their tenancy agreement (for registered housing associations this is written in by the tenant's guarantee). Tenancies are swapped by deed of assignment (see **3.34** above).

To register for an exchange, tenants must approach their landlord organisation and complete the relevant forms, indicating what sort of property they are looking for and in which location. This scheme is customer-led, ie the tenant needs to check regularly through the details of those households which could be potential swaps.

In practice, the tenant identifies a potential swap property and is introduced to the current tenant of that property by the housing authority. Both parties will be given the opportunity to view each other's property, by mutual consent, and if both parties are in agreement for the exchange to go ahead both will apply to the council for a deed of assignment.

It is important to note that on acceptance of an exchange of property, each party to the exchange accepts the swap property in its current state. The new tenant will not have the right to demand alterations to the property once *in situ*. For instance, if an interior door of the exchange property is damaged due to the previous tenant's neglect or ill treatment, the council will not be responsible for replacing the door when the new tenant moves in. If the previous tenant has fitted a shower into the property, the new tenant must take responsibility for the repair and upkeep of the shower – it is not the property of the council and they are under no obligation to repair, remove or replace it.

It is therefore important that tenants carefully check the exchange property under consideration and request comprehensive details of alterations/ appliances the current tenant has made or put in place. This might include kitchen units, taps, showers, light fittings, interior doors, etc.

The *Housing Act 2004* added a new power to housing authorities to suspend certain rights relating to mutual exchange in connection with anti-social behaviour. Landlords may withhold consent to an exchange where a suspended possession order or injunction is in place, or an application for an order is pending, on the basis of anti-social behaviour.

CHAPTER 4

Enforcement of Rent Arrears

Overview of rent arrears management

4.1 The management of rent arrears is a large operation within most social housing organisations because of the need to maximise rental income as the main income of the housing service. Additionally, there are a number of performance indicators which both RSLs and local authority housing departments are required to measure their performance against, giving rent arrears management a high profile within the organisation.

In best value terms, the control of rent arrears is seen as a key factor, featured under the cost and efficiency element of the best value regime. The performance indicators include:

- a proportion of rent collected;

- rent arrears of current tenants as a proportion of the authority's rent roll; and

- rent written off as non-collectable, as a proportion of the rent roll.

Early warning

4.2 Most social housing organisations have policies and procedures for the collection of rent arrears; this generally involves a computer system which 'manages' the arrears process and generates standard letters when arrears appear on a tenant's account.

The most effective way to manage arrears is to warn tenants about arrears as early as possible. At this time it can easily be established whether the tenant falls into one of two categories: that he cannot pay his rent; or that he will not pay his rent. At this stage, there is a range of help the organisation can give.

- Assistance in applying for housing and other social security benefits.

- Debt counselling, either by in-house staff or by referral to a specialist agency such as the Citizens Advice Bureau or a money advice centre.

- Making an arrangement to reduce arrears by paying an additional amount each week to clear the debt (this can be deducted directly from benefit).

- Arrangements can be made for rent and arrears payments to be made direct by the local authority or the Benefits Agency. It is good practice to obtain the tenant's approval before doing so, but this is not always necessary; provided the tenant is eight weeks or more in arrears with his rent, a request can be made for payments to be made direct to the Benefit Authority.

Seeking possession

4.3 If the arrears persist and the tenant is not keeping to an arrangement to pay the additional weekly amount, the next stage is to serve a notice seeking possession (NSP), which is the first stage in possession proceedings against the tenant on the grounds of rent arrears. This notice must be in a prescribed format with prescribed information (see **CHAPTER 6 POSSESSION PROCEEDINGS**), and it must give the tenant a clear four weeks' notice of the authority's or RSL's intentions. The grounds for possession must be clearly stated and explained; these grounds are set out in the table below.

Grounds for possession for rent arrears cases

Housing association	Local authority
Ground 8 – the tenant owed at least eight weeks' rent when the landlord gave notice seeking possession and at the date of the court hearing.	*Ground 1* – rent arrears were due at the time court proceedings were started.
Ground 10 – the tenant was behind with his rent both when the landlord served his NSP and when court proceedings were begun.	
Ground 11 – even if the tenant was not behind with his rent when the landlord started possession proceedings, the tenant has been persistently late in paying his rent.	

If the arrears are cleared within the four week notice period, no further action can be taken, although the NSP itself still remains valid for 12 months. (This is because the tenant has already demonstrated non-compliance with his tenancy agreement.)

However, if upon expiry of the NSP the arrears are still outstanding or increasing, the next stage in possession proceedings will be taken. This involves an application to the county court for a hearing. At the hearing, one of a number of types of order will be made. These are outlined in **CHAPTER 6 POSSESSION PROCEEDINGS**.

If the possession action in court is successful, the landlord is likely to ask for court costs at the hearing; in the majority of cases these are awarded. The costs requested are usually the issue fee, plus any costs of a lawyer attending to present the case. Court costs awarded by court order are enforceable, and if left unpaid may themselves result in eviction.

If, after the court order is made, the tenant finds that he is unable to meet the terms of a suspended possession order due to a change in circumstances, he may apply to the court for a variation to the terms of the order, provided proof and an explanation of the change in circumstances is produced.

If the terms of the court order are breached, the landlord must apply again to the county court for a bailiff's warrant. The court will issue a date at which a bailiff will attend the property to carry out an eviction; both the landlord and tenant will be advised of this. The tenant may request a stay of execution via the county court in order to suspend eviction action; at this hearing the judge will decide whether or not the eviction should go ahead. If the eviction is suspended then a new order with new terms will be made.

Summary of process

4.4   In summary, the following procedure outlines the rent arrears management process.

1. Tenant is discovered to be in arrears, highlighted by arrears management system.

2. First contact from landlord, followed up by letter.

3. Warning of service of NSP, but arrears still increase.

4. Service of NSP, but arrears increase.

5. Application for county court hearing.

6. Court hearing. Landlord asks for a possession order and the judge may (at his discretion) agree to suspend this order, if the arrangement is in place and working, or the landlord might ask for an outright order for possession.

7. Tenant fails to comply with the terms of the order; landlord threatens eviction.

8. Arrears increase, application for eviction warrant.

9. Eviction, or stay of execution with revised terms.

Although these are the clear legal stages in rent arrears recovery, they do not always happen in this linear fashion. For example, a tenant may be in arrears, reach court, and clear the debt in full. A year later, the same tenant may fall into arrears again, and the process starts afresh. A lot of tenants with rent arrears will only reach the stage of NSP, and then arrears are either cleared in full, or by the operation of a satisfactory arrangement.

Rent arrears management: a practical guide

4.5 Management of rent arrears should become an integral part of the housing organisation's work. The landlord should consider adopting a formal policy to control rent arrears.

The policy's objective should be to:

*   provide tenants with the opportunity to pay, and provide accurate statements of the rent account;

*   provide a sympathetic but firm and consistent approach to the collection of rent arrears;

*   respect the tenant's confidentiality; and

*   compile accurate reports and statistical returns.

Rent control starts at the commencement of a tenancy and therefore should be applied to all new tenants. On-site sign-ups that include the completion of housing benefit claim forms can be extremely helpful.

Example of a rent arrears policy

Introduction

4.6 This is an arrears policy for housing management of properties and temporary accommodation. The purpose of the document is an introduction to the more detailed procedure notes to assist the induction of new staff and to inform external agencies of the policies on the collection of rental income and to ensure that statutory obligations in relation to rent collection/arrears collection are complied with. These obligations include:

- providing tenants with the opportunity to pay and accurate statements of account;

- providing a sympathetic but firm and consistent approach to the collection of rent arrears;

- respecting tenant confidentiality; and

- compiling accurate reports and statistical returns.

New tenants

4.7 Recognise that new tenants, especially introductory tenants who have recently moved house, are more likely to have financial problems. To assist new tenants or those tenants transferring, consider giving pre-tenancy advice on the following issues as part of a 'welcome pack' at the time of signing a new tenancy:

- payment of rent;

- conditions of the tenancy;

- housing maintenance;

- termination of the tenancy;

- standard of service;

- tenants' and residents' associations;

- introductory tenancies;

- tenants' rights;

- the tenants' participation scheme.

Note: All the above information should be summarised in leaflets available to the public. Allocation officers may find it helpful to use a checklist of issues to discuss with tenants when they sign for a new tenancy.

The pack might also include:

- information relating to Housing Benefit;

- a standard Housing Benefit claim registration letter which must be completed, signed and retained, then passed immediately to the Housing Benefit department.

- an authority for the tenant to sign to allow housing services to obtain information from Housing Benefit in the event of a benefit problem arising. (See **APPENDIX A** (Letter 4) for an example letter.)

Methods of payment

4.8 You need to provide details of where and how rents can be paid and the frequency with which they should/could be paid. For example:

- at the area office (provide address and opening hours);

- by standing order at the bank;

- through Post Office Giro account; or

- by post.

Always give the landlord's account number; advise the tenant to quote his tenancy reference number and direct him to where he will find this.

Rent arrears policy: 'firm but fair'

4.9 The landlord takes rent arrears very seriously and expects all tenants to pay the rent due each week/fortnight/month. This is an important condition of tenancy.

However, we recognise that occasionally tenants may have financial difficulties and are unable to pay the rent due. In these cases our aim is to be firm but fair, and to provide all tenants in arrears of rent with sound financial advice and to offer clear practical repayment plans wherever possible.

In all rent arrears cases, we will:

- take early action in every case;

- make personal contact with tenants, supported by letters if there is no response;

- provide up-to-date rent account balances;

- document all actions and conversations;

- provide pre-tenancy advice on the payment of rent, and who to contact if difficulties arise;

- write rent arrears letters in plain English;

- agree negotiated payments based on the tenant's income and reasonable expenditure;

- offer first stage money advice. In serious cases of debt, refer the tenant to the debt counselling service provided by the Citizens Advice Bureau or other like agency;

- take stronger action when no payment or agreement is reached; and

- where necessary, recover arrears via DSS direct payments.

Arrears actions for properties

STAGE ONE

4.10   Once arrears are owed over two weeks, a first reminder letter is sent. (See **APPENDIX A** (Letter 6) for an example letter.)

STAGE TWO

4.11   If no arrangement is agreed or an arrangement is breached, send a letter/appointment for the tenant to attend an interview at the office.

If the tenant does not attend an interview or an agreement is breached, a home visit should be carried out the following week. You should write again to the tenant to advise him that you will be making a home visit.

At a home visit, any reasons for the arrears should be clearly identified and recorded. (See **4.20** below.)

STAGE THREE: NOTICE

4.12   If arrears are over six weeks and an arrangement has been breached, or no contact has been made with the tenant after your attempts to do so, you should serve notice seeking possession. (See **APPENDIX A** (Letter 8) for an example.)

After 28 days' notice, if there is no response or the response is unsatisfactory, send a letter giving standard notice of impending court proceedings. (See **APPENDIX A** (Letter 9) for an example notice.)

If the account is still not cleared or the debt not reduced, you should proceed with court action, but you must check that the NSP is still valid and that you have a record of what has happened throughout.

STAGE FOUR: SUMMONS

4.13 Two weeks later, if there is no response, you should complete the summons and particulars of claim and send them to the county court. (See **APPENDIX B** for an example.)

You should then write to the tenant advising him of the court hearing date.

You may need to attend the court hearing, but you must ensure that you have authority to negotiate a reasonable payment package with the tenant, informally or in chambers, if this has not already been done.

Every effort should be made to contact and liaise with Social Services and other support agencies regarding tenants who may benefit from additional counselling, including debt advice.

Once the court hearing has taken place, you must arrange for all files to be updated. Court costs are added to the account and a letter is sent to the tenant advising him of the outcome of the court hearing. (See **APPENDIX A** (Letter 10) for an example letter.)

You should monitor the rent account on a fortnightly/monthly basis. If the tenant breaches the court order you may decide to inform the tenant in writing, giving him an opportunity to bring the account back into line with the court order.

STAGE 5: EVICTION PROCEDURE

4.14 Once a tenant has been taken to court and the judge has made an order for payment, the tenant must ensure that payment of the ordered amount is made on the dates specified. If any one payment is missed or payment is less than the amount in the court order, the tenant is in breach of the order.

Before proceeding with an eviction request, every effort should be made to ensure that the opportunity has been given to the tenant(s) to bring their account into line with the court order. This is because if you proceed with an eviction, you will need to be able to explain all your actions/decisions to the court.

At this point, a letter should be sent to the tenant advising of your intention to make an application for a warrant to evict. (See **APPENDIX A** (Letter 11) for an example letter.)

When the eviction date is received from the court, notification should be sent to the tenant (the court also informs the tenant) confirming the eviction date and advising him to clear the property of all his belongings and return the keys of the property to you before the eviction date and time.

Social Services and/or other support agencies should be contacted to be advised that a resident is threatened with homelessness. The referral might include the anticipated date of homelessness, the reasons and the composition of the household. The household is also warned at an early stage that they have the right to apply to this authority as homeless, but they may be deemed intentionally homeless, in which case no alternative accommodation will be offered.

You should update all files and pass details of the eviction to the responsible housing officer. The housing officer/manager should then arrange for access to the property to be gained, perhaps with a locksmith/carpenter who will gain entry and change the locks. You might also consider arranging for storage of any belongings left in the property. A contractor with van(s) might also be made available for transfer of items from the property to the place of storage.

The police should only be asked to attend any eviction if there is knowledge of potential violence. (The court bailiff oversees the eviction on the day.)

On the eviction day, you should arrange for at least two officers to attend the eviction. If the tenant is still at the property he will be asked to leave by the bailiff. If he refuses, the police will be called and he will be removed.

Your housing officers should advise the tenant to take all belongings with him. If he is unable to do this, and you are able to arrange for storage of belongings, the tenant should be informed in writing that an inventory will be taken and that the items will be stored, where they will be stored and for how long. He should also be informed that if he does not arrange to collect all his belongings within this period, the belongings will be disposed of. A forwarding or contact address should also be obtained.

If the tenant is not at the property, entry will be gained, and the bailiff will hand the property back to you, the landlord. You should then take a written inventory and photographs of all remaining items. This must be kept on the former tenant's file along with the keys to any place used for storage. Written confirmation of this procedure must be immediately issued to the tenant's forwarding contact address if this is known.

Notes should also be made on your computer system to show where the goods are stored. This should enable any officer of your organisation to deal with an enquiry.

You should pass the keys to the (now vacant) property to the allocations officer along with the file, in order that the property can be made ready for reallocation.

INTERVIEWS

4.15 All interviews at the tenant's home or in the office must be carried out in a sensitive and non-threatening manner. They should take place in private and are confidential. If there are any persons present when the tenant is interviewed, checks should be made that the tenant is happy to have the interview in the presence of that party before continuing. If the tenant is not happy, alternative arrangements must be made (this is to ensure compliance with the *Human Rights Act 1998*). (See **CHAPTER 10 HUMAN RIGHTS IN HOUSING.**)

For interviews without prior appointments at the tenant's home or in the office, the tenant should be made aware that a rent interview is to take place. If it is not convenient for the tenant to discuss the rent account, an alternative appointment should be agreed.

All interviews should be documented and key points confirmed in writing to the tenant.

HOME VISITS

4.16 For interviews in the tenant's home, housing staff must:

- introduce and identify themselves with ID cards (where these are available);

- explain the purpose of the visit;

- ensure there is adequate privacy for the tenant;

- take and retain notes of matters arising during the visit; and

- at the end of the visit go through with the tenant any information obtained and agreement to ensure understanding (in preparation for any potential issues raised by *HRA 1998, art 10*). (See **CHAPTER 10 HUMAN RIGHTS IN HOUSING.**)

If at all possible, visits should be carried out during stages one and two to ascertain the reason for the arrears. A visit must be carried out during stage three to serve the NTQ, and make arrangement to pay if possible. During this process, contact should be made with the Housing Benefit department regarding any claim for Housing Benefit the tenant may have made. Where the tenant has not previously authorised housing services to obtain information from the Housing Benefit department, a signed authority must be obtained from the tenant. (See **APPENDIX A** (Letter 4) for an example.)

LETTERS

4.17 All letters should be:

- in plain English;

- correctly addressed; and

- have the direct line phone number of the sender wherever possible.

Letters following an interview or home visit should:

- summarise the key points of the meeting;

- show a current rent balance including the most recent payment; and

- request that the tenant pays the outstanding debt by a designated date or offers a suitable payment plan.

CHECKLIST

4.18

Checklist	Yes	No
Is the interview by appointment?		
If other persons are present is the tenant happy for the interview to be conducted?		
Does the tenant know what the interview is about?		
If vulnerable*, would the tenant prefer to have someone with him?		
Would the tenant prefer to make an alternative appointment?		
Has a new time and date been issued? Time .... Date		
Have the key points of the interview been identified and confirmed with the tenant at the interview?		
Have the key points been further confirmed in writing to the tenant?		

*   If the tenant appears confused, upset, has communication difficulties which are apparent, check whether he would prefer to have someone with him, i e friend, relative, social worker, etc.

The tenant's means

4.19 Most housing organisations do not look into the tenant's means and ability to reach an affordable agreement for repayment of rent arrears until the arrears are placed before the court.

However, 'good practice' would be to identify financial difficulties at the earliest possible stage in rent arrears. This could well be the first interview or home visit stage.

If at this stage the housing officer ensures that the tenant is receiving all benefits he is entitled to and conducts an assessment of financial resources, the tenant's arrears may well never reach the stage where possession proceedings are necessary.

GUIDES FOR CONSIDERATION

The claimant is not in work, is capable and available for work, is not a full-time student, is single or with a partner

4.20 Consider:

- if the claimant has previously worked:
    - contributory Jobseeker's Allowance;
    - income-based Jobseeker's Allowance (if he has dependants);
    - Council Tax Benefit; and
    - Housing Benefit.

- if the claimant has not previously worked:
    - income-based Jobseekers Allowance;
    - Council Tax Benefit; and
    - Housing Benefit.

The claimant is incapable of work, single or with a partner

4.21 Consider:

- if the claimant has previously worked:
    - Statutory Sick Pay or Incapacity Benefit (short-term lower rate for the first 28 weeks); followed by
    - Incapacity Benefit (short-term higher rate for the next 24 weeks); followed by
    - Incapacity Benefit (long-term rate);
    - Income Support (if the claimant has dependants);
    - Disablement Benefit (if the incapacity was caused by an industrial accident or disease);

- Disability Living Allowance (if the claimant needs attention, supervision, or has problems with mobility);
- Council Tax Benefit; and
- Housing Benefit (also consider Carer's Allowance for anyone looking after the claimant).

- if the claimant has not previously worked:
  - Income Support (via a claim for Incapacity Benefit);
  - Disability Living Allowance (if the claimant needs attention, supervision, or has problems with mobility);
  - Council Tax Benefit; and
  - Housing Benefit (also consider Carer's Allowance for anyone looking after the claimant).

The claimant is working more than 16 hours per week, is single or with a partner

4.22 Consider:

- if the claimant has dependent child/ren:
  - Child Tax Credit;
  - Council Tax Benefit; and
  - Housing Benefit.

- if the claimant is disabled, with or without children:
  - Child Tax Credit and/or Working Tax Credit;
  - Disability Living Allowance (if the claimant needs attention, supervision, or has problems with mobility);
  - Council Tax Benefit; and
  - Housing Benefit.

The claimant is a widow/widower

4.23 Consider:

- if the claimant has child/ren:
  - Bereavement Payment;
  - Widowed Parent's Allowance;
  - Income Support;
  - Social Fund payment;
  - Council Tax Benefit; and
  - Housing Benefit.

- if the claimant has no child/ren:
  - Bereavement Payment;
  - Widow's Pension (Bereavement Allowance);

- Income Support;
- Social Fund payment;
- Council Tax Benefit; and
- Housing Benefit.

The claimant is a pensioner

4.24 Consider:

- Retirement Pension;

- Income Support (if income is below £92.15 for a single person or £140.55 for a couple?);

- Social Fund payments;

- Disability Living Allowance (if the claimant is aged under 65 and needs attention, supervision, or has problems with mobility); or

- Attendance Allowance (if the claimant is aged 66 or over and needs attention or supervision);

- Council Tax Benefit; and

- Housing Benefit (also consider Carer's Allowance for anyone looking after the claimant).

FINANCIAL ASSESSMENTS

4.25 Check that the tenant can afford to pay the offer he is making. There is little point in reaching an arrangement with the tenant which he cannot afford to sustain. This might be achieved by obtaining a financial assessment as early in the arrears stage as is possible.

EXAMPLE FINANCIAL STATEMENT

4.26

To help you assess your financial situation, complete the following statement. You must record *all* income and expenditure no matter how large or small, for an accurate assessment.

(Delete as necessary) **Weekly/monthly net income** £p	**Weekly/monthly expenditure** £p
Wages (tenant)	Rent
Wages (partner)	Council Tax
Tax Credit payments	Electricity
Income Support	Gas
Jobseeker's Allowance	Telephone
State Pension	Catalogue
Widows/Bereavement	Life insurance
Pension	Contents insurance
Private Pension	TV rental and licence
Child Benefit	Maintenance
Incapacity Benefit	Travelling expenses
Sickness Benefit	Clothing
Industrial Injuries Benefit	Housekeeping
War Pensions	Cigarettes/alcohol
Maintenance	School meals, etc
Income from children	Childminding fees
Income from lodgers	Court orders
Disability benefits	Others
Other income	Others
Other income	
Total £ _____	**Total £** _____
Under/overspend £	

Who can help me?

If you find, after completing the statement, that you do have problems (however large or small), contact your housing officer (telephone number …).

If you prefer, you can make an appointment with your local Citizens Advice Bureau, who may be able to assist you with completing this form.

In order to reach an agreement to reduce your rent arrears, you should complete all the details above, which will help us in negotiating a payment arrangement to clear your arrears without putting your home at risk of being repossessed. Once you have completed this form your housing officer will contact you to discuss the arrangements for payment.

I/We undertake to pay a weekly/fortnightly/monthly basis *all* current rent and other charges to the account plus a sum of £… … … … … ..
to reduce and eventually clear the arrears.

Signed … … … … … … Date … … … … … … … … … … …
…

Name … .

Address … … … … … … … … … … … … … … … … … …
…

… ..

… … … … … … … … … .Tel no … … … … … … … … … …
…

CHAPTER 5

Tenancy Management Issues

Tenant involvement

5.1 *HA 1980* was the first piece of legislation that introduced a statutory framework for tenant participation, although this was fairly limited in its scope. The rights of tenants were largely rights to be consulted on a variety of management issues – maintenance, improvements/demolition and the provision of certain services. These were simply obligations to consult; there was no duty in law to take any notice of the tenant's opinions.

Statutory duties for landlords

5.2 Landlords of secure tenants have certain statutory duties to consult and inform tenants on housing management matters. *Section 105* of *HA 1985* requires public sector landlords to have arrangements to inform and consult secure tenants who are likely to be substantially affected by some proposed changes in housing management matters. *Section 105* goes on to define a housing management matter as one relating to the management, maintenance, improvement or demolition of properties let on secure tenancies, or the provision of services to such properties.

Rents and service charges are specifically excluded from the definition. It is up to each landlord to decide whether the conditions for consultations apply. Failure to consult by the landlord may lead to an application for judicial review. Decisions on consultation by a local authority must be that of a 'reasonable landlord' and must have regard to all the relevant facts (*R v Brent LBC ex parte Morris (1996)*). The landlord must consider any representations made to it before making a decision on a matter subject to consultation. Local authorities and housing action trusts (HATs) which have introductory tenancy schemes in operation have a statutory duty to consult introductory tenants on certain aspects of housing management; this is covered in *Part V* of *HA 1996*.

MINIMUM STANDARDS

5.3   RSLs must provide a copy of consultation arrangements to the housing corporation and to the local authority where the landlord has dwellings let on secure tenancies. There is no statutory duty on RSLs to consult their assured tenants. However, they are expected to adopt minimum standards in accordance with the Tenants' Charter under *section 36* of *HA 1996*. The Charter has broadly similar provisions to those that apply to secure tenants, except that it goes further in terms of consulting on the cost of services paid for out of tenants' service charges. The Tenants' Guarantee 1994 sets out guidance for housing associations on how tenants should be able to become involved in managing their own homes and the associated housing services.

CONSULTATION

5.4   There are other instances where landlords are legally required to consult and involve tenants on decision making as set out below.

- A local authority gets involved in a management agreement with another agency to manage all or some of its stock under *section 27* of *HA 1985*, as amended by the *Leasehold Reform, Housing and Urban Development Act 1993*. The authority is obliged to involve tenants in the selection of contractors. This also applies to management agreements made under the compulsory competitive tendering regime.

- The local authority is considering disposing of its housing stock to a private or registered social landlord (LSVT) – tenants must be given the opportunity to vote either to transfer or to remain.

- There is a proposal from a HAT to take over the ownership of properties to upgrade the area – tenants must be informed and able to vote in a ballot (if the majority of tenants say no to the proposal, then the transfer to the HAT cannot go ahead).

Non-statutory ways of increasing tenant involvement

5.5   In addition to these legal requirements, there are a number of mechanisms that landlords may consider to facilitate greater tenant involvement. These include:

- tenant representation on decision-making committees;

- funding tenants' groups;

- provision of tenant participation grants.

TENANT PARTICIPATION COMPACTS

5.6 The legislative framework aside, local authorities and RSLs are expected to encourage and enable tenants to influence their operations. This has been a steady trend over the last decade or so. For local authorities, the housing investment programme rounds will establish and give credit for progress on the development of tenant participation compacts. The Housing Inspectorate will also be interested to see how tenants are involved.

Increasing tenant involvement and influence is part of the government's wider community empowerment agenda. *The National Framework for Tenant Participation Compacts* was published by the Office of the Deputy Prime Minister (ODPM) in June 2000. It lists core standards setting out the minimum expected standards of provision, which were effective from 1 April 2000. The Framework makes it clear that compacts will enable tenants to be involved in planning, improving and monitoring housing services provided by local authorities and will encourage tenants to choose how they get involved in these activities.

The document states that compacts are a tool to help ensure councils become more efficient, transparent and accountable. They are also a tool for implementing best value by enabling tenants to make an informed view on their housing services.

Tenant compacts are agreements between local authorities and its tenants that set out:

- how tenants can get involved with local decisions on housing matters;

- what the council and its tenants want to achieve locally through compacts, such as better ways of working together, improving services, etc;

- how the compacts will work and be monitored for effectiveness.

Dealing with anti-social behaviour

5.7 Anything that an individual does which interferes with the peaceful enjoyment of a tenant's home and/or the surrounding area that makes a tenant feel threatened, vulnerable, uncomfortable or uneasy could be deemed to be anti-social behaviour.

The Home Office established the Anti-Social Behaviour Unit in January 2003 to lead the drive from central government to tackle anti-social behaviour. This Unit works across the government to co-ordinate new initiatives and approaches to tackling anti-social behaviour.

In October 2003, the Home Office launched the TOGETHER campaign and published an Action Plan *Together: Tackling Anti-Social Behaviour*. The aim of the campaign is to help improve responses to tackling anti-social behaviour (ASB). This campaign works hand in hand with the *Anti-Social Behaviour Act 2003*. This Act effectively streamlines measures that were available in other pieces of legislation to tackle ASB. In particular, it develops the measures already introduced in the *Crime and Disorder Act 1998* (ASB Orders) and the *Criminal Justices and Police Act 2001* (fixed penalty notices for disorder).

The Anti-Social Behaviour Act 2003

The purpose of the Act is to provide the tools for practitioners and agencies to effectively tackle ASB. Practitioners working within local authority housing departments and from RSLs will inevitably be involved with the legislation as part of their wider role in tenancy management. The main powers in the Act are set out below.

- Widening the use of Fixed Penalty Notices for noise, nuisance, truancy and other ASB acts such as graffiti. These can now be applied to 16–17 year olds.

- Providing new action to close down 'crack houses'.

- Powers to disperse groups where areas suffer severe ASB.

- Restricting the use of replica guns and air weapons to prevent these being used as firearms.

- Mechanisms for enforcing parental responsibility where children behave in an anti-social way in school or in the community – introducing parenting contracts and penalty notices for parents in cases of truancy.

- Creating a new offence to sell spray paints to anyone under 16 years of age.

- Improvements to Anti-Social Behaviour Orders (ASBOs).

The pieces of legislation contained in the *Anti-Social Behaviour Act 2003* that are most relevant to housing organisations are examined below. There are other provisions that require sanction by the Police; those outlined here are the provisions most relevant to housing organisations. Staff working within housing departments should be aware of all of these powers, and members of the public who are suffering from ASB in their area should talk to their housing officers about the actions that they are able to take to tackle it.

PART 2 – NEW POWERS FOR SOCIAL LANDLORDS TO TACKLE ANTI-SOCIAL TENANTS

These powers are contained in sections 12–17. Section 12 of the Act requires all social landlords (local housing authorities, RSLs and Housing Action trusts) to publish policies and procedures on how they deal with ASB. Section 13 gives RSLs and HATs the same powers as local authorities to obtain injunctions from the court without notice. Sections 14 and 15 introduce demotion orders for use where a tenant (or member of his family or visitors) behaves anti-socially. These allow a social landlord to apply to the court for a demotion order ending the tenants existing tenancy and replacing it with a less secure tenancy. This also removes the tenants Right to Buy and security of tenure for at least a year. Section 16 of the Act relates to possession proceeding; it requires courts to consider the impact of ASB on victims, witnesses and the wider community when hearing nuisance related cases.

PART 4 – DISPERSAL: DEALING WITH INTIMIDATING GROUPS

This can be a common complaint especially on housing estates where there are communal areas such as shopping parades, green areas, parks and so on. Sections 30–36 of the Act give new powers to enable the police and local authorities to identify problem areas that can be targeted to remove intimidation and ASB. In practice, a senior police officer can designate an area, with the agreement of the local authority; this designation must be published and then lasts for six months. Within that area the police have powers to disperse groups and exclude people for up to 24 hours. If individuals refuse to comply with this they will be committing an offence. The commencement date for these measures was January 2004.

PART 6 – ENVIRONMENT: CLEANER AND SAFER COMMUNITIES

This contains sections 40–56 of the Act, and covers ASB that affects the wider environment such as graffiti, fly posting and litter. The Act allows for a local authority officer to be accredited by the chief constable to issue fixed penalty notices in relation to graffiti and fly posting offences. This allows for the local authority to keep the proceeds of this fixed penalty notice (of £50). The Act also enables local authorities to require others (statutory undertakers such as a railway authority, owners of street furniture and educational institutions) to remove graffiti from their property; if it is not cleaned within 28 days the local authority can clean it and reclaim their costs. Section 54 of the Act makes it an offence to sell spray paint to someone under 16 years of age. Section 55 gives local authorities powers to tackle fly tipping, which previously were only available to the Environment Agency. The commencement date for these measures was March 2004 but the measures are currently only applicable in 12 pilot local authorities. The Home Office will then assess how the provisions will be rolled out.

PART 8 – HIGH HEDGES

Some neighbour disputes stem from disagreements about property that is not well maintained and sections 65–84 of the Act provide new powers for local authorities to tackle this. The Act gives local authorities the power to deal with complaints about high hedges where they are having an adverse effect on neighbours; a formal notice can be issued and failure to comply with its requirements is an offence. The local authority is able to carry out the work itself if necessary and to recover the costs of doing so from the hedge owner. The commencement date for these measures was October 2004.

It is clear from the Act that the government expects joined-up working between key agencies in tackling ASB. Most of the powers contained within the Act require effective joint arrangements to be in place to ensure ASB is tackled on housing estates.

MAKING COMPLAINTS ABOUT ASB

Where cases of anti-social behaviour are reported to the landlord, there will be a duty on the landlord to address and deal with such reports/allegations.

Upon receipt of any such complaint the landlord must endeavour to investigate thoroughly and to respond in writing to the complainant as to the outcome of the investigation.

The investigation should include:

- interviewing the complainant;

- interviewing the person(s) complained about;

- collecting evidence and information to support any decision;

- taking careful notes which should be retained if they are to be relied upon in the decision-making process; and

- obtaining witness statements which should be dated and signed by the witness if they are to be used to support any decision of the landlord.

Landlord control

5.8 The landlord should control problems of anti-social behaviour/nuisance by taking proactive action from the onset of the complaint. This should include the following.

- Commencing the investigation within seven days of the complaint being registered.

- Identifying 'victims' in any given situation.

- Establishing what, if any, action should be taken.

- Ensuring that the persons complained of are aware of the complaint and how this action constitutes a breach of any tenancy agreement. This may require the landlord to explain the tenancy agreement and relevant clauses to the persons complained about.

  In the event of court action being initiated, the tenant complained of may well have a defence if he did not know that his actions amounted to a breach of his tenancy agreement.

- Ensuring that, wherever possible, there is an authority from the tenant to obtain information from third parties in relation to matters directly related to the tenant's conduct of the tenancy. (This of course is always best obtained at the sign-up of a tenancy and held on file for use if and when required.)

  Such authorities will allow any landlord to obtain more detailed formal information from agencies such as the police, Social Services, etc. (See **APPENDIX A** (Letter 5) for an example authority.)

- Ensuring that other agencies that may be able to assist in resolving a problem are contacted and involved as early as possible in any investigation.

  This is of particular importance if the complainant or the person who is complained of is a vulnerable person, perhaps with special needs, alcohol/drug-related problems, is elderly or physically or mentally disabled.

- Ensuring that complaints files are easily accessible and separate from the tenancy file for the purposes of monitoring situations, evaluating progress, maintaining contact with other agencies and ensuring outcomes of other agency involvement are obtained and being aware of where and when stronger action might be required.

Common causes of complaints

NOISE

5.9 This may be due to loud music, televisions, shouting, banging, drilling and hammering at unreasonable hours, etc.

VERBAL ABUSE

5.10 This may come in many forms, for example making a resident feel uncomfortable by making what, on the face of it, may initially appear to be harmless comments, but when constantly repeated may make a resident feel insecure or vulnerable; or swearing, racial, sexual or discriminatory remarks.

UNRULY CHILDREN

5.11 This is very often problematic because the tenant may not have a clear understanding that he is responsible for every person living in his home or visiting his home. Behaviour may include damage to property, noise, verbal abuse or even violence or threatened violence.

VIOLENCE

5.12 Actual or threatened violence should be considered under this heading.

DRUGS/DRINK

5.13 Where offences under this heading are alleged, care should be taken to ensure wherever possible that third party involvement from other agencies is obtained, ie the police, Social Services, the probation service, etc.

RUBBISH/LITTER

5.14 Obtaining proof that a person has deposited rubbish or litter can often be difficult. Therefore, care must be taken to photograph evidence of such offences and to obtain evidence that the offending person(s) have deposited such rubbish/litter, even if only by witness statements.

PETS

5.15 There may be a problem with persistent barking, pets fouling or dangerous pets being kept.

RACIAL HARASSMENT

5.16 Fortunately, racial harassment is a less common problem than one might expect, but should be investigated thoroughly with third party involvement wherever possible.

Remedies

EARLY INTERVENTION

5.17 Early intervention will assist in resolving minor problems such as personality clashes, clash of lifestyles, etc. An example of a situation where a common problem was resolved easily by early intervention occurred where one tenant complained that his neighbour's television and radio were so loud that it disturbed his sleep and general peaceful enjoyment. On early intervention, the housing officer in the case was able to establish that the neighbour was almost deaf and had not realised that his television and radio were so loud. In this situation, the housing officer was able to explain about the hearing difficulties to the complainant tenant; and to provide appropriate advice and referral for the tenant with the hearing problem for him to obtain aids to assist him with his hearing problems.

In this situation, had the landlord simply written to the tenant with the hearing problem about the complaint (instead of making a visit to establish the problem) this matter may well have escalated and caused unnecessary friction between the two tenants.

Also, early intervention, by way of a visit to the person complained of, may establish that the problem is not with the person complained of, rather the tenant making the complaint. It is often the case that, upon enquiry, a housing officer will find that the person complained of has resorted to action (by way of nuisance) following long periods of endurance of the complainant's behaviour. In such instances mediation may well be the effective remedy.

MEDIATION

5.18 Mediation can often be effective in resolving minor anti-social behaviour problems. However, for it to be effective all parties to the complaint must be agreeable to mediation taking place. Through mediation, affected parties will gain a greater awareness of how their behaviour impacts on other tenants, which may not have been apparent previously.

Both early intervention and the use of mediation services can reduce the need for landlords to resort to legal action to resolve problems, and can reduce any animosity amongst tenants.

ANTI-SOCIAL BEHAVIOUR ORDERS

5.19 The *Crime and Disorder Act 1998* introduces the anti-social behaviour order (ASBO) to combat threatening and disruptive anti-social behaviour which causes people harassment, alarm and distress. ASBOs, which have been available since April 1999, are promoted by the government as a vital measure in its drive to control disorder on estates and in communities. An order contains conditions prohibiting the offender from specific anti-social acts or entering defined areas, and is effective for a minimum of two years. For example, an ASBO may prohibit an offender from associating with other named people or from going near a house where they have caused problems. ASBOs are civil orders made in court and are likely to involve local people in the collection of evidence and in helping to monitor breaches of the order. Professional witnesses can also be used to give evidence in court and this helps to protect those who are subject to or affected by the ASB.

The main aim of the ASBO is community safety; allowing people to live their lives free from fear and intimidation, by preventing ASB by named individuals.

ASBOs are appropriate for dealing with:

- harassment;
- verbal abuse;
- criminal damage;
- vandalism;
- noise nuisance;
- writing graffiti;
- congregation of youths and threatening behaviour therefrom;
- joyriding;
- substance misuse;
- begging;
- prostitution;
- kerb crawling;
- throwing missiles/fireworks;
- assault;

- vehicle crime; and

- abuse of the elderly and disabled.

The following are grounds for granting an ASBO.

- The individual's behaviour is anti-social, ie it causes harassment, alarm or distress to one or more people not in the same household as him/herself.

- The Order is necessary to protect persons from further anti-social acts.

Magistrates have to be sure 'beyond reasonable doubt' that the past acts of ASB alleged against the defendant are proven. Although the Orders are civil ones, a breach is a criminal offence.

The minimum duration for an Order is two years. There is no specified maximum but the court should make the Order only for so long as it considers that it is necessary for the protection of the community from the individual in question.

Children aged ten and upward can be made the subject of an Order and their case will be dealt with in the Magistrates' Court acting in its civil capacity. Because these are civil proceedings, they are not dealt with in the Youth Court.

A breach of an Order is a serious criminal offence and should be tackled quickly and effectively. The Crown Prosecution Service (CPS) will conduct prosecutions.

They are, however, only workable as part of a partnership between local authorities and the police. They can be applied for by local authorities, police forces (including the Transport Police) and by RSLs. An ASBO will prevent the defendant from doing anything specified in the Order. A breach of the Order is a criminal offence and as such will attract a penalty of up to five years imprisonment.

There are six main stages to obtaining an ASBO. These are set out below.

- *Anti-social behaviour occurs* – the definition of anti-social behaviour as set out in *section 1(1)* of the *Crime and Disorder Act 1998* is 'a manner that caused or was likely to cause harassment, alarm, or distress to one or more persons not of the same household as himself'. Examples may include some of the following:
    - intimidating neighbours with threats and violence;
    - persistent unruly behaviour;
    - organised bullying of children;

- – racial or homophobic behaviour; or
- – persistent anti-social behaviour as a result of drug or alcohol misuse.

- *Police, local authority or RSL decide to apply for an order* – orders should only be applied for when there is a need to intervene to protect members of the community from further acts of anti-social behaviour and other remedies are not appropriate. The police and local authority *must* consult each other before any application is made.

- *Application for an order* – this is by way of complaint to the Magistrates' Court. The court acts in its civil capacity which requires the civil standard of proof; this is on the balance of probabilities.

- *Procedure in court* – the Magistrates' Court will arrange a date for the hearing. The defendant is able to contest the case. If an order is awarded, the minimum duration will be two years. The order will essentially contain prohibitions to have effect within the local authority area and possibly adjoining local authority areas too. The order should be served in person on the defendant and a copy of the order given to those concerned including the police, local authority and other organisations. The complainant should be notified of the outcome of proceedings.

- *Appeal against an order* – this is made to the Crown Court.

- *Breach of an order* – breach of an order is a criminal offence and must be treated seriously. The normal procedures for prosecution of criminal offences apply, and the standard proof is beyond reasonable doubt. Prosecutions are conducted by the Crown Prosecution Service.

INJUNCTIONS

5.20 Injunctions can be extremely effective in tackling ASB. Injunctions can be obtained against both tenants and non-tenants (ie those visiting a tenant's home). Injunctions can be obtained more rapidly than possession, or as an interim measure to prevent further problems in cases where possession is considered to be a viable option.

Sections 153 to 158 of HA 1996 provide for injunctions prohibiting a person from:

- engaging or threatening to engage in conduct causing or likely to cause a nuisance or annoyance to a person residing in or visiting such premises or engaging in lawful activities in the vicinity of the premises;

- using or threatening to use the premises for immoral or illegal purposes; or

- entering the premises or being found in the vicinity of such premises.

The exact wording of the injunction will be determined by the court, and prepared immediately following the hearing. The Order may also state how long it remains in force. The housing organisation's solicitor will arrange for the order to be served on the perpetrator within 24 hours of it being granted.

Interim injunctions are appropriate as the first step in most cases. A power of arrest can be attached if the judge is convinced that the perpetrator has or has threatened to use violence. Perpetrators are advised of the hearing and can attend to defend themselves.

The same evidence is required for injunctions and possession hearings; evidence can be given in the form of an affidavit. However, the judge is likely to want to question the complainant or witnesses, who must therefore attend court.

Injunctions frequently result in the behaviour of the tenant or visitor to the tenant ceasing. In cases where this does not occur, an injunction with the power of arrest attached will at least enable the police to arrest the person in question. Breaching an injunction is very serious. The perpetrator is in contempt of court and can be imprisoned as a result (this is usually between 7 and 14 days for a first offence).

In all cases, the injunction must be sought against the offending person, rather than the actual tenant.

ACCEPTABLE BEHAVIOUR CONTRACTS

An acceptable behaviour contract (ABC) is a voluntary written contract between a person who has been involved in ASB and one or more local agencies such as the local authority, an RSL or the police. They are most commonly used for young people but can also be used for adults.

The aim of the ABC is to:

- act as a deterrent to the young person concerned, in an attempt to stop their continuing involvement in unruly and anti-social behaviour;

- reduce the incidence of crime and disorder in the neighbourhood;

- act as a general deterrent to other young offenders in the community;

- improve the quality of life for those who live in the area;

- inform the young person/s and his/her family of the consequences of breaching the contract;

- act as a precursor to an ASBO, should the behaviour continue;

- provide supporting evidence if legal action is required at a later date; and

- improve the performance of the Association in dealing with ASB.

Legal action in the form of an ASBO or possession order should be stated on the contract where this is the potential consequence of the breach. The threat of legal action provides the incentive for the contract to be complied with.

EVICTION

5.21 In order to obtain possession of a property the landlord must follow the process set out in *HA 1996* by service of a notice of intention to seek possession at the appropriate time and in the appropriate manner. This can be a long process, but often service of a NSP will result in the person complained of desisting with his behaviour. Furthermore, the notice is effective for 12 months and can be enacted at any time, and is seen by most housing officers to be a useful deterrent.

Where a NSP proceeds to possession action the landlord must demonstrate that the behaviour of the tenant is 'so bad that it warrants taking his home away from him' (see **CHAPTER 10 HUMAN RIGHTS IN HOUSING**).

In order to do this, the landlord must have carried out a thorough investigation of the matter, compiled information and evidence that he will rely on in his application to the county court, and have made available such information to the tenant complained of in order that the tenant can mount an appropriate defence (*HRA 1998, Art 6*).

Unfortunately this can often be very difficult, in particular where complainant tenants are reluctant to be witnesses in the case, or where witnesses are reluctant to be identified to the person complained of for fear of intimidation and/or reprisals. However, support offered by the landlord by way of regular contact, keeping the witnesses informed, introducing them to other witnesses, etc. can be a successful resolve to such barriers. Landlords may also rely on injunctions to protect the witness from reprisals and intimidation; or a more extreme measure might be to offer witnesses alternative accommodation (either temporary until the matter is resolved or permanently where reprisals are likely to occur after the matter has been settled by the court).

Further problems may arise where information of relevance to the complaint is not formalised in particular by a third party. For instance, the housing officer may have checked with the police in relation to the number of times they have been called out to the property and may have been advised that the police have been called out due to neighbour nuisance on five occasions over a two-month period and have cautioned the person complained of. However, the police may have been reluctant to formally confirm this in writing, which may happen if the housing authority does not have any signed authority from the tenant complained of to obtain this written confirmation from a third party.

Filmed evidence

5.22 Further evidence may be obtained with the use of a camcorder or CCTV footage. If cameras are directed at general public places, this would not run the risk of breaching *Article 8* of *HRA 1998* (the right to privacy). Such evidence can be admitted into court. However, care must be taken in using aids such as a camcorder: for example, it is fine to direct it on to the street, where actions of the person complained about might be caught in a public area, but to direct it on to a person's home would be likely to result in a breach of *Article 8* of *HRA 1998*. Often if CCTV and/or camcorder evidence is shown to the person complained of prior to the court hearing, he may agree to terminate his tenancy or alternatively not defend possession proceedings.

Likely outcomes

5.23 Once a case for possession has come to court, there are four likely outcomes, given the fact that possession in cases of anti-social behaviour is discretionary (see **3.11**) on the part of the court. The four outcomes are as follows.

- *Dismissal* – this rarely occurs, but is likely to happen where the housing authority has not prepared its case or evidence in a manner that is acceptable to the court, or where the housing authority has relied on evidence that it has failed to make available to the person complained of.

- *Adjournment* – this might occur where the tenant has not had sufficient time to consider the evidence of the case; or where the tenant, on consideration of the case, decides that he needs legal representation; or where the tenant makes reference to contradictory matters which need further consideration; or even where the tenant has indicated that he wishes to be present at the hearing, but does not turn up on the day; or where the tenant alleges that the requirements of *HRA 1998* have not been adhered to in the action relating to possession (see **CHAPTER 10 HUMAN RIGHTS IN HOUSING**).

- *Suspended possession* – this might occur where the tenant attends court and pleads his case for a second chance to control his behaviour; or where it is established that the behaviour complained of was not common place and only occurred as a result of extenuating circumstances; or where perhaps the behaviour complained of was the behaviour of a visitor to the tenant's property and that visitor no longer goes to the property.

- *Outright possession* – this is the most common outcome in cases of anti-social behaviour, but is less common if possession is sought on grounds of arrears joined with anti-social behaviour.

It must be noted, however, that each case is looked at by the courts and considered on its individual merits. Any case which does not result in outright possession will frequently lead to negative reactions from the complainant, witnesses and the community as a whole, as the view may be that the person complained about can get round the court system and that all their efforts in supporting an application are wasted.

CHAPTER 6

Possession Proceedings

Introduction

6.1 Where a landlord wishes to recover his property from a tenant and the tenant will not vacate the property, he must take possession proceedings in the county court. A possession order cannot be granted by the court unless the correct procedure has been followed. Any possession obtained without a court order will be deemed to be unlawful eviction for which the landlord can be ordered to pay substantial damages to the tenant, or in certain cases may result in the landlord being imprisoned.

Recovery without a court order

6.2 There are very limited cases where the landlord can recover property without a court order, but in any case the landlord who uses force or violence in recovery of a property will most likely be guilty of a criminal offence.

These limited cases are:

- where the landlord or a member of his family shares the property with the tenant/licensee and have done so since the commencement of the tenancy/licence;

- where the property is a holiday let;

- where the accommodation is made available to the tenant or licensee free of charge;

- where the accommodation is let as hostel accommodation; and

- where the accommodation was given as a temporary measure to a squatter or trespasser.

Reasons for seeking possession

6.3 The most common reason for seeking possession of a property is that the tenant has in some way breached his tenancy agreement. However, the landlord may want his property back for other reasons, for example:

- he may not wish to renew an expired tenancy agreement;

- he may want his property back to live in;

- he may need his property back to undertake essential works; or

- he may want to sell the property.

This chapter looks at the correct procedure and time limits for the recovery of property.

Initial procedure

6.4 Initially the landlord must serve on the tenant, in writing, a notice of intention to seek possession (NSP), or a notice to quit (NTQ) (in the case of the tenancy having come to an end). This should clearly state time limits, for example, one month/two months from the date of issue.

The NSP or NTQ should:

- be delivered to the tenant's home or last known address stating the address of the property to which the notice relates;

- outline the grounds on which possession is being sought, providing the actual wording of that ground as set out in *HA 1988* or *HA 1996*;

- provide a full explanation of why each ground stated is being relied upon;

- provide the date on which proceedings might be commenced; and

- be signed and dated by or on behalf of the landlord.

Grounds for possession of council properties

6.5 The court can only make an order for possession in respect of a secure tenancy on specified grounds which are set out in *HA 1985*, as amended by *Part V* of *HA 1996*.

Grounds 1 to 8

6.6 Under Grounds 1 to 8, the court may only make an order for possession where it is reasonable to do so.

GROUND 1 – RENT ARREARS OR BREACH OF TENANCY AGREEMENT

6.7 Rent arrears must relate to the rent due at the time when court proceedings were started by the council. The amount of rent arrears is not specified, but the landlord must ensure that the action he is taking in seeking possession is necessary and that full and due consideration has been taken of *Article 8 of HRA 1998* and *Article 1* of the *First Protocol*. Matters taken into consideration by the court will be the frequency of rent arrears or non-compliance with the terms of the tenancy. Note that arrears can only include rent that is lawfully due, so if a tenant has arrears which consist only of Housing Benefit clawback payments, on receipt of the initial Housing Benefit payment, the rent that was lawfully due is paid and cannot become lawfully due again. Such Housing Benefit clawback payments on a rent account must be identified separately from the rent that is lawfully due and contributes to the arrears.

GROUND 2 – NUISANCE OR ANNOYANCE OR CONVICTION FOR USE OF PREMISES FOR IMMORAL OR ILLEGAL PURPOSES

6.8 This applies where a tenant, a person residing in the property or a visitor to the property has been guilty of conduct causing a nuisance or likely to cause a nuisance to people engaged in lawful activities in the locality. Possession may also be sought if the same person is convicted of using the property for unlawful purposes or has committed an arrestable offence in the locality of the property. Again the landlord should ensure that his actions are proportionate in relation to *HRA 1998*. This ground is almost identical to Ground 14 in assured tenancies under *HA 1996*.

GROUND 2A – DOMESTIC VIOLENCE

6.9 This applies where a married or cohabiting couple have occupied the property, one or both of the partners is a tenant, and one partner has left the property because of violence or threats of violence by the other, either towards the partner or a member of the family. The court must be satisfied that the partner who has left is unlikely to return until such time that the violent partner is removed from the property. The reason behind this ground is to enable the landlord to obtain possession from the violent partner with a view to providing a safe home for the other partner.

GROUND 3 – DETERIORATION OF PREMISES OR COMMON PARTS

6.10 The condition of the property must have deteriorated owing to the neglect or the default of the tenant or a person living in the property. If the neglect is by a lodger or sub-tenant and the tenant has not taken such steps as he ought reasonably to have taken to remove the lodger or sub-tenant from the property, this ground still applies.

GROUND 4 – DETERIORATION IN THE CONDITION OF THE FURNITURE PROVIDED BY THE LANDLORD

6.11 The condition of the furniture provided by the landlord has deteriorated owing to ill treatment by the tenant or a person residing in the property. Again, if the ill treatment is by a lodger, the tenant should have taken reasonable steps to remove him or her from the property. It is, of course, within the court's remit to try to establish whether the removal of a person from the property was an option which was reasonably available to the tenant, ie would it be reasonable for a parent to remove a child causing damage? An alternative and frequently less troublesome solution to issues of this nature might be to obtain an order for the cost of damage/repair rather than possession.

GROUND 5 – GRANT OF TENANCY INDUCED BY FALSE STATEMENT TO THE LANDLORD

6.12 This may occur where the landlord was induced to grant the tenancy either by the tenant or by a person acting on the tenant's behalf. The landlord will have to show that the false statement influenced the granting of the tenancy and that the person providing the false statement did so knowingly or recklessly.

GROUND 6 – PREMIUM PAID IN CONNECTION WITH ASSIGNMENT

6.13 This relates to assignment by way of mutual exchange, where a premium was paid in connection with it.

GROUND 7 – PREMISES LET IN CONNECTION WITH EMPLOYMENT RELATED TO NON-HOUSING PURPOSES AND CONDUCT INCONSISTENT WITH THESE PURPOSES

6.14 This ground applies where the property forms part of other premises and is held mainly for purposes other than housing, and the property was let in connection with the person's employment. The tenant or person residing in the property must have been guilty of conduct that means it would not be right for him to continue to occupy the property.

GROUND 8 – TEMPORARY RE-HOUSING DURING WORKS AND FORMER PREMISES ARE NOW AVAILABLE

6.15 The property was made available for occupation by the tenant whilst works were carried out to the property that the tenant previously occupied as his main or principal home, and it was agreed that occupation of the new property would be given up when the previous tenancy was available again. This ground can be used when the works have been completed and the other property is available to occupy.

Grounds 9 to 11

6.16 Under Grounds 9 to 11, the court must make a possession order where alternative suitable accommodation is available.

GROUND 9 – THE PROPERTY IS OVERCROWDED TO THE EXTENT THAT THE OCCUPIER IS GUILTY OF AN OFFENCE

6.17 The property is statutorily overcrowded.

To establish whether the property is statutorily overcrowded the bedroom allocation is one room for:

- a couple living together as man and wife;
- a single person aged 16 or over;
- two children under the age of ten of the opposite sex;
- a child under the age of 16;
- two children under the age of 16 of the same sex.

GROUND 10 – THE LANDLORD INTENDS EITHER TO DEMOLISH OR RECONSTRUCT OR DO WORKS TO THE PROPERTY AND NEEDS POSSESSION IN ORDER TO DO SO

6.18 The landlord intends, within a reasonable time of gaining possession, to demolish or reconstruct the building, and cannot reasonably do so without gaining possession of the property.

GROUND 10A – THE PROPERTY IS TO BE SOLD BY THE LANDLORD TO ALLOW REDEVELOPMENT TO TAKE PLACE

6.19 The property is within a redevelopment area approved by the Office of the Deputy Prime Minister or housing corporation and the landlord intends to dispose of the property within a reasonable time of gaining possession.

GROUND 11 – THE LANDLORD IS A CHARITY AND IT WOULD CONFLICT WITH THE CHARITABLE OBJECTIVES OF THE CHARITY FOR THE TENANT TO REMAIN IN OCCUPATION

6.20 This would also occur where the property is required because the person in occupation is causing the charity to be in conflict with its objectives.

Grounds 12 to 16

6.21 The court may make a possession order only if it is reasonable to do so and suitable accommodation is available.

GROUND 12 – PREMISES LET IN CONNECTION WITH EMPLOYMENT RELATED TO NON-HOUSING PURPOSES AND REQUIRED FOR A NEW EMPLOYEE

6.22 The property forms part of a building which is held mainly for non-housing purposes and consists of accommodation other than housing accommodation, or is situated in a cemetery, and the tenancy was let as a consequence of employment and that employment has now ceased. The landlord now requires the property for another employee where it is a condition of the employment that a property has been provided.

GROUND 13 – THE PROPERTY HAS BEEN ADAPTED OR SPECIFICALLY DESIGNED TO ACCOMMODATE A PHYSICALLY DISABLED PERSON AND THERE IS NO ONE LIVING IN THE PROPERTY WHO IS DISABLED

6.23 The property has been adapted and is now required for someone else who needs that particular type of accommodation. However, this ground can only ever be applied where neither the current tenant nor a member of his family have needs for disabled facilities.

GROUND 14 – CONFLICT OF PURPOSES OF SPECIALIST HOUSING ASSOCIATION OR TRUST

6.24   The landlord is a housing association or housing trust which lets properties to people with special circumstances (other than merely financial circumstances) and either there is no longer someone living in the property who meets that criteria or the tenant has received an offer of secure move-on accommodation from a local authority. The landlord requires the property for someone who does meet the special circumstances criteria.

GROUND 15 – THE PROPERTY IS NORMALLY LET AS SPECIAL NEEDS HOUSING AND THERE IS NO ONE LIVING IN THE PROPERTY WITH SPECIAL NEEDS AND THE LANDLORD REQUIRES THE ACCOMMODATION FOR SOMEONE WITH SPECIAL NEEDS

6.25   This applies where the property is one of a group of properties, which the landlord lets to people with special needs; and a Social Services or special facility is provided close by in order to assist the people with special needs. However, this ground can only be relied upon where the property is no longer occupied by someone with special needs, and the landlord requires it for someone who does have special needs.

GROUND 16 – THE CURRENT TENANT SUCCEEDED TO THE PROPERTY AS A MEMBER OF THE PREVIOUS TENANT'S FAMILY AND THE PROPERTY IS NOW UNDER-OCCUPIED

6.26   The accommodation is larger than is reasonably required by the tenant and it is occupied by virtue of a succession by somebody other than the spouse of the deceased. A notice for proceedings of possession must have been served under *section 83* of *HA 1996* (or where it has not been, the proceedings for possession must have begun more than six months but less than 12 months after the date of the previous tenant's death).

Grounds for possession of an assured tenancy

Mandatory grounds

6.27   Grounds 1 to 5 require the landlord to have provided prior notice to the tenant at the commencement of the tenancy of the possibility of such action being taken (this requirement can be waived at the discretion of the court).

GROUND 1 – OWNER-OCCUPATION

6.28   Two months' notice of proceedings is required. There are two different situations where this ground could apply:

- the landlord at some time before the start of the tenancy lived in the property as his main or principal home; and

- the landlord requires the property for himself as a main or principal home, provided he did not purchase the house during the tenancy.

GROUND 2 – REPOSSESSION BY LENDER

6.29   Two months' notice is required. This applies where the property is subject to a mortgage or charge which was granted before the start of the tenancy and the lender is entitled to exercise a power of sale under *section 101* of the *Law of Property Act 1925*, and the lender requires vacant possession to sell the property.

GROUND 3 – OUT OF SEASON HOLIDAY LET

6.30   Two weeks' notice is required. The tenancy must be for a fixed term of not more than eight months, and at some time during the 12 months prior to the start of the tenancy it must have been occupied for a holiday.

GROUND 4 – VACATION LETS OF STUDENT ACCOMMODATION

6.31   Two weeks' notice is required. The tenancy must be for a fixed term of not more than 12 months, and during the 12 months prior to the start of the tenancy, the accommodation was used as a student letting.

GROUND 5 – MINISTER OF RELIGION

6.32   Two months' notice is required. This applies where the property is held for occupation by a minister of religion as a residence from which to perform his duties of office. The landlord must have given notice at the beginning of the tenancy that the property may be required for this purpose; and the property is actually required for this same purpose by a minister of religion.

GROUND 6 – REDEVELOPMENT

6.33   Two months' notice is required. The landlord, who is a registered social landlord or a charitable housing trust, must intend to demolish, reconstruct or carry out substantial works to the whole or majority of the property and is unable to do this with the tenant in residence, or the tenant is not willing to allow such works to be carried out while he is in residence. Landlords who purchased the property during the tenancy cannot use this ground.

GROUND 7 – DEATH OF PERIODIC ASSURED TENANT

6.34 Two months' notice is required. This applies to a periodic or statutory periodic tenancy which has been passed on in the will of the former tenant. Possession proceedings must have started not later than 12 months after the death of the former tenant, or of the landlord first becoming aware of the death. Any acceptance of rent by the landlord from the person resident in the property after the death of the tenant will not constitute the creation of a tenancy unless such arrangements are confirmed in writing by the landlord to the resident of the property.

GROUND 8 – SERIOUS RENT ARREARS

6.35 Two weeks' notice is required. At the time of the notice and at the time of the hearing, there must be arrears lawfully due of at least:

- eight weeks' rent if paying weekly or fortnightly;
- two months' rent if paying monthly;
- one quarter's rent three months in arrears if paying quarterly; or
- three month's rent if paying annually.

Note: Rent arrears resulting from any clawback of Housing Benefit entitlement will not constitute rent lawfully due and therefore cannot be relied upon as grounds for possession. This is because, upon the landlord's receipt of any Housing Benefit, that due payment will be rent lawfully due at the time that the payment of Housing Benefit is made (therefore, this element of rent could not be lawfully due again). For this reason, any clawback of Housing Benefit attributable to any arrears must be shown as a separate issue in possession proceedings.

Discretionary grounds

6.36 Under Grounds 9 to 17 the court may make an order for possession if it considers it to be reasonable to do so.

GROUND 9 – SUITABLE ALTERNATIVE ACCOMMODATION

6.37 Two months' notice is required. Suitable alternative accommodation must be available for the tenant, or will be when the court order takes effect.

GROUND 10 – RENT ARREARS

6.38 Two weeks' notice is required. Some rent must be in arrears at the time of serving the notice and at the start of court proceedings.

GROUND 11 – PERSISTENT DELAY IN RENT PAYMENTS

6.39 Two weeks' notice is required. There need not be any rent arrears at the time of the court hearing but the landlord must prove a history of late payment.

GROUND 12 – BREACH OF TENANCY OBLIGATION

6.40 Two weeks' notice is required. This applies where a breach of any term has occurred, other than rent.

GROUND 13 – DETERIORATION IN THE CONDITION OF THE PROPERTY OR COMMON PARTS

6.41 Two weeks' notice is required. The tenant or member of his family or lodger must be guilty of an action or inaction, which has caused the condition of the property or common parts to deteriorate. If the lodger has caused the condition, then the tenant must have failed to take reasonable action or steps to remove the lodger. The court will look to ascertain whether the tenant has done all that he reasonably could have done in reaching a decision as to whether or not to grant an order for possession.

GROUND 14 – NUISANCE, ANNOYANCE, ILLEGAL OR IMMORAL USE OF PROPERTY

6.42 Two weeks' notice is required but the landlord can specify in the notice a date for the commencement of proceedings that is less than two weeks away. The tenant, or anyone living in the property or visiting it, must have been guilty of behaviour likely to cause a nuisance or annoyance or has been convicted for using the property for an illegal or immoral purpose or has been convicted of an arrestable offence in or around the property.

GROUND 14A – DOMESTIC VIOLENCE

6.43 Two weeks' notice is required. This ground only applies to assured tenancies granted by RSLs or charitable housing trusts. It can be used where a married or cohabiting couple has occupied the property and one partner has left and is unlikely to return because of violence or threats of violence.

GROUND 15 – DETERIORATION OF FURNITURE

6.44 Two weeks' notice is required. This ground is similar to Ground 13 (see **6.41** above) except that it applies to furniture.

GROUND 16 – EMPLOYEE OF LANDLORD

6.45 Two months' notice is required. This applies where the property was let because of the employment, but that has now ceased.

GROUND 17 – RECOVERY OF POSSESSION WHERE GRANT IS INDUCED BY FALSE STATEMENT

6.46 Two weeks' notice is required. The tenant or a person acting on his behalf must have made a false statement knowingly or recklessly, which led to the offer of accommodation.

POSSESSION OF INTRODUCTORY TENANCIES

6.47 During the first 12 months of an introductory tenancy the landlord may seek possession of a property where he has correctly served notice on a tenant and provided that tenant with a right of appeal against such notice within reasonable time.

Notice of proceedings for possession for introductory tenancies

6.48 If a local authority wishes to bring the tenancy to an end it must still do so with a court order (*HA 1996, s 128*). However, there is no requirement on the local authority to prove any grounds for possession; it must prove that it has followed the correct procedure. As with secure tenancies, a NSP must be served on the tenant. However, the information contained in this NSP is different. The NSP must:

- inform the tenant of the council's intentions to seek possession;
- give reasons for the landlord's decision to apply for a court order;

- give the earliest date for proceedings to begin;

- inform the tenant of the right to request a review and the time limits and manner for doing so; and

- inform the tenant where to get advice about the notice, ie from the Citizens Advice Bureau, a housing aid centre, a law centre or solicitor.

At the expiry of any notice in introductory tenancy cases, if the application is made to court, the court *must* grant an order for possession; the court does not have any discretion in these matters.

Applying to the court for possession

6.49   Upon expiry of the NSP, the local authority must apply to the county court for a possession order if it still wants occupation of the property. Particulars of claim should be completed, stating the property to be recovered, the rent and the grounds under which possession is sought. The court will issue a summons giving a date for the hearing, which will be at least 21 days from the date the summons was issued.

From October 2001, all applications to court for possession have to demonstrate that consideration has been given to *HRA 1998* in possession proceedings (County Court Rules, Practice Direction 15) (see **CHAPTER 10 HUMAN RIGHTS IN HOUSING**). Therefore social landlords must adhere to *HRA 1998* principles when seeking possession otherwise they might have what appears to be a concrete case dismissed because correct procedures have not been complied with. Additionally, and even in the event of the case being considered by the court, they may not obtain an order for costs against the tenant.

The housing officer will attend the hearing as a witness. This is usually led by a legal representative from the landlord but this is not always the case as experienced housing officers can confidently present their own case where it is straightforward. The tenant will also be awarded an equal right of audience in the court on the basis that both parties have an equal right to state their case and to be heard.

If the tenant does not attend the hearing, the case can be heard in the tenant's absence, but this decision is entirely at the discretion of the district judge.

Court order for possession

6.50   At the hearing, the court may do any of the following.

- *Dismiss the case.* Particularly where the landlord cannot demonstrate that he has complied with the required procedure prior to resorting to the court.

- *Adjourn the hearing.* This may happen where the tenant does not attend the hearing, particularly where the tenant has indicated that he intends to attend but does not turn up. Additionally, adjournments may also become commonplace where evidence is presented to the court that all parties have not had the opportunity to consider and defend or question. This of course would be a requirement of *Article 6 of HRA 1998*, which the court must adhere to.

- *Make an order for possession.* This order has various ways of taking effect. It may have immediate effect (known as possession forthwith); it may be suspended for a while (eg 28 or 14 days, or in exceptional cases 56 days, usually to allow the tenant to vacate). The most common result would be to suspend the order pending payment of arrears, either by lump sum or by instalments. The judge has a fairly wide discretion as to how a possession order will be put into effect. In housing possession actions the most common form of order is the suspended order.

Suspended orders

6.51 A suspended order does not end the tenancy unless the tenant breaches the terms. Once this happens the tenancy has ended and the landlord can apply for a bailiff's warrant. The former tenancy can be revived by an application to the court to vary the possession order – such an application would be made by a well-advised tenant. If a breach has occurred but the landlord does not act to evict the tenant, the tenancy is not revived but rather the occupant is treated in law as a 'tolerated trespasser'. A new tenancy is not created unless it is the intention of both parties to do so.

It must, however, be noted that previously most RSLs have entered court with a view to obtaining a suspended possession order, thus using the courts to make money arrangements. This is not good practice and may constitute a breach of *Article 8 of HRA 1998* and *Article 1* of the *First Protocol.*

In order to avoid such a breach, the landlord should seek to make an arrangement with the tenant prior to resorting to court action. In doing so, the landlord should award full consideration to the tenant's ability to pay by way of obtaining financial statements from the tenant in the early stages of arrears control.

Landlords must have a greater awareness that resorting to court action should only be applied as the last resort and will need to demonstrate that they have done all that could possibly be done without resorting to the court. It is only when options available to the landlord have been exhausted that an application to the court should be made.

See **APPENDIX B** for court forms.

CHAPTER 7
Defending Possession

Introduction

7.1 When possession proceedings are issued against a tenant, the most important thing is that he does not ignore them, regardless of how helpless the tenant may feel. There are a number of agencies that can assist with this problem, for example, the Citizens Advice Bureau, law centres and housing advice offices. If the tenant is on a low income, he may qualify for Legal Aid.

In order to evict the tenant, the landlord, in most cases, will have to show that the tenant has done something so wrong that it warrants taking away his home. This might include persistent failure to pay rent, or any other ground set out in possession proceedings (see **CHAPTER 6 POSSESSION PROCEEDINGS**).

Summons

7.2 Whatever the landlord intends to rely on to obtain possession must be contained in the summons and it is therefore important that the tenant reads this thoroughly; if there is anything he disagrees with he must point this out.

When the summons is issued, the tenant has 14 days in which to reply, and will also have the right to attend the possession hearing to state his case.

Even if the tenant intends to attend the court hearing, he should, wherever possible, respond to the summons, even if he does not have a defence. In responding, he may wish to point out why the situation giving rise to the summons occurred and what he has tried to do, or intends to do about it. The tenant may also consider putting some information forward as to how losing his home is going to affect him and his family.

If the tenant has not responded to the summons but is going to appear at court, it will also help if he writes down the information suggested above so that he does not forget anything important, which is quite easily done when faced with the formalities of the court hearing.

Preparing a defence

7.3 The issuing of a summons does not automatically mean that the tenant will lose his home. The court will take all the circumstances into account when considering the application, provided that the tenant puts them forward.

Rent arrears

7.4 In cases where the summons is for rent arrears, the tenant might explain why he is in arrears with the rent. He should also always complete the information requested by the court in relation to the provision of the details of income and expenditure. He might also include information in relation to the following.

- Has he made any offer of repayment to the landlord? If so what was the offer and why did the landlord refuse this offer?

- If he has not made an offer of repayment, why not?

- Can he afford the actual rent plus an amount off the arrears?

If he can afford the current rent, plus an amount off the arrears (which is affordable and sustainable), the court is likely to make an order for possession of the property, but suspend the order on the condition that the tenant keeps up with any arrangement agreed by the court.

It is very important that the tenant does not panic and make an offer to pay the arrears that he cannot realistically afford; otherwise it will be inevitable that he defaults on the court order and risks losing his home.

Nuisance

7.5 In cases where the summons is for nuisance or annoyance, the tenant might include information in relation to the following:

- his version of events;

- what he has done to try to resolve this problem;

- what he will do to try and resolve this problem; and

- will eviction resolve the problem?

Information relating to the circumstances of the tenant and his family will be important. It might also be helpful if the tenant has anyone to support his version of events.

Deterioration

7.6 In cases where the summons is for the deterioration in the condition of the property or the furniture provided by the landlord, the following should be considered.

- Read what is said about this very carefully. Does the tenant agree with it all? If not, he should explain why.

- Are there photographs? These might be helpful in the defence, in particular where the written account sounds much worse than it actually is.

- Has the tenant been accused of damage that was there when he moved in that he is not responsible for, and did he take this up with the landlord at the start of the tenancy? If not, why not?

- If the deterioration or damage is the tenant's fault, what has he done or tried to do or intend to do to resolve this problem?

Former property available again

7.7 In cases where the summons is because the tenant has been in temporary housing and his former property is now available, he might include information in relation to the following.

- Why does he not want to move back into the old property? Is there a good and legitimate reason?

- What problems did he have in the old property? Have these problems reduced or been extinguished in the current home?

If there is anyone to support this, for example a social worker or doctor, etc, it may be helpful to obtain a letter of support from him or her. Remember that in these circumstances the landlord needs to show that there is suitable alternative accommodation for the tenant to move into. (In most cases this will be the previous property, so the tenant must show the reason that it is not suitable now as it clearly was when he took up the tenancy.)

Under-occupation

7.8 In cases where the summons is because the tenant succeeded to the property as a member of the previous tenant's family and the property is now under-occupied, he must be able to argue why the alternative property which has been made available is not suitable. This information might include issues like family ties in the area, children being in school nearby, having established community links, being near to work, etc.

Procedure

7.9 The landlord cannot recover the property in most cases without showing a very good reason. He must also follow the correct procedure, by issuing notices at the correct time and allowing notices to expire before taking the next step in recovery.

Therefore it is important to check that the landlord has followed the procedure that the law requires him to take. If he has not, then the tenant must rely on this in the defence. He can also apply to the court for any legal costs that he may have incurred against the landlord.

At the hearing

7.10 Whatever is set out in the summons as grounds for possession will be relied on in court. However, the landlord can add additional grounds at the court hearing. If this happens, the tenant must be prepared to respond. Alternatively, if he needs to seek advice about these grounds he should tell the court, or he may want time to consider these new grounds and request an adjournment. This should always be granted by the court as *Article 6* of *HRA 1998* requires a fair hearing. The tenant will have been deprived of such a right unless he has had the time to consider the implications of any allegations made against him which may result in losing his home.

Costs

7.11 Finally, where possession cases are brought to court, the summons will include an amount in respect of court costs. Usually the party who succeeds in the case will be responsible for the court costs. However, if the tenant feels that the case could have been resolved without having to involve the court, he should request that the court consider whether he should be liable for the court costs. This is particularly relevant where, for example, he has made a reasonable offer to pay rent arrears, but the landlord would not accept the offer, whereas the court has done so. The question as to who will be responsible for the costs is entirely at the discretion of the court.

CHAPTER 8

Housing Benefit

Part 1: Introduction

8.1   People who have a low income and pay rent for their home can claim Housing Benefit. This is always paid by the local authority. This chapter will deal with Housing Benefit claims for those in the social rented sector. Local authority tenants claim rent rebate and housing association tenants claim rent allowance; unless stated otherwise the following applies to claims for both rent rebate and rent allowance.

Basic rules

8.2   The main legislation on Housing Benefit is as follows.

- *Housing Benefit (General) Regulations 1987 (SI 1987 No 1971).*

- *Social Security Administration Act 1992 (SSAA 1992).*

- *Social Security Contributions and Benefits Act 1992 (SSCBA 1992).*

- *Child Support, Pensions and Social Security Act 2000 (CSPSSA 2000).*

- *Housing Benefit and Council Tax Benefit (Decisions and Appeals) Regulations 2001 (SI 2001 No 1002).*

No entitlement to benefit

8.3   In certain circumstances, a claimant will not be entitled to Housing Benefit. The main reasons are that the claimant:

- has more than £16,000 in capital (see **8.4** below);

- is a full-time student (there are some exceptions to this rule) (see **8.5** below);

- has no liability to pay rent or is treated as having no liability (see **8.6** below);

- has agreed to pay rent to take advantage of the Housing Benefit scheme (see **8.6** below);

- lives with their landlord who is a close relative (see **8.7** below);

- is receiving Income Support, income-based Jobseekers Allowance, or Guarantee Credit, and housing costs (for things like a mortgage or home improvement loan) are included in his or her benefit (see **8.8** below).

MORE THAN £16,000 IN CAPITAL

8.4   [SI 1987 No 1971, reg 37]

Where a claimant, or a couple living together as husband and wife, has savings or capital of more than £16,000, they will not be entitled to Housing Benefit. The £16,000 capital limit is the same for a single claimant as it is for a couple (see **8.49**ff below).

If, however, the claimant or either of them is over 60, this rule may not apply. The introduction of State Pension Credit from 6 October 2003 has affected the capital rules for those over 60. The capital limit does not apply where the claimant or the claimant's partner is over 60 and entitled to claim Guarantee Credit. However, the capital limit continues to apply to claimants over 60 who are not receiving Guarantee Credit, even if they are receiving Savings Credit.

FULL-TIME STUDENTS

8.5   [SI 1987 No 1971, reg 48A]

Claimants who are full-time students in higher education will not be entitled to Housing Benefit in most cases. However, if the student has a partner who is not a full-time student, that partner can claim Housing Benefit for both of them. Other full-time students may be entitled to Housing Benefit, for example where the student:

- has dependent children;

- is aged over 60; or

- is disabled or has been incapable of work for more than 28 weeks, provided that the claimant is not in student accommodation, such as halls of residence.

NO LIABILITY TO PAY RENT/TREATED AS NOT LIABLE TO PAY RENT

8.6   [*SSCBA 1992, s 130 (i)(a); SI 1987 No 1971, reg 6 and 7*]

Claimants who are not legally bound to pay rent for their accommodation are not entitled to Housing Benefit. This includes, for example, claimants who live in accommodation which they will not have to leave if no rent is paid. However, there are some claimants who may not be legally liable to pay rent for their home, but it is reasonable to treat them as responsible for paying rent. This would apply, for example, where the resident's former partner was the tenant of the property, but that former partner no longer resides in the property (see **8.23** below).

Claimants and/or their partners are treated as not liable to pay rent (and are not entitled to Housing Benefit) in the following circumstances.

(a)   The tenancy is not on a commercial basis (ie it is not legally enforceable, or the relationship between the landlord and the tenant is not a proper business arrangement).

(b)   The landlord is a person who lives in the same dwelling and is a close relative of the claimant or their partner.

(c)   The landlord is a former partner who used to live in the same property as the claimant or their current partner (see **8.7** below).

(d)   The landlord is the parent of a child for whom the claimant or their partner is responsible.

(e)   The landlord is a company or a trust of which:
   (i)   the claimant;
   (ii)   his or her partner;
   (iii) a close relative of the claimant or his or her partner; or
   (iv)   the former partner of the claimant's current partner

   is a director or employee (in the case of a company) or a trustee or a beneficiary (in the case of a trust).

(f)   The landlord is a trustee of a trust of which a child of the claimant or his or her partner is a beneficiary.

(g)   Before the claimant was liable to pay rent, he or she was a non-dependant (see **8.58**) of someone who lived and who still lives in the same property.

(h)   The claimant or his or her partner owned the property within the last five years. This does not apply where the claimant or his partner could not have continued to live in the property without giving up ownership, eg home rescue schemes.

(i)   The occupation of the property is a condition of the claimant's, or the claimant's partner's, employment. This might include caretakers, wardens, etc.

(j)   The claimant is a member of, and is wholly maintained by, a religious order.

(k)   The liability was created to take advantage of the Housing Benefit scheme.

[SI 1987 No 1971, reg 7]

Paragraphs (e) and (g) do not apply where the Housing Benefit department is satisfied that the liability was not created to take advantage of the housing benefit scheme.

CLAIMANT LIVES WITH THEIR LANDLORD WHO IS A CLOSE RELATIVE OF THE CLAIMANT OR THEIR PARTNER

8.7   [SI 1987 No 1971, reg 7]

Claimants who live with a close relative (of themselves or their partner) to whom they are liable to pay a rent are specifically excluded from the Housing Benefit scheme. A close relative is defined in *regulation 2 of SI 1987 No 1971* as being a parent, step-parent, child, step-child, brother, step-brother, sister, step-sister or partner of any one of these. Where the claimant is divorced, they are no longer regarded as a close relative of their parents-in-law or children-in-law.

HOUSING COSTS FROM OTHER SOURCES

8.8   [SI 1987 No 1971, reg 8]

Claimants who receive another income-based benefit which includes housing costs are not normally entitled to Housing Benefit. However, a claimant living in a shared ownership scheme with a registered social landlord may be able to claim Income Support, Guarantee Credit or income-based Jobseeker's Allowance in respect of his or her mortgage interest payments and claim Housing Benefit for any rent element.

Ineligible payments

8.9 Some charges which are included in the rent are not eligible for Housing Benefit (*SI 1987 No 1971, Sch 1*). These are set out in **8.10** to **8.17** below.

Fuel

8.10 Fuel charges for the claimant's own room are not eligible for Housing Benefit. However, fuel charges for communal areas are eligible where these are included in the claimant's rent.

Where the rent includes a charge for fuel, the Housing Benefit department will deduct either the actual charge (if identified by the landlord) or an amount as prescribed by regulations. Where a claimant only has one room and the use of shared common areas, a single room fuel deduction is applied (*SI 1987 No 1971, Sch 1, para 5*).

Service charges

8.11 Most service charges included in the rent are not eligible for Housing Benefit. However, service charges for the following items are eligible.

- Furniture and household equipment, provided that it will not become the property of the claimant.

- The use of laundry facilities on the premises by the claimant.

- Cleaning of communal areas.

- Cleaning of the exterior windows (where the charge is not funded by the Supporting People scheme), but only where the claimant and all members of his or her household are unable to do this for themselves because of disability.

Garden maintenance, the provision of a children's play area, lifts, entry phones, rubbish removal, television aerials and so on are all eligible provided they are connected with the provision of adequate accommodation.

Service charges for people in supported accommodation were originally left to the Housing Benefit scheme. The deficiencies in this approach were recognised by the decision to introduce a separate scheme to cover these charges with effect from April 2003. This scheme is known as the Supporting People scheme. During the period from April 2000 until April 2003, these charges were covered by a scheme known as Transitional Housing Benefit, which came to an end in April 2003 when the finance allocated to this scheme was transferred to the new Supporting People budget.

Payments made under the Transitional Housing Benefit scheme ended on 6 April 2003 (where rent is paid weekly or in weekly multiples) and on 31 March 2003 in all other cases. From these dates, certain charges are no longer eligible for Housing Benefit and the responsibility for funding them has been taken over by Supporting People. These are:

- charges for general counselling and support services;

- certain arrangements for cleaning rooms and windows where neither the claimant or any member of the household is able to do it themselves; and

- charges for the provision of an emergency alarm system.

The new system covers those who live in sheltered or supported housing. Those who live in normal accommodation can have certain charges paid for as part of their rent, under the Housing Benefit scheme.

More information can be found at the Supporting People website which is at www.spkweb.org.uk.

8.12 Where the rent includes a payment for meals, the payment is not eligible for Housing Benefit. The amount deducted is prescribed by regulations. There is no deduction for anyone who is not charged for meals, eg a baby (*SI 1987 No 1971, Sch 1, paras 1, 1A*).

Water rates

8.13 Water rates included in the claimant's rent are not eligible for Housing Benefit. To assess the amount to be deducted from the claimant's rent, the Housing Benefit department will either take the actual charge, or a percentage of the water rates bill for the whole property based on the proportion of the whole property occupied by the claimant (*SI 1987 No 1971, reg 10(3), (6)*).

Parts of the property used for business purposes

8.14 Any part of the property which is used exclusively for business purposes will not be eligible for Housing Benefit (*SI 1987 No 1971, reg 10(4)*).

Payments under a shared ownership scheme

8.15 Payments made under a co-ownership scheme, which are payments for the claimant's purchase of part of a property, are not eligible for Housing Benefit. However, any rent element payable to a registered social landlord is eligible for Housing Benefit (*SI 1987 No 1971, reg 10(2)(a)*).

Payments under a hire purchase agreement

8.16 Payments made under a hire purchase, credit sale or conditional sale agreement which are payments for the claimant's purchase of part of a property are not eligible for Housing Benefit, for example where the claimant is living in a mobile home which is subject to a hire purchase or credit agreement.

Payments for local authority residential homes

8.17 Payments for living in local authority residential or nursing homes are not eligible for Housing Benefit.

Referral to the rent officer

Rents exempt from referral

8.18 [*SI 1987 No 1971, Sch 1A as amended*]

It is the responsibility of the rent officer to fix rents for housing benefit claims. There is a complex procedure for referral to the rent officer and the determination of the rent eligible for housing benefit.

Rents for local authority tenancies are never referred to the rent officer. In some cases, the rent charged by a registered social landlord may be referred to the rent officer to establish the amount of rent that will be used in the benefit assessment. However, the regulations provide exemptions from referral for most RSL rents.

From 2 January 1996, the following are exempt from referral to the rent officer.

- Tenancies entered into before 15 January 1989.

- Regulated tenancies under the *Rent Act 1977* (protected tenancies, statutory tenancies and restricted contracts) and similar agricultural tenancies under the *Rent (Agriculture) Act 1976*.

- Home Office bail hostels and probation hostels.

- HAT tenancies.

- Lettings of local authority or new town housing stock which has been transferred to a new owner under *HA 1985* or the tenant's choice provisions of *HA 1988* unless:
  - there has been a rent increase since the date of the transfer; and
  - the authority considers the accommodation to be unreasonably large or the rent to be unreasonably high. For tenancies that have been transferred by LSVT on or after 7 October 2002, local authorities are no longer required to refer rents to the rent officer if they consider that the accommodation is unreasonably large (*SI 2002 No 2322*).

- A housing association letting, unless the authority considers the accommodation to be unreasonably large or the rent to be unreasonably high.

Discretion to refer

8.19 The Housing Benefit department has discretion to refer Housing Association rents to the rent officer in cases where it considers the accommodation too large or the rent too high. The authority must state this when referring to the rent officer (*SI 1987 No 1971, reg 12A*).

The DWP has issued guidance to local authorities that they must bear in mind that this is a discretionary power, which means that each case must be considered on its individual merit. There must not be a blanket policy to refer all rents of this nature.

In exercising its discretion to refer such cases to a rent officer, the authority may use the rent officer's criteria (see **8.20** below) as a guide but it is not obliged to do so. The DWP advises that local authorities should look at the circumstances of each case (DWP HB/CTB Circular A28/2002).

Other relevant factors could be:

- the claimant being allocated the property when he had a larger family which has now moved away;

- the claimant having relinquished a protected tenancy of a larger house to make it available for another family; or

- the claimant being allocated a larger property to accommodate any special needs due to a disability, or to accommodate an additional child soon to be born, etc.

It is good practice for the authority to make further relevant enquiries of the tenant or landlord to ascertain the reason for the allocation of a larger property before referring a case to the rent officer.

The rent officer's size criteria

8.20 [*SI 1997 No 1995, Sch 2*]

The rent officer should address the requirements of the family when assessing whether a property is too large and will allocate the following.

- Bedroom allocation – one room for:
  - a couple living together as man and wife;
  - a single person aged 16 or over;
  - two children under the age of 10;
  - a child under the age of 16; or
  - two children under the age of 16 of the same sex.

- Living room allocation:
  - one living room where there are between one and three occupiers;
  - two living rooms where there are between four and six occupiers; or
  - three living rooms where there are seven or more occupiers.

8.21 The government has announced its intention of moving towards standard rents for particular areas. Nine 'Pathfinder Areas' are operating a pilot scheme in which a set amount is allocated to each tenant for their rent. If the tenant can find a cheaper property, they can keep the excess. If they have to pay more rent than the standard rent, they must find the difference. The nine pilot areas are Blackpool, Brighton and Hove, Conwy, Coventry, Edinburgh, Leeds, Lewisham, North East Lincolnshire, and Teignbridge. The pilot schemes began in 2003 and will run for two years.

Part II: Claiming Housing Benefit

8.22 A person who makes a claim for Housing Benefit must complete an application form.

The claimant must provide details of all those people who are living in the house and details of their income, savings and investments; he or she will also be required to provide proof of this income. The claimant must also supply details and proof of the rent payable, which must include details of any amounts included in the rent for non-eligible costs (see **8.10** to **8.17** above). This proof can be by the way of a letter from the landlord or in the form of a tenancy agreement.

Who can claim?

8.23 Any person who is required to pay rent as a condition of occupying his or her dwelling as a home can make a claim for Housing Benefit (*SI 1987 No 1971, reg 6*). Paragraph **8.3** above lists the main groups that are excluded from entitlement.

Where a couple are living together as husband and wife then either partner can make the claim for Housing Benefit. It is usually best for the partner who may attract most benefit to make the claim. For example, if one of the partners is incapable of work through sickness or disability, he or she may attract an extra disability premium.

Where a person is incapable of managing his or her own affairs because of a disability, the local authority will accept a claim from someone legally appointed to act on their behalf such as under a power of attorney. Where no such person has been appointed, the local authority itself can appoint someone to deal with the claim (*SI 1987 No 1971, reg 73*)).

Where a person who is not liable to make payments for a property makes a claim because the person who is actually liable to make those payments no longer lives in the property, his or her claim may be accepted, provided that it is reasonable to treat him or her as liable, in order that he or she can continue to occupy the dwelling as his or her home (*SI 1987 No 1971, reg 6*).

This could arise, for example, where a claimant's partner was the tenant of the property, but they have separated and the tenant has left the accommodation, which was also the claimant's home; or where the claimant has lived in the property as his or her home and the legal tenant has died, or is in hospital, residential care or prison, etc.

Where the claimant is a joint tenant with another person who is not the claimant's spouse or partner, entitlement to Housing Benefit will be assessed on the claimant's share of that joint liability.

Date of claim

8.24 A claim for Housing Benefit can be made up to 13 weeks before the date of occupation. All claims must be made in writing (*SI 1987 No 1971, reg 72*).

Generally, the date of claim is the date on which the authority first receives the claim form (or a letter asking to claim Housing Benefit) from the claimant. Claims can be made either by completion of an application form or a letter of application. If it receives a letter of application, the local authority will normally send the claimant an application form. If this is returned within four weeks of the date when the initial letter of application was received, the earlier date is normally treated as the date of claim (see **APPENDIX A**).

People who claim Income Support or income-based Jobseeker's Allowance get a combined HB/CTB form (HCTB1) with their claim pack for that benefit. They return the completed form to the local authority. People claiming Pension Credit are asked whether they also want to claim Housing Benefit, and if they do, they are sent a claim form by the local authority.

When a person has made a successful claim for Income Support or income-based Jobseeker's Allowance, provided he makes a claim for Housing Benefit within four weeks of that claim, he will be entitled to Housing Benefit from his first day of entitlement to Income Support/income-based Jobseeker's Allowance.

Where a claimant has made an unsuccessful claim for Income Support, income-based Jobseeker's Allowance or Guarantee Credit, then the date of claim will be the date the claim for Housing Benefit is received by the Housing Benefit department or the DWP, whichever is earlier.

In each case Housing Benefit will normally be payable from the Monday following the date of receipt of the claim by the relevant authority. For example, for a claim received on Thursday 6 March, Housing Benefit will be payable from Monday 10 March.

Where the claimant becomes liable to pay rent for the dwelling occupied as the home in the week in which the claim is made (or treated as made), he or she is entitled to benefit from that week. For example, for a claim received on Thursday 6 March, where the claimant is liable to pay rent from Monday 3 March, Housing Benefit will be payable from Monday 3 March.

If the claim is from a recipient of Income Support, income-based Jobseeker's Allowance or Guarantee Credit who has a new liability to pay rent on a dwelling which he or she occupies as his or her home, then provided that the claim is received by one of the appropriate authorities within four weeks of the claimant first becoming liable, Housing Benefit will be payable from the first date of liability.

Further information required or form not fully completed

8.25   Once a claim form is received, the authority may request further information in writing from the claimant, for example proof of rent and income details, details of non-dependants, capital, etc, or it may return the form because it has not been signed or fully completed. The local authority should be reasonable in the information it requests. For example, it would not be reasonable to expect a claimant to supply their last five payslips if they have just started work. The claimant should provide the requested information or the completed form within four weeks of the date of the request. The local authority may allow longer than four weeks if it considers this reasonable. Provided that the authority receives the information or the form within this period, the date of claim will be the date on which the application was treated as having been made (see **8.24** above).

A claimant is expected to provide a national insurance number with their claim, unless they are living in a hostel.

If the claimant does not provide the required information or the completed form within this period, the local authority may take one of the following courses of action.

It may decide to treat the claim as 'defective'. As no decision has been made the claimant has no right of appeal.

Alternatively, the Housing Benefit office will make a decision in respect of that claim in the absence of the evidence. In most cases this will result in an unfavourable decision. The claimant must be notified of this decision, and has a right of appeal.

If the required information is provided late (outside of the four-week time limit) the Housing Benefit department will make a new decision. If it does not consider it reasonable to allow extra time, then the effective date of the new decision will be the Monday following the receipt of that further information. The Housing Benefit department must also issue this decision in writing to the claimant explaining the right of appeal.

If the claimant provides the missing information after the four-week time limit and the Housing Benefit department has not allowed any extra time, he or she may request, in writing, that the claimed is backdated. He or she will have to show continuous good cause for not having provided that information within the original four-week time limit (see **8.59** below).

Rapid reclaim

8.26 Where claimants are reclaiming Housing Benefit within 12 weeks of the ending of a previous Housing Benefit claim, they can complete a shortened claim form provided:

- they are also making a rapid reclaim for Income Support or income-based Jobseekers Allowance; and

- they are entitled to this benefit; and

- their circumstances have not changed.

Local authorities can allow rapid reclaim in cases where the claimant is reclaiming contribution-based (but not income-based) Jobseekers Allowance.

Decision

8.27 The authority is required to make a decision in respect of a claim within 14 days (or as soon as is reasonably practicable) of the receipt of a claim and all the information and evidence required to carry out that assessment.

For rent allowance claims, if the local authority is not able to make a decision within 14 days and this is not due to any failure on the part of the claimant (eg the local authority did not request the information or it has a backlog of claims) then it is obliged to make an interim payment on account.

Decisions are also made during a claim, for example when circumstances change. Most decisions are appealable to a tribunal (see **8.80**). In addition, a decision may be revised or superseded (see **8.60**).

Notification

8.28 The authority is required to notify the person affected of a decision in writing within 14 days of that determination, or as soon thereafter as possible (*SI 1987 No 1971, reg 77, Sch 6*). A person affected includes the claimant, an appointee and a landlord to whom payments of benefit are made directly.

The Housing Benefit Regulations list the information that must be included in notification letters. Depending on the circumstances of the individual claim, this should include:

- the weekly eligible rent;

- the amount deducted for fuel;

- the amount and category of any deductions for non-dependants living in the house;

- the amount of benefit to which the claimant is entitled;

- the claimant's duty to notify of a change of circumstances;

- details of any assessment of income and how it is calculated;

- details of the applicable amount and how it is calculated;

- where the claimant receives the Savings Credit, but not the Guarantee Credit, of Pension Credit, the amount of any savings and benefits for children taken into account; and the amount of any income and capital notified to the local authority by the DWP which has been taken into account;

- the amount and date from which benefit is to be paid, where it is paid direct to the landlord;

- confirmation of the landlord's duty to notify the authority of any changes in circumstances known to him;

- the claimant's or landlord's right to request a written statement of reasons for the decision and time limit for doing so; and

- the claimant's or landlord's right to request an appeal and the time limit for doing so.

Where the claimant or person affected (this includes the claimant, an appointee and the landlord where payments of benefit are made directly to the landlord) requests, in writing, a written statement of any matter included in the determination, the authority must send a written statement within 14 days of the request, or as soon as possible thereafter. Days between the date of the request for a statement of reasons and the date on which it is supplied are ignored in calculating the time limit for an appeal.

Where the request is made by someone other than the claimant (eg a solicitor, welfare rights officer, etc), such requests should either be signed by the claimant or be made by a person whom the claimant has authorised to make such representations (SI 1987 No 1971, reg 77).

Benefit period

8.29 Benefit was until recently paid for a fixed period, not exceeding 60 weeks, after which the claimant had to reclaim. For those aged 60 or over who are not claiming Income Support or income-based Jobseekers Allowance, benefit periods were abolished from 6 October 2003. For those under that age, benefit periods were abolished from 5 April 2004. A claimant is obliged to report changes of circumstances but will no longer be expected to renew a claim after a certain period has elapsed (*The Housing Benefit and Council Tax Benefit (Abolition of Benefit Periods) Amendment Regulations 2004, SI 2004 No 14*).

Part III: How Housing Benefit is calculated

8.30 Where the claimant receives Income Support, income-based Jobseekers Allowance, or Guarantee Credit, they are entitled to Housing Benefit consisting of the full amount of their eligible rent. Where this is not the case, the following calculation must be carried out. (*SI 1987 No 1971, regs 16, 17, Sch 2*).

Applicable amount

8.31 A claimant's Housing Benefit is calculated by first of all working out the applicable amount. For those aged under 60, this is made up of personal allowances and premiums.

PERSONAL ALLOWANCES

8.32 Personal allowances are amounts intended to cover a person's day-to-day living expenses (eg food, fuel, clothing, etc). These amounts are worked out on a fixed scale depending on age and circumstances.

For those aged 60–64, there are higher applicable amounts which reflect the appropriate minimum guarantee calculated for the individual or couple under the Pension Credit scheme. For those aged 65 or more, the applicable amount also includes the maximum Savings Credit to which a single person or couple is entitled, to ensure that they are not penalised by claiming Savings Credit.

There are additional personal allowances paid in respect of dependent children. Since April 2003, there is only one rate for both children (generally under 16s) and 'young persons' (generally 16 to 19 years old for whom Child Benefit is still payable). Unlike other means-tested benefits, the additions for children in the applicable amounts will not be replaced by the Child Tax Credit.

PREMIUMS

8.33 Premiums are additional amounts which will be allocated to claimants with specific circumstances relating to family, age, disability, etc. They are allocated in addition to personal allowances.

Family

8.34 This is paid to any family with a child or children for whom they claim Child Benefit. Lone parents who have received Housing Benefit or Council Tax Benefit continuously since April 1998 receive a higher rate of the Family Premium. There is only one premium payable regardless of the number of children. This is always paid in addition to any other premium.

Disabled child

8.35 This premium is payable for each child who is blind or who receives Disability Living Allowance, and is only paid if the child has less than £3,000 capital. This is always paid in addition to any other premium.

Pensioner premiums

8.36 With effect from 6 October 2003, there are no pensioner premiums included in the calculation of housing benefit for people aged 60 or over. This is because entitlement to Housing Benefit is determined by reference to the more generous Pension Credit rules. For details, see below at **8.42**.

Disability

8.37 This is payable if the claimant or his or her partner is aged under 60 and:

(a)   either the claimant or the claimant's partner is registered blind;

(b)   either of them has an invalid carriage, car or private car allowance from the DWP;

(c)   either of them receives Attendance Allowance, the long-term or the short-term higher rate of Incapacity Benefit, Disability Living Allowance, Working Tax Credit (including a disability element) or Severe Disablement Allowance (for themselves); or

(d)   the claimant (but not their partner) has been incapable of work for at least 52 weeks.

There is one rate payable for single people and a higher rate for couples. Only one premium is payable even if both partners qualify. If the claimant is also entitled to the bereavement premium then he or she will receive whichever premium is the higher.

Enhanced disability

8.38 This premium is payable if the claimant, their partner, (aged under 60), or any child receives the highest rate of the care component of Disability Living Allowance, unless:

- the DLA is paid for a child who has capital in excess of £3,000; or

- the claimant (or in the case of a couple, both members) has been in hospital for more than 52 weeks.

This is always paid in addition to any other premium provided that these conditions are fulfilled.

Severe disability

8.39 This is payable to a single claimant who is severely disabled, provided that:

- he or she is receiving the middle or higher rate Disability Living Allowance care component (for him or herself); and

- he or she is defined as living alone; and

- no one is receiving Carer's Allowance (previously known as Invalid Care Allowance) for him or her.

'Living alone' means there are no non-dependants over the age of 18 living in the house (non-dependants who are registered blind or who get certain disability-related benefits are not counted). Any boarders with a liability to make payments to the claimant on a commercial basis will also be ignored.

If both partners in a couple fulfil all three conditions, they qualify for the double rate.

If both partners in a couple fulfil the first two conditions but only one fulfils the third, they will receive the single rate.

If the claimant (note it must be the claimant) fulfils all three conditions and their partner is registered blind, they will receive the single rate.

This premium is always paid in addition to any other premium.

Where the claimant or their partner is aged 60 or over, the same conditions give entitlement to an additional amount for severe disability as part of their applicable amount for Housing Benefit. Entitlement also arises where the benefit claimed is Attendance Allowance rather than Disability Living Allowance.

Carer

8.40   This is payable if the claimant or their partner gets Carer's Allowance (previously known as Invalid Care Allowance) or would be entitled to Carer's Allowance but is getting another benefit instead.

It is always payable in addition to any other premium. Couples will receive one carer premium if only one of them fulfils the conditions; if they both do, they will receive two.

Where the claimant or their partner is aged 60 or over, the same conditions give entitlement to an additional amount for a carer as part of their applicable amount for Housing Benefit.

Bereavement

8.41   This is payable to single claimants who:

- on 9 April 2001 had reached the age of 55, but were still under 60;

- had received bereavement allowance for a husband or wife who died on or after 9 April 2001, and

- claimed Housing Benefit or Council Tax Benefit as a single person within eight weeks of the last day on which they were entitled to a bereavement allowance.

Entitlement to a bereavement premium continues provided that the person is still claiming Housing Benefit or Council Tax Benefit as a single person and that there are no breaks in their entitlement to these benefits of more than eight weeks.

If the claimant is also entitled to the disability premium then he or she will receive whichever premium is the higher.

Applicable amounts for pensioners

8.42   A person aged 60 or over, or a couple one of whom is aged 60 or over, who are being paid Guarantee Credit is automatically passported on to the maximum amount of Housing Benefit and no calculation is necessary.

A person aged 60–64, or a couple one of whom is aged 60–64, who is not receiving Guarantee Credit will have an applicable amount which consists of their appropriate minimum guarantee. This consists of the standard minimum guarantee for a single person or couple, as appropriate, plus additional amounts where the person is a carer (see **8.40**) or is severely disabled (see **8.39**). The amounts of the additional payments are the same as for those premiums.

A person aged 65 or above, or a couple one of whom is aged 65 or above, also has an applicable amount consisting of their appropriate minimum guarantee, together with the maximum amount of savings credit payable (£15.50 for a single person, £20.25 for a couple).

Income

EARNED INCOME

8.43   The second step in calculating Housing Benefit is to work out the claimant's (and any partner's) income. The amount of earned income taken into account is the gross income, less tax, National Insurance and 50% of pension contributions (*SI 1987 No 1971, regs 28, 29, 30, 31, 36, Sch 3*).

The amount is usually assessed on earned income received for the period immediately preceding the week in which the claim is treated as having been made. The assessment period will be as follows.

- Paid weekly – the earnings will be assessed over the preceding five weeks.

- Paid monthly – the earnings will be assessed over the preceding two months.

- Earnings fluctuate – the assessment period will be any preceding period which may be representative of the claimant's earnings, determined at the authority's discretion.

- Where the claimant has not worked for the prescribed period, the assessment can be carried out on estimated income.

HOW INCOME IS CALCULATED

8.44   Income includes any of the following:

- earnings;

- other income, including maintenance and other benefits; and

- tariff income from capital.

Certain amounts are disregarded from earned income, as follows:

- The first £20 of earnings is disregarded where the claimant is aged 60 or over and eight weeks prior to reaching the age of 60 he or she qualified for a disability premium.

- The first £20 of earnings is also disregarded where the claimant qualifies for a disability premium or carer premium.

- If the claimant is a lone parent, the first £25 of the claimant's earned income is disregarded provided they are not also claiming Income Support or income-based Jobseekers Allowance.

- In all other cases, for single claimants the first £5 of earned income is disregarded, and for couples the first £10 is disregarded.

Child care costs

8.45 Some parents who are working may be entitled to disregard certain amounts of child care costs from their income. The amount of the disregard is up to £175 a week in child care costs where there is one child under the age of 15 (or 16 if the child is either registered blind or receiving Disability Living Allowance) or up to £300 a week where there are two or more children under the age of 15 (or 16 for any child who is either registered blind or receiving Disability Living Allowance).

The child care disregard from earned income is applied where child care costs are paid to an organisation or registered childminder, and where either the claimant is a lone parent, or the claimant is one of a couple and both members of the couple are working or one member is working and the other is incapacitated (*SI 1987 No 1971, regs 21, 21A*).

Disregard for those working for more than 30 hours

8.46 There is a further disregard from earnings for certain people working 30 hours a week or more. This rule applies only where the claimant (and their partner, if any) is aged under 60 or is receiving Income Support or income-based Jobseekers Allowance.

The sum of £14.50 is disregarded from the claimant's earnings where the claimant or their partner works for 30 hours or more per week and:

- they attract the 30-hour element in the assessment of Working Tax Credit; or

- they receive the family premium and, if a couple, work a total of 30 hours per week between them, with at least one working 16 hours or more per week; or

- if they do not receive the family premium, the claimant or their partner is aged at least 25 and works an average of 30 hours or more a week; or

- the claimant (or their partner) works at least 30 hours per week, and their applicable amount includes the disability or higher pensioner premium; and (if the claim is from a couple) the partner for whom the premium is awarded must work for 16 hours or more per week.

Other income

8.47 Any award of Attendance Allowance or Disability Living Allowance is disregarded (*SI 1987 No 1971, reg 33, Sch 4*).

Maintenance

8.48 Where Housing Benefit includes a family premium, the first £15 per week of any maintenance payment received is disregarded.

See *Schedules 3* and *4* to *SI 1987 No 1971* for full details of all other disregarded income.

Capital

8.49 [*SI 1987 No 1971, regs 37–45, Sch 5*]

If the claimant's (and any partner's) total savings are assessed at more than £3,000 for claimants under the age of 60 and £6,000 where the claimant or any partner is aged 60 and over, then a tariff income will be applied in respect of these savings. For those under 60, this tariff income is assessed at £1 per week for every £250 (or part) by which the claimant's capital exceeds £3,000. Where the claimant or their partner is over 60, the tariff income is assessed at £1 per week for every £500 (or part) by which the capital exceeds £6,000 (*SI 1987 No 1971, reg 37; SI 2002 No 1792, reg 15(6)*).

Note: There is no capital cut-off rule for those over 60 receiving Guarantee Credit (see **8.4**).

DISREGARDED CAPITAL

8.50 Certain types of capital can be totally disregarded so that they do not come into the calculation at all. These are listed in full in *Schedule 5* to *SI 1987 No 1971*, but the most important of them are as follows.

- The dwelling occupied as the claimant's home, regardless of its value.

- The value of premises purchased by the claimant that he intends to occupy as his or her home within 26 weeks or such longer period as may be needed to obtain possession.

- The sale proceeds of any previous home of the claimant that he or she intends to use to buy a new home within 26 weeks or such longer period as may be needed to complete the purchase.

- Any property occupied by a partner or relative of the claimant or his or her family as their home, where that person is either over 60 or incapacitated; or a former partner of the claimant from whom the claimant is neither estranged nor divorced, or from whom he or she is estranged or divorced but who is a lone parent.

- The assets of any business owned wholly or partly by the self-employed claimant, so long as the business is still going. If the business ceases, the assets can continue to be disregarded for a reasonable period to allow for sale.

- Any arrears of benefit but only for 52 weeks from receipt. Arrears of benefit of £5,000 or more which were caused by official error are disregarded indefinitely provided Housing Benefit or Council Tax Benefit remains in payment continuously.

- Money received (for example under an insurance policy) for the purpose of replacing, or repairing damage to, the claimant's home or personal possessions, or any loan or other sum acquired for essential repairs or improvements to the home. For those receiving Pension Credit, or aged 60 or above and not in receipt of Income Support or income-based Jobseekers Allowance, the disregard is for one year or until the end of the assessed income period, if that is longer; for other claimants, the disregard lasts for 26 weeks or such longer period as is reasonable.

- Any personal possessions of the claimant except those acquired by the claimant with the intention of reducing his or her capital for the purpose of obtaining benefit or increased benefit. For example, if a claimant spends £10,000 on a diamond ring for his wife and then claims benefit, the ring is unlikely to be disregarded.

- Damages recovered for personal injury, which have been placed in trust.

- The surrender value of an insurance policy.

- Where payment of capital is being made by instalments, the right to receive any outstanding instalments, but only where the claimant and their partner, if any, is aged under 60, or is claiming Income Support or income-based Jobseekers Allowance.

- Any Social Fund payment.

CAPITAL TAKEN INTO ACCOUNT

8.51 If the capital does not fall within any of the disregards set out in the schedules to the regulations, the next question is whether it is of such a nature that it has to be taken into account. Capital includes all assets of any kind owned by the claimant and will thus include money saved in the home, bank or building society accounts, premium bonds, stocks and shares, unit trusts, items of value such as paintings, stamp collections etc. Also included will be items such as debts or other choses in action which have a market value and can be sold, even though they may not be payable until some future date. For example, in *R(SB)31/83* the claimant sold a house and left £4,000 outstanding on a private mortgage to be redeemed in six months time. It was held that the mortgage had a value which must be taken into account as a capital resource.

Personal possessions such as wedding rings, clothes, ornaments, etc are disregarded as stated above unless they have clearly been purchased in order to reduce capital.

Ownership

8.52 Only capital which is beneficially owned by the claimant or the claimant's partner is taken into account. If the claimant holds property as a trustee, whether the trust is formal or informal, it should not be held to be part of his or her capital resources.

Money held by another for the account of, or for the benefit of, the claimant will be counted. Therefore, money held by a solicitor or any other third party will be capital owned by the claimant if the claimant can call for it to be transferred to him or her.

If the claimant transfers a share in the matrimonial home to a child of the family as part of a divorce settlement, that will be treated as a capital resource belonging to the child which, depending upon valuation, might bar a subsequent claim by that child for any means-tested benefit unless it can be disregarded (for example because the child is living there).

Valuation

8.53 Capital is to be valued at its current market or surrender value less:

- a fixed amount of 10% where any expenses are incurred in the sale; and

- the amount of any incumbrance (ie mortgage or other charge) secured upon it.

(SI 1987 No 1971, reg 41(a))

The value of any property owned but not occupied by the claimant will be ignored for up to six months if the claimant:

- has left the property following the breakdown of a marriage or other relationship;

- has sought legal advice or commenced legal proceedings with a view to occupying the property as his or her home;

- is taking reasonable steps to dispose of the property;

- is carrying out essential repairs or renovations in order to occupy the property as his or her home;

- has received a payment of compensation in respect of a damaged or destroyed property which is intended to be used for repairs;

- has sold the home and intends to use the proceeds to purchase another home for personal occupation;

- has obtained money for the express purpose of essential repairs and improvements to the home;

- has deposited money with a housing association as a condition of occupying a home;

- is a local authority tenant and has obtained a grant to buy the home or to carry out essential repairs or alterations to the home.

In the last three cases, the disregard does not apply where the claimant or their partner is aged 60 or over and is not receiving Income Support or income-based Jobseekers Allowance.

Although the above disregards are generally applied for only six months, there is discretion to extend them for longer periods if it is reasonable to do so. At the end of the period they must be taken into account in full when assessing the claimant's capital.

Notional capital

8.54 As well as actual capital, notional capital affects a person's benefit entitlement (*SI 1987 No 1971, reg 43*).

Notional capital is capital which the claimant does not actually possess but is deemed to possess. Subject to certain exceptions, a claimant is treated as possessing capital of which he or she has deprived him or herself for the purpose of securing entitlement to benefit.

Two matters must be established. The first is that there has been an actual deprivation, and the second is that such deprivation was for the purpose of securing entitlement or increased entitlement to benefit.

Before the claimant can be shown to have deprived him or herself of an asset it must be established that they owned it. If it is established that the claimant owned the asset, it is then for the claimant to show what has happened to it. If no satisfactory explanation is forthcoming, then it is likely that he or she will be held still to own it, and the amount will form part of their capital.

So if, for example, it is shown that the claimant has recently received a payment of £10,000, and apart from £2,000 spent on a car there is no satisfactory explanation of where the rest went, the claimant is treated as still having capital of £8,000.

If it is shown that there has in fact been deprivation (which includes not only giving away but also exchanging, for example, goods for a cash sum), the question then arises as to the claimant's purpose, and of course here there are obvious difficulties. Few claimants are likely to admit to a deprivation for the purpose of securing an entitlement to benefit, so it is necessary for the purpose to be inferred from the surrounding circumstances. It is for the local authority to show deprivation and purpose, not for the claimant to refute it.

Diminishing capital

8.55 Where a claimant is fixed with a sum of notional capital, it is not the case that he or she is deprived of benefit for ever. There is a formula for reducing notional capital over a period of time. The theory is that the claimant will spend part of the capital each week in order to live, and so the capital will steadily diminish (*SI 1987 No 1971, reg 43A*).

For example, where a claimant is paying more rent because the notional capital rule prevents him or her from receiving Housing Benefit, then the claimant is treated as spending some of the notional capital on rent. This will therefore diminish the amount of notional capital which the claimant has. Where the claimant does not qualify for any other means-tested benefit because he or she has too much capital, then the amount of that means-tested benefit which he or she would have been awarded but for the capital will also diminish the capital, as in theory the claimant would have to subsidise living expenses from the capital.

An initial assessment of diminishing capital would not have to be carried out until the claimant makes a further claim for benefit at least 26 weeks after the initial assessment. However, after this point, the diminishing capital rule should be applied at intervals of not less than 13 weeks where so requested by the claimant.

Assessment of entitlement

8.56   [*SI 1987 No 1971, regs 61–64*]

First work out the claimant's weekly eligible rent (normally actual rent less any ineligible service charges).

Assessment of weekly rent

8.57   Where the claimant's rent falls to be paid weekly, provided there are no rent-free periods, the rent used to assess Housing Benefit is normally the actual rent less any service or other charges not eligible for Housing Benefit.

Where rent is paid four weekly, then the four-weekly rent figure is divided by four to give a weekly rent (*SI 1987 No 1971, reg 69*).

Where rent is paid monthly, the local authority will usually calculate a weekly rent as follows: the rent is multiplied by 12, divided by 365 (or 366) days, and multiplied by 7 to give a weekly rent.

> ## Example
>
> Rent of £500 per month × 12 = £6,000 ÷ 365 = £16.44 × 7 = £115.07 per week

Housing Benefit is not payable for rent-free periods.

Entitlement to Housing Benefit for claimants with rent-free periods is calculated differently. For the periods that rent is payable their applicable amount, income, minimum amount payable, non-dependant deductions and amenity deductions are increased by a factor to ensure that the claimant does not receive more benefit than he should during the rest of the year as a result of having rent-free weeks.

Where rent is paid weekly or in multiples of a week the factor is the number of rent weeks in the year (52/53), divided by the number of weeks for which rent is actually payable. Where rent is paid monthly the factor is the number of days in the rent year (365/366) divided by the number of days for which rent is actually payable.

Note: The factor is *not* applied to the rent. The term 'rent-free periods' does not include cases where the landlord has waived liability in respect of works or repairs carried out by the tenant.

The next step in the calculation is to find the difference between the claimant's assessed income and his or her applicable amount.

If the income is less than the applicable amount then 100% of the eligible rent will be paid in Housing Benefit (less any non-dependant deductions).

If the income is greater than the applicable amount then the next step is to find 65% of the difference between the applicable amount and the income (*SI 1987 No 1971, reg 62*).

The resulting figure is deducted from the eligible rent less any non-dependant deductions.

The claimant will have to pay any shortfall.

The minimum Housing Benefit that can be paid is 50p per week.

Example

The claimant pays rent of £320.00 per month, all of which is eligible rent:

£320 × 12 = £3,840 ÷ 365 = £10.52 × 7 = £73.64 per week eligible rent (see **8.57** above).

The claimant is a lone parent earning £510 per month net (£117.69 per week) for working 32 hours per week. She receives £25 per week in maintenance and £150 per week in Tax Credits, in addition to Child Benefit of £39.80. She has three dependent children aged 5, 11 and 16. Her claim is made in June 2004. Her eldest child attained the age of 16 in August 2003 and is staying on at school. She also pays £35 per week for after-school care to an organised club.

Applicable amount	£	Income	£
Personal allowance	56.20	Earnings	117.69
Family premium	22.20	*Less* disregard	25.00
Child aged 5	43.88	*Less* child care	35.00
Child aged 11	43.88	*Less* 30-hour disregard	14.50
Child aged 16	43.88	Income from earnings (less disregards)	43.19
		Tax Credits	150.00
		Maintenance	25.00
		Less disregard	15.00
		Child Benefit	39.80
Total	£210.04	Total	£242.99

Difference = £32.55 (£242.99 − £210.04) × 65% = £21.16

Maximum eligible rent: rent £73.64 less £21.16 = £52.48 per week Housing Benefit.

Non-dependants

8.58 If there are any non-dependants living in a claimant's home, ie non-tenants over the age of 18 (children, relatives or friends), deductions will be made under *regulation 63* of *SI 1987 No 1971* from any award of Housing Benefit in respect of these non-dependants at the following rates. This does not apply where the claimant is registered blind, or receives Attendance Allowance or any of the care components of Disability Living Allowance.

Aged 18 or over and in remunerative work	£
Gross income £332 or more per week	47.75
Gross income £258–£321.99 per week	43.50
Gross income £194–£257.99 per week	38.20
Gross income £150–£193.99 per week	23.35
Gross income £101–£149.99 per week	17.00
Gross income less than £101 per week	7.40
Others 18+ and not in remunerative work or 25+ and on Income Support or income-based JSA	7.40

Note: In this context 'remunerative work' means working an average of 16 hours or more per week.

If a claimant has not given details on his application form of a non-dependant's income, then the Housing Benefit officer must apply the highest non-dependant deduction. It is therefore in the claimant's interest to supply accurate information if it is obtainable.

If the non-dependant is:

- under 18;

- on a youth training scheme;

- in full-time education;

- a full-time student;

- a person under 25 receiving Income Support or income-based Jobseeker's Allowance;

- someone who has been in hospital for more than 52 weeks; or

- a prisoner,

then no non-dependant deduction will be made for that non-dependant.

Where the non-dependant is one of a couple, there is a single deduction based on their joint weekly income.

If the claimant is a joint tenant, then a non-dependant deduction will usually be equally apportioned between the number of joint tenants, unless the non-dependant clearly 'belongs' to only one or some of the joint tenants.

Backdating

8.59   Benefit can only be backdated for a maximum of 52 weeks from the date the request for backdating was made.

In order to make a successful claim for backdating, the claimant must show that he or she has continuous good cause for not having claimed for all the time from the date that the claim should have been made until the date that the application for backdated benefit is received by the authority (*SI 1987 No 1971, reg 72(15)*).

If, therefore, a claimant wants benefit to be backdated for six months, there will have to be good cause shown for the whole period up to the date of the application for backdating. If good cause is shown for (say) the last three months of the period, benefit can be backdated for three months but not for six. On the other hand, if there is no good cause covering the period immediately leading up to the application (for example, the claimant was ill for the first three months of the period) the local authority cannot backdate at all.

A claimant who is unaware of his or her right to claim cannot usually show good cause for a late claim as claimants are expected to make enquiries about their entitlement. If, however, the claimant is misled by enquiries, then good cause will be shown. Some examples of good cause are that the claimant was too ill (mentally or physically) to make a claim and no one could claim on their behalf, or the claimant was not aware that a partner had not made a claim, or the claimant was left to understand that another organisation (such as the Citizens Advice Bureau or a solicitor) would register a claim.

Part IV: Changes in entitlement

Revisions and supersessions

8.60   Where the local authority changes its decision it can do this in one of two ways – by revising its original decision, or by superseding it.

- *Revision* – the local authority changes its decision from the original date, replacing the original decision.

- *Supersession* – the local authority changes its decision from a date later than the original date, eg because the claimant's circumstances have changed since the original decision was made.

Revisions

8.61 Where a claimant (or a person affected by the decision) is not happy with a decision made by the authority in respect of Housing Benefit, that person can request a revision or an appeal. The request must be in writing, and the written request must be received by the local authority within one month of the date on which notification of the decision was sent out.

While appeals should normally be signed by the applicant, a request for a revision may be signed by someone acting on the claimant's behalf, such as an advice worker or a solicitor.

The authority should then carry out a review within 14 days, or as soon thereafter as is possible, and a further written decision should be issued to the applicant (*SI 1987 No 1971 Sch 6*).

If the claimant (or person affected by the decision) appeals, the authority must look at the claim again, and if they can change their decision in favour of the applicant, they must do so. If they cannot change their decision in favour of the applicant, they must pass the application over to the Appeals Service for processing for an appeal tribunal (see **8.80**ff below).

If the claimant (or person affected by the decision) requests written reasons for a decision, the time limit of one month will not include any time taken by the Housing Benefit department in providing these written reasons.

Example

The Housing Benefit department makes a decision on 11 July and sends this to the claimant on the same date. The initial date by which the request for a revision must be received is 11 August.

The claimant requests written reasons for the decision. The request is received by the department on 26 July. The department takes ten days to provide the written reasons.

The date that the request for revision must be received by the Housing Benefit department is now 21 August, ie the department must extend the time limit by ten days because this is how long it took to provide the written reasons.

Where the applicant is not happy with the outcome of a revision, he or she can appeal. The appeal must be in writing and signed by the claimant, and must be received by the local authority within one month of the issue of the revision decision (see **8.80ff** below).

Late applications for revision

8.62 A late application for a revision may be made in certain circumstances, but must be made within 13 months of the date of the decision in respect of which the application for revision is made (ie one month from the date of initial decision plus a 12-month extension).

Applications must be made in writing by the person affected, and must contain the grounds for the late application and identify the decision to which the late application relates.

An extension of time can only be allowed where the Housing Benefit department is satisfied that:

● it is reasonable to grant the late application;

● the application has a reasonable chance of success; and

● there are special circumstances which meant that it was not practicable for the application for revision to be made in time.

In deciding whether it is reasonable to grant the late application, the Housing Benefit department must consider the time which has elapsed since the expiry of the time limit for an application, and how compelling the special circumstances are.

The department cannot take account of the applicant's misunderstanding or ignorance of the law, regulations or time limits, nor of the fact that a more recent decision of a Commissioner or court has changed the view of what the law was understood to be at the time of the decision.

An application for an extension of time which has been refused may not be renewed.

Supersessions and changes of circumstances

8.63 Where a claimant has a change in circumstances, or in the circumstances of any member of the household, then he or she has a duty to notify the authority in writing as soon as the change is known to him or her. If a change of circumstances is not notified in time, a claimant may be overpaid or may not receive all the benefit to which he or she may otherwise be entitled.

Changes in circumstances are usually deemed to take effect from the Monday following the date of the change. Where the change is a rent increase, this takes effect from the week in which the rent increases.

If the effect of the change is disadvantageous to the claimant, the reduction in benefit takes effect from the date of the change of circumstances. (This may result in an overpayment if the claimant has delayed reporting the change.) If it is advantageous (ie the claimant's benefit will increase) it must be reported within one month of the date of the change. Otherwise benefit will be changed from the date the change was reported, unless the claimant can show 'special reasons' for the delay.

The decision resulting from the change of circumstances must be notified to the claimant in writing. He or she then has the right of appeal.

Landlords who are receiving direct payments of rent allowance also have a duty to report changes in their tenants' circumstances which they 'might reasonably be expected to know might affect the claimant's right to, the amount of or the receipt of housing benefit' (*SI 1987 No 1971, reg 75*). Where the Housing Benefit department has been alerted in writing by the landlord to a suspected overpayment of rent allowance and it decides that the landlord has not contributed to the overpayment, the overpayment is not recoverable from the landlord (*SI 1987 No 1971, reg 101(1)*).

Overpayments

8.64   [*SI 1987 No 1971, regs 98–105*]

Overpayments of Housing Benefit arise where a change in circumstances has not been reported promptly or the local authority has not acted upon the reported change. In most circumstances the Housing Benefit regulations require local authorities to try to recover these overpayments.

New rules introduced in October 1997 have allowed recovery of overpayments from ongoing payments made to a landlord in respect of other tenants who have not been overpaid.

The main types of overpayment are as follows.

- *Claimant error/fraud* – the claimant does not include relevant information on the claim form or delays reporting a change in circumstances. This may be a genuine mistake or may be a deliberate withholding of information. Depending on the circumstances, the local authority may decide to treat the overpayment as 'claimant error' or 'fraud'. In both cases, the local authority will decide if the overpayment is recoverable, whether they are going to recover it and from whom. The local authority may decide to take further action (eg prosecution or sanction) if they consider that the overpayment is due to fraud.

- *Local authority error* – the local authority has made a mistake or has failed to act on information received in respect of a claim at an appropriate time. All overpayments are recoverable from the claimant or the landlord unless the overpayment is a local authority error and it was not reasonable for the claimant to know at the time in question that he was being overpaid.

Very often there is a combination of reasons for the overpayments, for example, on 4 July the authority receives notification from the local DWP office that the claimant ceased to claim Income Support on 8 June. However, the authority fails to do anything with this information until 14 July. In this case the overpayment which has arisen from the period up to 4 July will be due to claimant error/fraud, as it is the claimant's responsibility to report changes in circumstances.

The overpayment which has arisen for the periods from 5 July to 14 July may be classified as local authority error. The local authority may decide to recover the whole overpayment or just the first part, depending on whether the claimant could have reasonably known he was being overpaid.

The regulations now provide for offsetting of notional entitlement to benefit against overpaid benefit. This means that if there has been an overpayment of benefit and the authority is able to establish sufficient information to determine what benefit the claimant would have been entitled to had he notified the authority, the authority must offset any overpayment against notional benefit entitlement.

For example, the claimant was in receipt of Income Support and starts work, but does not tell the authority. The authority then becomes aware of this, and is provided with the claimant's proof of income from the time he started work. The old benefit paid was £50 per week but the reassessment is £10 per week. This means that £10 per week will be offset against that £50 per week, therefore the overpayment to be recovered is £40 per week.

Extended payments

8.65   *[SI 1987 No 1971, reg 62A, Sch 5A]*

A claimant is eligible for an extended payment of Housing Benefit where the Secretary of State has certified to the Housing Benefit department that the claimant or their partner was entitled to Income Support or income-based Jobseeker's Allowance or Training Allowance for a continuous period of at least 26 weeks, and that entitlement has ceased in consequence of the claimant or partner having taken up employment or increased their income or their hours in that employment which is expected to last for five weeks or more (in either an employed or self-employed capacity).

Qualifying conditions

8.66 The question as to whether the claimant satisfies the qualifying conditions for the benefit or for the qualifying benefit period is a question which must be determined by the Secretary of State.

There is no scope in the regulations for the Housing Benefit department or indeed the tribunal to determine whether the claimant has satisfied this condition of entitlement to the extended payment. If the local DWP office does not confirm to the authority that the claimant has been in receipt of the relevant benefit for the prescribed period of time, then the Housing Benefit department cannot make any award of extended payment to the claimant.

Claims

8.67 To claim an extended payment, the claimant must notify the local DWP office or the local authority within four weeks of the claimant or their partner starting work. (This notification may be in any form, eg written or a phone call.) The claimant will be able to continue to receive Housing Benefit paid at the rate which he was receiving when in receipt of Income Support/income-based Jobseeker's Allowance for a continuous period of 28 days. This extended payment will be paid whether the claimant is earning £200 per week or £2,000 per week.

Discretionary Housing Payments

8.68 Discretionary Housing Payments (DHPs) are discretionary payments made from a cash limited budget. They are not housing benefit payments, and decisions on an application for DHPs do not carry a right of appeal.

A local authority can pay DHPs to anyone who:

- is entitled to Housing or Council Tax Benefit: and
- appears to need financial help in addition to their benefit.

(*CSPSSA 2000*, s 69; *Discretionary Financial Assistance Regulations 2001, SI 2001 No 1167, reg 2(1)*)

DHPs cannot be paid where the hardship is because of:

- rent or council tax for which the claimant was liable before 2 July 2001;
- ineligible service charges;
- water or sewerage charges;
- council tax, if the claimant is eligible for Housing Benefit but not for Council Tax Benefit, or is eligible for the second adult rebate of Council Tax Benefit;
- increases of rent to cover arrears of rent, or service or other charges;
- a reduced benefit direction for failing to co-operate with the Child Support Agency;
- a reduction in benefit because of leaving a job voluntarily without just cause, or being dismissed for misconduct, or failing to attend a work-focussed interview;
- suspension of benefit;
- a benefit restriction imposed by a court for failure to comply with a community penalty, or a sanction resulting from committing certain benefit offences.

It is for the local authority to decide on the amount of any payment, and how long it will be paid for. The claim procedure is a matter for the authority.

Suspending and terminating benefit

8.69 *[SI 2002 No 1002]*

The authority may suspend payments and awards of housing benefit in whole or in part where:

- there is a question relating to the claimant's entitlement to benefit, for example, where he or she has failed to supply sufficient information and evidence with the original claim;
- it appears that the decision on benefit entitlement may have to be revised or superseded;
- it appears that there may be a recoverable overpayment of benefit; or
- an appeal is pending against an appeal tribunal, Commissioner or court decision (whether it is the claimant's appeal or an appeal in a different case), and it appears that the effect of the decision subject to appeal would have an impact on the decision made in the particular case.

Restoring suspended payments

8.70 Once the authority is satisfied there are no outstanding issues that remain to be resolved and the benefit suspended is properly payable, it must restore any or all of the payments that are suspended within 14 days of the decision to make or restore the payments.

Suspending for failure to provide information and evidence

8.71 The Housing Benefit department may suspend benefit in whole or in part where a person is required to provide information and/or evidence which is reasonably required by the authority for the purpose of reaching a decision.

The following persons are required to satisfy the information provisions:

- the person whose benefit has been suspended;

- a person affected who has made an application for revision or supersession; or

- the person who has made the claim for benefit.

In suspending benefit, the authority must issue a notification to the claimant to the effect that he or she must supply the information or evidence within one month of the issue of that notification (though an extension may be awarded where the claimant is able to satisfy the Housing Benefit department that that an extension of time is reasonably required).

Where evidence is requested that either does not exist (for example, because the claimant's home has burned down and a document has been lost), or that it is impossible for the claimant to obtain (even with an extension of time), perhaps because the claimant cannot gain access to the home due to domestic violence, etc, the Housing Benefit department may reach a decision in the absence of the required evidence.

Where this is the case, the claimant must advise the Housing Benefit department that the evidence does not exist or that it is impossible for him or her to obtain it, giving as much detail as possible as to why this is the case. This must be done within one month of the request for information or evidence.

Termination for failure to provide information

8.72 Where a claimant fails to comply with any of the requirements for information, evidence or time limits, and payment of benefit has been suspended in whole (but not in part), the claimant's entitlement to the benefit claimed will be terminated from the date on which the payment was suspended.

Part V: Treated as occupying a dwelling

Temporary absence from home

8.73 Where a claimant is temporarily absent from home in certain specified circumstances (eg in prison on remand or in hospital), he or she can continue to receive Housing Benefit for up to 52 weeks. In the case of any absence which does not fall within the specified circumstances, the claimant can receive benefit for a maximum of 13 weeks. The conditions in both cases are that the claimant intends to return to the property, that it is not let or sublet during his or her absence, and that the period of absence is unlikely to exceed 13 or 52 weeks (depending on the reason for absence) (*SI 1987 No 1971, reg 5(7B), (7C), (8), (8A), (8B), (8C)*).

The absence must be continuous. Consequently, if the claimant returns home for a period exceeding 24 hours then the period of absence will start to run again (*R v Penwith District Council Housing Benefit Review ex parte Burt, 22 HLR 292*).

52 WEEKS

8.74 Claimants who can continue to receive Housing Benefit during absences of up to 52 weeks, provided their absence is not expected to exceed this period, include those who are:

- in hospital;

- providing or receiving medically approved care, or convalescing (in the UK or abroad);

- caring for a child whose parent/guardian is receiving medically approved care;

- in prison on remand;

- on a government training course;

- a student not excluded from Housing Benefit;

- away from home through fear of violence (see **8.77**).

13 WEEKS

8.75 In other cases, Housing Benefit may only be paid for a maximum of 13 weeks, where the claimant is unlikely to be away for longer than this. The Housing Benefit Regulations do not specify the reasons for absence, but these might be:

- working away from home;

- on holiday (in the UK or abroad); or

- convicted prisoner serving a sentence of 13 weeks or less.

Claimants in residential care – temporary absence from home/trial basis

8.76 Housing Benefit can be paid to a claimant who is temporarily in residential care. Where a claimant has a partner who is not in residential care, Housing Benefit will continue to be paid for the person occupying the home.

There are two categories of claimants who are treated quite differently under this rule.

- Where a claimant goes into residential care for reasons *other than* on a trial basis (for example, for a period of respite care) he or she can receive Housing Benefit for up to 52 weeks during the period of absence. Housing Benefit can only be paid in these circumstances where the claimant intends to return home within 52 weeks and the home is not occupied by another person (other than the claimant's partner) or sublet.

- Where a person goes into residential care on *a trial basis* Housing Benefit can be paid for up to 13 weeks. Housing Benefit can only be paid in these circumstances where the claimant intends to return home if the residential accommodation does not meet their needs within 13 weeks, and the home is not occupied by another person (other than the claimant's partner) or sublet.

In both cases, Housing Benefit can be paid if the claimant intends to return home within the specified period, namely 52 or 13 weeks as appropriate.

Once the claimant makes a decision not to return home, entitlement to Housing Benefit will cease.

Liable for rent on two homes

8.77   [*SI 1987 No 1971, reg 5(5)*]

Where a claimant is liable to make payments in respect of two homes, Housing Benefit can be paid for both in the following circumstances:

- For up to 52 weeks, where the claimant has moved out of one home because of a fear of violence in that home, or of violence by a former member of the family (provided the absence is reasonable and the claimant intends to return). If they do not intend to return, Housing Benefit can be paid for up to four weeks only.

- Where one member of a couple is a student and it is unavoidable that they occupy two separate dwellings.

- Where a large family has been housed by a housing authority in two separate dwellings.

- For a period not exceeding four weeks, where a claimant has moved into a new property and for some reason is still liable to pay rent for a former property, and the duplication of liability is unavoidable, he or she may be entitled to Housing Benefit on both properties.

- Where the claimant has to remain in his or her former home while the new home is being adapted to meet his or her disablement needs, or those of a member of the family. In this situation, Housing Benefit may be paid for up to four weeks on both homes.

Entitlement before moving in

8.78   [*SI 1987 No 1971, reg 5(6)*]

Housing Benefit can normally only be paid once a person has moved into a dwelling and is occupying it as his or her home. However, in the case of certain specified delays in moving, namely:

- the delay is necessary in order to adapt the property to meet the requirements of a disabled person;

- the claimant is not receiving Housing Benefit on a current property and the move to the new property has been delayed because the claimant is waiting for the outcome of a Social Fund application. The claimant must also have a child under the age of five, or must qualify for a disability premium, pensioner premium, disabled child premium or severe disability premium, or must be aged 60 or over and not be claiming Income Support or income-based Jobseekers Allowance; or

- the claimant was a hospital patient or in residential care, and it is reasonable to meet his or her rent liability before he or she moves into the property,

Housing Benefit may be awarded in respect of the new rent liability prior to moving in for a period not exceeding four weeks. The claimant must have claimed Housing Benefit before moving in, and must be liable to pay rent on the new property before moving in.

Note: This is not a payment on 'two homes'. If Housing Benefit is already being paid on the former home this regulation does not apply.

Subsidy

8.79 The local authority can claim back from central government most of the benefit it pays out.

In some circumstances it will not receive full subsidy on benefit paid, eg where the Housing Benefit department has overpaid benefit because of a local authority error it cannot get any subsidy back for the benefit it has paid. Therefore, if the overpayment is not recovered, it will cost the authority money. If the local authority decides to backdate a claim, it will receive subsidy of 50% of the backdated payment.

Part VI: Appeals

8.80 An appeal must be in writing and must be signed by the claimant. It must identify the decision appealed against.

If the Housing Benefit department is able to revise its earlier decision to the advantage of the claimant on the basis of the appeal itself and any further information or evidence which it receives, it revises the original decision and notice to that effect is issued to all persons affected.

If it is not able to revise the decision to the advantage of the appellant, it must issue a decision stating that it is unable to revise the decision and send this to the persons affected. The date of the appellant's appeal will now be the date of the Benefit department's decision not to revise.

Decisions which are advantageous to the appellant include decisions to:

- increase the amount of Housing Benefit awarded;
- reinstate suspended payments;
- lift a disqualification of benefit entitlement in whole or in part;

- reverse a decision to pay benefit to a third party; and

- reduce, or not recover, a recoverable overpayment.

Decisions against which no right of appeal lies

8.81 Most decisions made by the Housing Benefit department can be appealed to a tribunal; the main exceptions are listed below. If an appeal is made against a decision from which no appeal lies, the appeal will be struck out by the clerk of the tribunal.

Decisions made under *Part X (Claims)*, *Part XII (Payments)* and *Part XIII (Overpayments)* of *SI 1987 No 1971* carry no right of appeal to a tribunal except a decision on:

- the date of claim (*SI 1987 No 1971, reg 72(5), (11), (15), (16), (17)*);

- a payment on account of rent allowance (*SI 1987 No 1971, reg 91(3)*);

- the circumstances in which payment is to be made to the landlord (*SI 1987 No 1971, reg 93*);

- the circumstances in which payment may be made to the landlord (*SI 1987 No 1971, reg 94*);

- recoverable overpayments (*SI 1987 No 1971, reg 99*);

- a person from whom recovery may be sought (*SI 1987 No 1971, reg 101*);

- diminution of capital (*SI 1987 No 1971, reg 103*); and

- sums to be deducted in calculating a recoverable overpayment (*SI 1987 No 1971, reg 104*).

Under regulations governing claims and payments for Income Support and Jobseekers Allowance, certain decisions carry no right of appeal. A Social Security Commissioner has held that the exclusion of appeal rights is contrary to *Article 6* of the *European Convention on Human Rights*. At the time of writing, it is understood that the case is to be considered by the Court of Appeal (CIS/540/2002).

Time limits for making appeals

8.82 Appeals to the appeal tribunal must be made within one month of the issue of the decision against which the appeal is brought. However, if the appellant asks for written reasons, any time taken from the date the Housing

Benefit department receives the request for written reasons to the date that it issues those reasons will not count towards the time limit of one month.

A late appeal may be made in certain circumstances, but must in all cases be made within 13 months of the date of the decision in respect of which the appeal lies. This provision extends the prescribed time for bringing an appeal by 12 months. However, an extension of time will not be allowed unless the decision maker, or a legally qualified panel member, is satisfied that:

● if the application was granted there would be reasonable prospects of success; or

● it is in the interests of justice that the application be granted because there are special circumstances which are relevant to the application.

The late application must be as a result of those special circumstances, which must have meant that it was not practical for the application to be made within one month of the decision. The longer the time which elapses before the application for a late appeal is made, the more compelling the circumstances must be for the application to be allowed.

Special circumstances are prescribed as:

● the applicant, or a spouse or dependant of the applicant, has died or suffered serious illness;

● the applicant is not resident in the United Kingdom;

● normal postal services were disrupted; or

● there are other circumstances which are 'wholly exceptional'.

When considering the interests of justice, no account is taken of the applicant's misunderstanding or ignorance of the law, regulations or time limits, nor of the fact that a Commissioner or court have taken a different view of the law than that applied at the time of the decision. An application for an extension of time which has been refused may not be renewed.

Making an application for appeal

8.83 Applications for appeals must be made by a person affected, or a representative to whom the appellant has provided his or her written authority.

The appeal must be made in writing, by the completion and signature of a prescribed appeal form (or by a signed letter) which states:

● the claimant's or applicant's name;

- their National Insurance number;
- the date of the decision;
- the benefit that the appeal is in respect of; and
- the grounds for the appeal.

The appeal must be delivered to the Housing Benefit office which issued the decision that is the subject of the appeal.

Where an appeal is made which does not contain the information set out above, the Housing Benefit department should request the further information from the appellant by issuing a prescribed form (or a letter requesting the specific information required) which must be completed and returned to the Housing Benefit department within 14 days of being issued.

The form (or the requested information) must be forwarded with any other relevant documents to The Appeals Service. A legally qualified tribunal member will decide whether the information provided meets the relevant requirements to continue with an appeal. The legally qualified member will then issue a determination to both the appellant and the authority.

The tribunal

8.84 *CSPSSA 2000, Sch 7, para 23* provides that an 'appeal tribunal' means an appeal tribunal constituted under *Chapter I, Part I* of the *Social Security Act 1998 (SSA 1998)*.

The appeal tribunal consists of one, two or three members. The number of members will be determined by the subject matter of the appeal. Panel members may be a:

- legally qualified panel member;
- financially qualified panel member;
- medically qualified panel member; or
- member with a disability qualification.

In practice, Housing or Council Tax Benefit appeals are usually heard by a one-person 'tribunal' unless there is also a need for a financially qualified member.

Financially qualified members sit on appeals which are, in the opinion of the President of The Appeals Service, difficult, and which relate to:

- profit and loss accounts, revenue accounts or balance sheets relating to any enterprise;

- an income and expenditure account in the case of an enterprise not trading for profit; or

- the accounts of any trust fund.

This may be relevant in appeals concerning self-employed applicants who provide accounts.

All tribunals include a legally qualified panel member. This is someone who has been practising as a solicitor or barrister and is experienced in social security law.

The tribunal may require one or more experts to provide assistance in dealing with a question of fact of special difficulty. The tribunal may ask the expert to provide a written report (a copy of which will be supplied to every party), attend the hearing, give evidence, and be cross-examined.

This could include a specialist in housing law in appropriate cases involving questions of, for example, construction of leases and liability to pay rent (*SSA 1998, s 7(4)*).

PROCEDURE

8.85 Tribunal procedure is informal and is a matter for the tribunal to decide. In every case, the tribunal is likely to want to:

- read the papers provided;

- assuming the parties are attending, clarify the issues with the parties at the outset of the hearing;

- hear submissions and evidence from the parties; and

- question the parties and witnesses.

In the event of a 'paper hearing', the decision will be reached on the written information and evidence before the tribunal.

In addition, the tribunal may elect to adjourn the case to obtain further written evidence or to arrange for the attendance of a witness. It is advisable to ensure that all witnesses attend the hearing and that all relevant documents are available for inspection.

After the conclusion of the hearing, the tribunal will deliberate in private and reach a decision. This may be announced on the day or sent to the parties later. In any case, a notice of the decision must be completed, giving the tribunal's findings and decision, and the reasons for it.

ISSUES

8.86 The types of issues that a tribunal will be asked to decide vary. They include the following.

- *Questions of fact* – for example, when did the claimant tell the Housing Benefit department that he had reduced his hours of work? He says he did this on a particular date; the department says he did not. The tribunal will want to see, for example, departmental records, the system of recording personal callers and telephone callers, information provided to the claimant informing him of the requirement to notify changes in circumstances.

  Note: The fact that a local authority has a system of recording incoming telephone calls does not mean that the claimant is not telling the truth if there is no record of an incoming telephone call which the claimant alleges that he or she made: CH/4065/2001.

- *Questions of law* – what constitutes 'occupying a home' within the meaning of *SI 1987 No 1971, reg 5(1)*? Is a situation where the claimant has moved all their belongings into the property and spends some time there each day sufficient to be classed as 'occupying the home' or must the claimant also sleep in the property? The answer to the question is a matter of legal construction.

- *Questions of mixed law and fact* – Who are the legal owners of the property? It is occupied by the tenant who pays rent to the landlord. However, the tenant's name appears on the Land Registry entry as the legal owner. The answer to this question requires consideration of the legal requirements for ownership of property and a check of the relevant benefit rules for the definition of ownership of the property. Having ascertained what the law is, the tribunal would make findings of fact by:
  - examining the documentary evidence for proof of ownership or otherwise;
  - obtaining oral evidence by asking questions and taking witness statements; and
  - making a judgment as to what, on a balance of probabilities, the evidence proves so far as ownership of the property is concerned.

Before the hearing

8.87 Usually the clerk to the appeal tribunal writes to the appellant to ask whether he or she would like to have an oral or paper hearing. The case may be dealt with on the papers if the appellant agrees, or does not respond to the enquiry. The parties will be given not less than 14 days' notice in writing of the date, time and location of the appeal hearing. If the appellant does not respond to the enquiry, the appeal may proceed in the absence of the appellant, or may be struck out.

If the notice of hearing has not been given to a person to whom it should have been given, the hearing may only proceed with the consent of that person. However, a party may waive his or her right to 14 days' notice by giving notice to the clerk to that effect.

If the case has been listed for a paper hearing, the tribunal may direct that it is necessary to hold an oral hearing to enable it to reach a decision.

If a party does not turn up to the hearing, the tribunal can decide, having regard to all the circumstances including any explanation offered for the absence, to proceed with the hearing in that party's absence or give directions for the determination of the appeal.

Postponements

8.88 Before the hearing starts, a party may write to the clerk seeking a postponement stating reasons for the request. The clerk has discretion to allow such a request or may ask the legally qualified panel member to exercise his discretion.

If a request for a postponement is refused, the clerk must inform the person making the request in writing (but need not state reasons) and must put the correspondence in front of the tribunal who deals with the hearing.

The clerk or a panel member may postpone an appeal of their own motion so long as they do so before the beginning of the hearing.

Adjournments

8.89 The tribunal may adjourn the hearing at any time if a party asks it to do so or of its own motion. If the hearing is adjourned the same tribunal need not necessarily hear the resumed case, which will be a complete re-hearing. If the tribunal refuses a request for an adjournment, it may be advisable for them to state their reasons.

WITHDRAWAL

8.90 A party seeking to withdraw an appeal can do so before the hearing or at the hearing. If they do so before the hearing, they must write to the clerk and state their intention to withdraw. No order will be drawn up – the appeal is simply withdrawn. The clerk will send a notice to both parties informing them that the appeal has been withdrawn.

At the hearing

8.91 The procedure in tribunals is determined by the legally qualified member, who normally also chairs the hearing. The proceedings are normally informal and the legally qualified member may seek the views of the parties at the outset as to the sequence of events in the case.

The usual routine is as follows.

- The panel and all those present are introduced.

- The tribunal will want to ensure that the appellant has received all the papers, whether there are any further documents for the tribunal, whether or not the appellant can understand the language or requires an interpreter, and whether he or she requires assistance in the form of representation.

- The tribunal invites the representative of the authority and the appellant to add to their written submissions.

- The appellant is invited to ask questions or make statements.

- The tribunal asks questions of the appellant and any witnesses.

- Representatives are given the opportunity to ask questions of witnesses, or to make further oral submissions.

Whilst conducting all of the above, the legally qualified member must also keep a written record of the proceedings which is sufficient to summarise all the evidence taken. This record is kept for six months after the decision and any party may ask for a written copy within that period.

POWERS OF THE TRIBUNAL

8.92 The tribunal has the power to take evidence on oath or by affirmation, but it is rare to do so. Where a witness gives evidence on oath or by affirmation, he or she commits the criminal offence of perjury if he or she does not tell the truth.

The tribunal also has the power to issue a summons to compel the attendance of a witness or the production of documents. There is a requirement that 14 days' notice of such summons shall be given to anyone so summonsed.

The tribunal '… shall take into account the need to protect any matter that relates to intimate personal or financial circumstances, is commercially sensitive, consists of information communicated or obtained in confidence or concerns national security'. Those summonsed may write and ask that the summons be set aside or varied.

REPRESENTATIVES

8.93 Representatives may attend. Any party to the proceedings has the right to be present and be heard at an oral hearing. They may bring a representative who may be professionally qualified or not but who will have all the rights and powers to which the appellant is entitled. This includes: addressing the tribunal, giving evidence, calling witnesses and cross-examining other witnesses.

DISCUSSION

8.94 If the tribunal needs to discuss any question of procedure after the hearing has started it may ask all persons in the tribunal room to leave while it does so. It may also ask them to leave for the purposes of arriving at the decision on the appeal.

After the hearing

8.95 A party may request a written statement of reasons for the decision. This request must be made in writing within one month of receiving the decision notice. There is a place on the decision notice for the clerk to mark the date on which the decision was given or sent. This part of the decision notice is also important for the calculation of the time for seeking leave to appeal.

Late applications for written statements will only be granted if the panel member is satisfied that it is in the interests of justice to do so. The interests of justice will not be met unless the panel member is satisfied that:

- the applicant or a spouse or dependant of the applicant has died or suffered serious illness;

- the applicant is not resident in the UK;

- normal postal services were adversely disrupted; or

- some other special circumstances applied.

No account shall be taken of the following in deciding whether the interests of justice will be served.

- The person making the application or his representative was unaware of or misunderstood the law applicable to his case, including time limits.

- A Commissioner or court has taken a different view of the law from that previously understood and applied.

The longer the time which has elapsed after the hearing and before the request for a statement, the more compelling the special circumstances need be for the request to be allowed.

A summary of the decision will be provided by the person making it and sent to all parties. Parties then have one month to request a written statement of that decision.

Correction of accidental errors

8.96   Clerks and legally qualified panel members have the power to correct accidental errors in any decision or the record of any such decision 'at any time'. Such corrections are part of the record and written notice of such corrections must be given to all parties.

Striking out appeals

8.97   The clerk and legally qualified panel member have the power to strike out an appeal:

- if it is outside the jurisdiction of the tribunal, and the appellant has been notified that an appeal against such a decision may be struck out; or

- for want of prosecution including being out of time.

The appellant will be notified in writing if the appeal has been struck out. He or she is offered the chance to ask for it to be reinstated.

Appeals that have been struck out can be reinstated if:

- the appellant makes representations within one month of the striking out order in support of the appeal, stating why the appeal should not have been struck out and the legally qualified panel member is satisfied that there are reasonable grounds for reinstating the appeal;

● the panel member is satisfied that the appeal is not an appeal which may be struck out within *regulation 46* of the *Social Security and Child Support (Decisions and Appeals) Regulations 1999, SI 1999 No 991*; or

● the panel member is satisfied that it is not in the interests of justice to strike out the appeal.

Natural justice

8.98 There are two principles inherent in natural justice:

● no person shall be a judge in their own cause – this means that the tribunal panel should not hear a case if they know the parties or witnesses;

● a person should not be condemned unheard – all parties have the right to be heard and to cross-examine.

Also relevant to considerations of natural justice are the provisions of *Article 6* of *HRA 1998*. This provides the right to a fair and public hearing within a reasonable time by an independent and impartial tribunal established by law. *Article 6* has been held in various international courts to include:

● the right of access to a court;

● the right to a fair hearing, which includes:
   – the right to a hearing in one's presence,
   – equality of arms (ie the appellant must have the same opportunity as the local authority to prepare and present their case),
   – evidence – the admissibility of improperly obtained evidence, hearsay, and the opportunity to cross-examine witnesses,
   – freedom from self-incrimination,
   – freedom from prejudicial publicity, and
   – a reasoned judgment;

● the right to a public hearing and a public pronouncement of judgment;

● the right to a hearing within a reasonable time; and

● the right to an independent and impartial tribunal established by law.

Decisions of appeal tribunals

8.99 The principal legislation and guiding regulations referred to are as follows.

- *Social Security Act 1998.*

- *Child Support, Pensions and Social Security Act 2000, s 68, Sch 7, para 8.*

- *Social Security (Transfer of Functions etc) Act 1999.*

- *Social Security (Recovery of Benefits) Act 1997.*

- *Social Security, Contributions and Benefits Act 1992.*

- *Social Security Administration Act 1992.*

- *Social Security and Child Support (Decisions and Appeals) Regulations 1999, SI 1999 Nos 991, 1466, 1623, 1670.*

- *Social Security Commissioners (Procedure) Regulations 1999, SI 1999 No 1495.*

- *Social Security Commissioners (Procedure) (Amendment) Regulations 2001, SI 2001 No 1095.*

- *Housing Benefit and Council Tax Benefit (Decisions and Appeals) Regulations 2001, SI 2001 No 1002.*

Decisions of the tribunal are recorded in summary and signed by the legally qualified member. All parties to the proceedings are advised of their right to request a statement of the reasons for the decision, which they must apply for in writing within one month of the date of issue of the decision. They may also request conditions governing appeals to the Commissioner.

The decision notice is very simple, and will include:

- whether the decision was a unanimous or majority decision;

- the decision itself; and

- a summary of reasons for the decision.

The decision is dated and sent to all affected parties. However, the tribunal does have the discretion to hand the decision to the affected parties at the appeal hearing.

See **APPENDIX C** for an example of a decision notice.

If any affected party requires a copy of the statement of reasons for the decision, an application must be made in writing to the legally qualified member within one month of the date of issue of the decision.

LATE APPLICATIONS FOR STATEMENT OF REASONS

8.100 A late application for a statement of reasons may be made in certain circumstances, but must in all cases be made in writing to the legally qualified member within three months of the date of the decision in the appeal in question. An extension of time will not be allowed unless the tribunal is satisfied that it is in the interests of justice that the application be granted because:

- the claimant, his or her spouse or a dependant, has died or suffered serious illness; or

- the appellant was not resident in the United Kingdom; or

- the normal postal services were disrupted; or

- there are other special circumstances relevant to the application.

The reasons for the late application must be as a result of those special circumstances, which resulted in it not being practical for the application to be made within one month of the decision. The later the application for a statement of reasons is made, the more compelling must be the special circumstances.

When considering the interests of justice, no account is taken of the claimant's misunderstanding or ignorance of the law, regulations or time limits; or of the fact that a Commissioner or court have taken a different view of the law from that applied at the time of the decision. An application for an extension of time which has been refused may not be renewed.

RECORD OF THE HEARING

8.101 The clerk to the tribunal will keep a copy of the record of proceedings from the appeal hearing for a period of six months from the date of the decision of the appeal. During this time any party to the proceedings may make a written request to the clerk to the tribunal for a copy of the record of the hearing.

It is recommended that any party who is considering appealing to the Commissioner requests a record of proceedings at the same time as requesting a statement of reasons.

See **APPENDIX C** for an example of a statement of reasons.

Setting aside decisions

8.102 [*CSPSSA 2000, Sch 7, para 7*]

An application to set aside a decision of the tribunal may be made in writing to the legally qualified member, who may set aside a decision where:

- a document was not sent to, or received at the appropriate time (i e 14 days before the hearing) by, a party to the proceedings; or

- a party to the proceedings or his or her authorised representative was not present at the hearing (this will only apply where the party and/or the representative actually indicated beforehand that they wished to be present at the hearing).

Applications to set aside any decision of the tribunal must be made within one month of the issue of the decision. Where the party requests written reasons for the decision, the prescribed time of one month will be extended by 14 days.

Where an application to set aside a decision is accepted, each party to the proceedings is issued with a copy of the application and invited to make further representations before the application is decided.

A notice of the decision and statement of reasons relating to the application to set aside a decision of the tribunal is issued to every party.

If the application to set aside the decision of the tribunal is granted, the appeal is considered afresh by a newly constituted tribunal.

Appeals to the Commissioner

APPLICATIONS FOR PERMISSION TO APPEAL TO THE COMMISSIONER

8.103   *[CSPSSA 2000, Sch 7, para 8]*

An application for permission to appeal to the Commissioner may be made by:

(a)   the Secretary of State;

(b)   the local authority;

(c)   any person affected who brought an appeal.

An application for permission to appeal to the Commissioner must be made directly to the legally qualified member, on the grounds that the decision of the tribunal was erroneous in point of law. The application must be made within one month of the date of the issue of the statement of reasons for the decision of the tribunal, and should include a copy of the statement of reasons for the decision.

An error in law may include cases where the tribunal:

- did not apply the correct law;

- wrongly interpreted the law;

- did not observe the rules of natural justice;

- did not have evidence or sufficient evidence to support the statement of its decision; or

- did not give adequate reasons for its decision.

In making an application for permission to appeal to the Commissioner, the person applying must clearly identify the tribunal's error of law.

If all affected parties agree that there is an error in law in the decision of the tribunal then the legally qualified member must direct that the appeal be re-heard by another appeal tribunal rather than grant permission to appeal to the Commissioner.

If the application for permission to appeal to the Commissioner is refused or rejected by the legally qualified member, the applicant may make an application for permission to appeal directly to the Commissioner.

Applications for leave to appeal to the Commissioner must be made within one month of the date of issue of the decision refusing leave to appeal (*SI 1999 No 1495, reg 9*).

An application to the Commissioner for leave to appeal must contain the following:

- the name and address of the applicant;

- the grounds on which the applicant intends to rely;

- if the application is late, the grounds for seeking late acceptance;

- the address for sending notices and documents;

- copies of the decision of the tribunal and reasons for the decision; and

- the legally qualified member's notice of refusal of permission to appeal.

Where the application is made by the Secretary of State or by the local authority, the applicant must send copies of the application, along with any supporting documents, directly to the claimant or other affected parties.

THE DECISION OF THE COMMISSIONER

8.104 An appeal lies to a Commissioner from any decision under *section 68* of and *Schedule 7* to *CSPSSA 2000* on the grounds that the decision of the tribunal was wrong in law (subject to the applicant having made an application for leave to appeal to a legally qualified member).

Each of the parties to the appeal is issued with a copy of the application for leave to appeal and afforded the opportunity to make further comment or representations before a decision is made.

If each of the principal parties to the case (the Secretary of State or the local authority and the appellant) consider the decision to be erroneous on point of law, then the Commissioner may set aside the decision and refer the case to a differently constituted tribunal with recommendations for its determination.

Where the Commissioner makes a decision in respect of the application for leave to appeal, he or she sends a copy of the decision to all affected parties.

If permission to appeal is granted (whether by the legally qualified member or by the Commissioner) the applicant must register a notice of appeal with the Commissioner.

Appeals to the Commissioner must be made within one month of the date of issue of the decision granting permission to appeal (SI 1999 No 1495, reg 13).

An appeal to the Commissioner must contain the following:

- the name and address of the applicant;
- the date on which the application for leave was granted;
- the grounds on which the applicant intends to rely;
- if the application is late, the grounds for seeking late acceptance;
- the address for sending notices and documents;
- a copy of the notice granting leave to appeal;
- copies of the decision of the tribunal and reasons for the decision;
- the legally qualified member's notice of refusal of permission to appeal (where appropriate).

Upon receipt of an appeal, the Commissioner will acknowledge receipt and notify all affected parties (SI 1999 No 1495, reg 16).

The Commissioner will invite affected parties to make written observations in respect of the appeal. These must be submitted within one month.

The written observations will then be sent to all affected parties, who will be invited to make their written observations in reply; again they will have one month following the issue of the invitation to do so.

The Commissioner may request any further documents, information or evidence from any affected party that he or she may reasonably require to assist in the decision-making process.

Where the Commissioner holds that the decision was wrong in law, he or she will either set the decision aside and give the decision which he or she considers to be correct without making fresh findings of fact, or make new findings of fact, or alternatively refer the case to a tribunal with directions for its determination (*CSPSSA 2000, Sch 7, para 8(4), (5), (6)*).

Most appeals to the Commissioner are considered without any parties to the appeal being present.

However, the Commissioner may order an oral hearing where it appears to be appropriate. All parties are invited to attend an oral hearing.

Any person affected may request an oral hearing before the Commissioner. The oral hearing will be granted unless the Commissioner feels that the proceedings can properly be determined without a hearing.

THE HEARING

8.105 *[SI 1999 No 1495, reg 24]*

Commissioner's hearings are generally public hearings, unless the Commissioner decides otherwise for special reasons.

Each affected party is notified of the time and place of the hearing, and will be given at least 14 days' notice of the hearing date.

If any party fails to appear at the hearing, the Commissioner may proceed in their absence.

The procedure at the hearing is much the same as the hearing before the tribunal. However, the hearing is a little more formal in so far as parties to the hearing will be able to address the Commissioner, and with the leave of the Commissioner, give evidence, and call and question witnesses.

As with tribunals, the Commissioner may summon witnesses to appear at the hearing.

All decisions of the Commissioner are in writing and signed by him or her and issued to all affected parties.

SETTING ASIDE THE COMMISSIONER'S DECISION

8.106 *[SI 1999 No 1495, reg 31]*

An application to set aside a decision of the Commissioner may be made in writing to the Commissioner, who may set aside a decision in the following circumstances:

- where a document was not sent or was received at the appropriate time (ie 14 days before the hearing) by a party to the proceedings, a representative, or the Commissioner;

- a party to the proceedings or their authorised representative was not present at the hearing;

- there has been some other procedural irregularity or mishap.

Applications to set aside any decision of the Commissioner must be made within one month of the issue of the decision, but where the party requests written reasons for the decision, the prescribed time of one month is extended by 14 days.

Where an application to set aside a decision is accepted, each party to the proceedings is issued with a copy of the application and invited to make further representations before the application is decided.

A notice of the decision and a statement of reasons relating to the application to set aside a decision of the Commissioner is issued to every party.

If the application to set aside the decision of the Commissioner is granted, the appeal may be considered afresh by the Commissioner, or the Commissioner may direct that it should be heard by a differently constituted tribunal.

There is no right of appeal against a refusal to set aside the decision of a Commissioner.

Appeals to the appellate court

8.107 An application must be made in writing to the Commissioner for permission to appeal to the appellate court (in England and Wales, the Court of Appeal) on a point of law. The application must be in writing, stating the grounds for the appeal, and must be made within three months of the date of issue of the Commissioner's decision (*SI 1999 No 1495, reg 33*).

If the Commissioner grants permission, an appeal to the Court of Appeal must be made within three months of the Commissioner having granted permission.

If permission is refused by the Commissioner, then an application to the court for permission must be made within three months of the date of issue of the Commissioner's decision refusing permission to appeal (*CSPSSA 2000, Sch 7, para 9; SSA 1998, Sch 5*).

An application to the court for permission to appeal must contain the following:

- the name and address of the applicant;

- the grounds on which the applicant intends to rely;

- the address for sending notices and documents;

- copies of the decision of the tribunal and reasons for the decision;

- the legally qualified member's notice of refusal of permission to appeal (where appropriate);

- copies of the Commissioner's decision; and

- the Commissioner's notice of refusal to grant permission to appeal.

Case law

8.108   The statutes and regulations are interpreted by Social Security Commissioners who hear appeals (on a point of law only) from local appeal tribunals. Reported Commissioners' decisions can be purchased from the Stationery Office, and all Commissioners' decisions are binding on appeal tribunals, but appeal tribunals are not bound by previous decisions of appeal tribunals.

Appeal lies from the Commissioners, on a point of law, to the appellate court and then the House of Lords.

For examples of welfare benefit appeals, see *Garlick v Oldham Metropolitan Borough Council [1993] 2 All ER 65* (an appeal to the House of Lords on housing) and *Chief Adjudication Officer v Foster [1993] 1 All ER 705* (an appeal to the House of Lords on Income Support).

The European Court of Justice has also dealt with a number of appeals relating to the UK benefit system; see for example *Jackson v Chief Adjudication Officer [1993] 3 All ER 265*.

There are also a number of Commissioners' decisions available on the Internet at www.osscsc.org.uk/decisions/decisions.htm. Commissioners' decisions relating specifically to Housing and Council Tax Benefit can be found at www.hbinfo.org/menu2/comdecs/cdindex.htm.

Commissioners' decisions are identified by case reference only. The case reference consists of a prefix identifying the benefit involved, followed by a file number, followed by the year the appeal was first registered with the tribunal. So for example, an Income Support case registered in 1999 would be identified as *CIS/5848/99*. A Housing Benefit case registered in 2001 may be identified as *CH/3776/2001*.

Checklist

8.109 All applications must be in writing.

> *If you are not happy with a decision of the tribunal.*
>
> Request a statement of reasons for the decision from the legally qualified member (time limit – one month from the date of issue of the decision).
>
> Request a record of proceedings from the clerk of the tribunal.
>
> *If you feel that the decision of the tribunal should be set aside.*
>
> Make an application to the legally qualified member to set aside the decision (time limit – one month from the date of issue of the decision, but may be extended by 14 days where a statement of reasons for the decision has been requested).
>
> *If you feel that the decision is wrong in law.*
>
> Make an application to the legally qualified member for permission to appeal to the Commissioner on a point of law (time limit – one month from date of issue of the statement of reasons).
>
> *If the legally qualified member refuses your application for permission to appeal to the Commissioner on a point of law.*
>
> Make an application to the Commissioner for permission to appeal on a point of law (time limit – one month from date of issue of the legally qualified member's decision to refuse permission).

If the legally qualified member grants your application for permission to appeal to the Commissioner on a point of law.

Appeal to the Commissioner on a point of law (time limit – one month from date of issue of the legally qualified member's decision to grant permission).

If the Commissioner grants your application for permission to appeal on a point of law.

Register your appeal to the Commissioner on a point of law (time limit – one month from date of issue of Commissioner's decision to grant permission).

If the Commissioner refuses your application for permission to appeal on a point of law.

Request permission to appeal to the Court of Appeal on a point of law; or apply for a judicial review of the Commissioner's refusal to grant permission (time limit – three months from the date of issue of the Commissioner's decision to refuse permission).

CHAPTER 9

Recent and Future Changes to Housing Benefit

Introduction

9.1 Some important changes to Housing Benefit (and Council Tax Benefit) are taking place at present. The introduction of Tax Credits, and particularly Pension Credit, in 2003 has already had an impact on Housing Benefit administrators and claimants.

Following a pilot exercise, RSLs are now able to verify documents on behalf of local authorities who are Verification Framework-compliant.

A welcome change is that from 21 May 2003 the length of time that people can be in hospital before their benefit is reduced has been increased from 6 to 52 weeks.

On 17 October 2002, the Secretary of State for Work and Pensions announced plans for the reform of Housing Benefit in a paper, 'Building choice and responsibility: A radical agenda for Housing Benefit'. The main changes are the introduction of a flat rate 'standard local housing allowance', which is now operating as a pilot scheme in nine areas. This is linked to a move away from direct payments of Housing Benefit to landlords, the simplification of the Housing Benefit claims process, and measures to tackle fraud and abuse.

The rest of this chapter will look at each of these changes in a little more detail, indicating the likely start date where this information was available at the time of writing.

Registered Social Landlords Verification Framework Scheme

9.2 The Verification Framework is a voluntary scheme whereby Housing Benefit departments agree to make specific checks on claims including verifying information by obtaining original documents. During the first few years of the Framework only staff working directly for the local authority or a Housing Benefit contractor could check information from original documents. This meant that claimants had to take original documents to the local authority to be checked and copied. Previously, many RSLs had photocopied documents for their tenants and forwarded them to the local authority, which had helped to reduce delays in dealing with their housing benefit claim.

During 2001–2002 a group of Verification Framework-compliant local authorities and their local RSLs (who were trained and then authorised to verify from original documents) piloted the Registered Social Landlords Verification Framework Scheme (for further information see the summary at www.dwp.gov.uk/housingbenefit/publications/2002/rsl-vf-eval.pdf). As a result of the pilot, this scheme has been extended on a voluntary basis to all Verification Framework-compliant authorities and their RSLs who have to make a joint application to participate. It started in Spring 2003.

The scheme is open to all RSLs (defined by the DWP as social landlords that are registered with the Housing Corporation, Communities Scotland and the Welsh National Assembly) and to ALMOs. The Operation and Good Practice Manual giving full details of the scheme can be found at http://www.dwp.gov.uk/housingbenefit/manuals/index.asp.

Tax Credits

9.3 Tax Credits were introduced in April 2003 and are administered by the Inland Revenue. They replace the Child Tax Allowance, the Working Families' Tax Credit and the Disabled Person's Tax Credit, and also the additions for children in Income Support and income-based Jobseekers Allowance, as well as in the non means-tested benefits such as Incapacity Benefit. Tax Credits are made up of two elements – Child Tax Credit and Working Tax Credit. Both credits are taken into account in full in the assessment of Housing Benefit (and Council Tax Benefit).

Unlike Working Families' Tax Credit and Disabled Person's Tax Credit, the new Tax Credits are not taken into account in the Housing Benefit and Council Tax Benefit assessment until they are actually paid to the claimant. Housing Benefit Departments must only take into account the actual amount of Tax Credit in payment, and must never assume a notional amount of Tax Credit (even if the claimant appears to be entitled to it). This means that local authorities cannot estimate how much a family who is not getting Tax Credits might receive in Tax Credits and use this figure when working out their Housing Benefit (and Council Tax Benefit). Lump sum arrears of Tax Credits are taken into account as capital in the Housing Benefit and Council Tax Benefit assessment.

The chapters on Housing Benefit explain more fully the effects which Tax Credits have on Housing Benefit.

Hospital patients

9.4 Previously, Housing Benefit (and Council Tax Benefit) applicable amounts were reduced (or downrated) after the claimant or their partner had been in hospital for six weeks. From 21 May 2003, the reduction does not take place until the person has been in hospital for 52 weeks. This applies to anyone entering hospital on or after 9 April 2003.

These changes also apply to other benefits, eg Income Support and Incapacity Benefit, but not to Disability Living Allowance and Attendance Allowance, which continue to be downrated after 28 days.

There is no reduction if a child or young person goes into hospital.

Note: The rules regarding people who are temporarily absent from home because they are in hospital have not changed (see **8.74ff**).

Pension Credit

9.5 Pension Credit, which was introduced on 6 October 2003, means important changes for pensioners and will have a major effect on Housing Benefit administration.

Pension Credit is administered by the Pension Service (part of the DWP) from Pension Centres around the country. It is made up of two elements – the Guarantee Credit and the Savings Credit.

It is planned that the Pension Service will collect and verify all the information for Pension Credit and work out the income to be used when making the calculation. If the pensioner has also claimed Housing Benefit (or Council Tax Benefit), the Pension Service will send an 'assessed income figure' to the local authority, which the authority must use as the income figure when working out the pensioner's Housing Benefit and Council Tax Benefit.

Pensioners will only have to reclaim Pension Credit every five years and during this time they do not have to report changes to their income or capital. However, they are required to report 'significant life events' such as separation, bereavement, marriage, living together, going into hospital, change of address, or absence abroad. Similar rules apply to pensioners getting Housing Benefit and Council Tax Benefit. In addition, they still need to report changes in their rent and in their non-dependants to the local authority.

This means some changes to the way Housing Benefit (and Council Tax Benefit) is worked out for pensioners. There are higher applicable amounts for pensioners aged 65 and over. Tariff income on capital over £6,000 is reduced to £1 for every £500. There is no capital cut-off point for pensioners receiving the Guarantee Credit. However, there is still a Housing Benefit capital limit of £16,000 for those pensioners who do not qualify for the Guarantee Credit but are still entitled to Housing Benefit. There will be five-year benefit periods for pensioners receiving Housing Benefit (instead of the previous maximum of 60 weeks).

Benefit periods

9.6 Following the changes for pensioners (which included the abolition of claim periods from October 2003 for those over 60), benefit periods for all Housing Benefit claimants were abolished with effect from April 2004 and claimants are now no longer obliged to re-claim at regular intervals. Local authorities may be required instead to make additional checks on claims where there may be a high risk of undisclosed changes of circumstances, fraud or error.

Flat rate 'standard local housing allowance'

9.7 The proposed flat rate 'standard local housing allowance' will apply initially to the deregulated private sector. The scheme is being piloted in nine Pathfinder Areas and the results will be evaluated before the scheme is introduced nationally. The Secretary of State for the DWP has stated that:

> 'Standard allowances cannot be introduced into social housing until rent restructuring and more choice-based lettings create the right conditions.'

The scheme provides for a standard allowance set by the rent officer based on rents in the local market and graduated to the size of the household, so higher allowances will be set for larger households.

Local authorities will no longer have to refer claims to the rent officer for an individual decision. Housing Benefit will be based on the standard allowance rather than the actual rent charged, and tenants who pay rent at a level below the standard allowance will be able to keep the difference.

The amounts of the standard allowance will be published to allow tenants and landlords to know in advance what Housing Benefit will be based on.

A 'move away from' direct payments of Housing Benefit to landlords will be linked to the standard allowance and tested by the Pathfinder authorities.

Housing benefit will be payable to a landlord in a Pathfinder area at the local authority's discretion where housing benefit was calculated on a local standard housing allowance which has not changed since it was set (which must have been within the last six months) and the claimant has been continuously entitled to housing benefit since that date. This can only be done where the local authority thinks it is improbable that the claimant will pay their rent, or has already made direct payments during the current award of housing benefit in any situations where direct payments must be made.

The nine Pathfinder authorities have been announced as: Blackpool, Brighton and Hove, Conwy, Coventry, Edinburgh, Leeds, Lewisham, NE Lincolnshire and Teignbridge. The pilots started in October 2003.

Simplification of the Housing Benefit claims process

9.8 Entitlement to Housing Benefit ends when someone on Income Support or income-based Jobseekers Allowance begins work, even if they are entitled to Housing Benefit on the basis of their wages. It is necessary to make a new claim, which may mean a delay in payment. Proposals to deal with the hardship caused by this problem have not yet been implemented, with the exception of 'housing benefit run-on' described below.

A person on Income Support, income-based Jobseekers Allowance, Incapacity Benefit, or Severe Disablement Allowance who starts work, or increases their hours or pay, or whose partner does so, is entitled to the same amount of Housing Benefit as they were receiving during the last week of that benefit, for a period of four weeks. The local authority must be notified of work starting, or circumstances changing, within four weeks.

A lone parent in this situation is entitled to a similar concession for 14 days after taking up full-time paid work. However, this concession will end in October 2004.

Driving down fraud and abuse

9.9 There is concern that 'rogue landlords' are abusing the system by letting property in poor condition and tolerating or encouraging anti-social behaviour by their tenants. The Housing Benefit reform paper *'Building choice and responsibility: A radical agenda for Housing Benefit'* states that this will be tackled 'as soon as parliamentary time allows'.

A Public Service Agreement target has been set to reduce benefit fraud by 25% by 2006. The proposed methods to tackle this include targeted data checking and investigation of high risk claims.

CHAPTER 10

Human Rights in Housing

Introduction

10.1 The *Human Rights Act 1998* (*HRA 1998*), which was introduced in English law in October 2000, has an impact on many issues relating to housing and services provided by public authorities. The local authority administering housing services falls within the remit of a public authority, as do the courts in providing a public service. Providers of social housing will also fall to be public authorities and must consider the implications of *HRA 1998* in their administration of such services.

10.2 Below the articles and protocols of *HRA 1998* are outlined – the main parts of the Act considered in this chapter are marked **.

The Articles:

- *Article 2* – Right to life
- *Article 3* – Prohibition of torture, inhuman or degrading treatment**
- *Article 4* – Prohibition of slavery and forced labour
- *Article 5* – Right to liberty and security
- *Article 6* – Right to a fair trial**
- *Article 7* – No punishment without law
- *Article 8* – Right to respect for private and family life**
- *Article 9* – Freedom of thought, conscience and religion
- *Article 10* – Freedom of expression
- *Article 11* – Freedom of assembly and association

- *Article 12* – Right to marry
- *Article 14* – Prohibition of discrimination**
- *Article 16* – Restriction on political activity of aliens
- *Article 17* – Prohibition of abuse of rights
- *Article 18* – Limitation on use of restrictions of rights

The *First Protocol*:

- *Article 1* – Protection of property**
- *Article 2* – Right to education
- *Article 3* – Right to free elections

The *Sixth Protocol*:

- *Article 1* – Abolition of the death penalty
- *Article 2* – Death penalty in time of war

Overview of HRA 1998

10.3 *HRA 1998* contains 22 sections and four Schedules. The rights are contained in Schedule 1. They include *Articles 2 to 12* and *14* of the *European Convention on Human Rights (ECHR)*, *Articles 1, 2* and *3* of the *First Protocol* and *Articles 1* and *2* of the *Sixth Protocol* as read with *Articles 16 to 18* of the *Convention*. These are protocols to the *European Convention on Human Rights*.

10.4 A summary of the provisions:

Section 1	Description of rights
Section 2	Interpretation of Convention rights
Section 3*	Interpretation of legislation
Section 4*	Declaration of incompatibility
Section 5*	Right of Crown to intervene
Section 6*	Acts of public authorities
Section 7*	Proceedings
Section 8*	Judicial remedies
Section 9	Judicial acts
Section 10	Power to take remedial action
Section 11	Safeguard for existing human rights
Section 12	Freedom of expression

Section 13	Freedom of thought, conscience and religion
Section 14	Derogations
Section 15	Reservations
Section 16	Period for which designated derogations have effect
Section 17	Periodic review of designated derogations
Section 18	Appointment to European Court of Human Rights
Section 19	Statements of compatibility
Section 20	Orders etc. under This Act
Section 21	Interpretation section
Section 22	Short title, commencement, application and extent

What are the rights?

10.5   There are three types of right:

- *Absolute – Arts 2, 3, 4, 7; Sixth Protocol, Arts 1, 2;*

- *Qualified – Arts 8, 9, 10, 11; and*

- *Limited – Arts 5, 6, 12; First Protocol: Arts 1, 2, 3; Sixth Protocol: Art 14.*

Absolute rights

10.6   An absolute right is one that permits no derogation – no inroads can be made into its protection and there are no limits to the right. A key issue with this type of right is: what is the appropriate threshold required to constitute a violation of it?

10.7   *Ireland v UK (1979–1980) 2 EHRR 25* was a case brought by the Irish government against the UK government arising out of events in Northern Ireland. The Irish government alleged that a policy of internment and detention which had been introduced in Northern Ireland between 1971 and 1975 constituted an infringement of *Articles 5* and *6* and that persons interned or detained had been subject to ill-treatment that constituted an 'administrative practice' in violation of *Article 3*. The decision of the European Court of Human Rights illustrates the high threshold that must be reached before inhuman treatment/punishment becomes torture. The ill-treatment was found to include five interrogation techniques:

- wall standing – forcing detainees to remain for periods of some hours in a 'stress position', namely standing spread-eagled against the wall with their fingers put high above their head against the wall, legs spread

73

apart and feet back causing them to stand on their toes with the weight of their body mainly on the fingers;

- hooding – putting a black or navy coloured bag over the detainees' heads and initially keeping it there all the time except during interrogation;

- subjection to noise – pending their interrogations, holding the detainees in a room where there was a continuous loud and hissing noise;

- deprivation of sleep – pending interrogations;

- deprivation of food and drink – reduced diet.

The court held that the above constituted inhuman treatment because they caused, if not actual bodily injury, at least intense physical and mental suffering to the person subjected thereto and also led to acute psychiatric disturbances during interrogation. They were degrading since they were such as to arouse in their victims feelings of fear, anguish and inferiority capable of humiliating and debasing them and possibly breaking their physical or moral resistance. The court held that the above did not constitute torture. The latter required a greater intensity than the suffering inflicted. Held: *Article 3* had been breached.

10.8 In a housing context, breach of *Article 3* (prohibition of torture, inhuman or *degrading treatment*) might be alleged where applicants for housing are questioned about very personal issues in a public area, or where the officer's manner of questioning the applicant is rude and abrupt, in particular where the applicant is already in a vulnerable situation, for instance he is homeless. Interviews carried out by the public authority should always be conducted in privacy and in a compassionate manner.

If these implications are not considered, there could well be potential for a *HRA 1998* action, in particular an allegation that the public authority subjected the applicant to degrading treatment.

Qualified rights

10.9 Qualified rights are those rights that are subject to a limitation or restriction clause, and while they still deserve protection one must also take the public interest into account. These rights have a two-stage structure: assert the right; and acknowledge that there are permissible qualifications to that right.

ARTICLE 8

10.10 Everyone has the right to respect for his private and family life, his home and his correspondence. There shall be no interference by a public authority with the exercise of this right except such as is in accordance with the law and is necessary in a democratic society in the interests of national security, public safety or the economic well-being of the country, for the prevention of disorder or crime, for the protection of the rights and freedoms of others.

The qualifications can be explained in the following way:

- Any restriction on civil and political rights must be prescribed by law. There must be some basis in national law and national law must be accessible and precise.

- The restriction must be justified by one of the aims recognised in the *ECHR*, i e public morals, national security.

- The restriction must be shown to be necessary in a democratic society – this imparts an objective standard which complies with pluralism and broadmindedness.

- Any qualification to rights cannot be applied in a discriminatory fashion.

10.11 In *Hatton and others v UK [2003] 37 EHRR*, the European Court of Human Rights was asked to consider whether the UK government had struck a fair balance (in context of *Article 8* rights) between individuals affected by night noise from Heathrow airport and the community as a whole. The UK government argued that the policy adopted on night-time flights was justified on the grounds of economic well-being of the airline operators and the economic interests of the country as a whole. The court held that there was no violation of the applicants' *Article 8* rights.

10.12 Where an applicant for housing has family considerations, for example, the shared care of a child who stays over with the applicant in his home during periods of contact, the applicant would have the right to consideration of his family life under *Article 8(1)* when making an application for housing. However, the public authority would equally be able to restrict this right if in its public duty it had to consider the rights of others in need of housing.

Therefore, if the applicant would normally be considered for a one-bedroom flat, but requests two bedrooms to accommodate a child staying overnight, the authority would be able to restrict the applicant's rights under *Article 8(1)* if there was a demand for two-bedroom properties in the area by those who had children living with them.

Limited rights

10.13 *Article 1* of the *First Protocol* guarantees the right to peaceful enjoyment of possessions but reserves to the State power to deprive individuals of their possessions, and to control the use of property, subject to certain qualifications.

Deprivation of property rights is only permissible where:

(a)   it is in the public interest;

(b)   it is provided by law;

(c)   it is subject to general principles of international law.

Control of property rights is only permissible where:

 (i)   it is in the general interest;

(ii)   it is necessary for the payment of taxes, contributions or penalties.

Proportionality

10.14 The principle of proportionality is concerned with defining the fair balance between the protection of individuals and the interests of the community at large. Where the principle is applied, the court will examine the legitimate purpose of the restriction of a right with protection of the rights themselves.

10.15 In *Open Door Counselling and Dublin Well Woman v Ireland (1993) 15 EHRR 411* the European Court found that an injunction preventing the dissemination of information about abortion was disproportionate to the aim of protecting morals because it was framed in absolute terms.

10.16 The following checklist should be applied when deciding whether a restriction of a right complies with the principle of proportionality:

- Have 'relevant and sufficient' reasons been advanced in support of the restriction?

- Is there a less restrictive alternative?

- Has there been some measure of procedural fairness in the decision-making process?

- Do safeguards against abuse exist?

- Does the restriction in question destroy the very essence of the right?

Where a decision to restrict a right involves a public authority exercising a discretion, the principle of proportionality requires that procedural fairness is exercised to ensure that the rights of those affected by such a decision are properly taken into account.

Article 1 of the First Protocol

10.17 In the housing context this might arise where a landlord is seeking possession of a property because the tenant is in rent arrears.

Where the landlord finds that there are rent arrears, he will in most cases be able to establish that such action is necessary to protect the rights of others (ie to make and keep available social housing for others in need); and his action will be in accordance with *HA 1996* (because of the established rent arrears).

However, can he establish that the action he is taking is proportionate and necessary in a democratic society?

If the landlord has done all that he can to try to resolve the matter, for example, by looking at the tenant's ability to repay arrears and attempting to reach an agreement with the tenant, but the tenant has failed to comply with such an agreement, then the court action for possession should comply with the requirement of being necessary in a democratic society.

If, however, the landlord has made unreasonable demands on the tenant to repay the arrears, and has not done all that he can do to reach an affordable agreement, perhaps by failing to consider the tenant's financial circumstances prior to resorting to the court (which is frequently the case), the landlord will not be able to show that his action in resorting to the court for possession complies with the requirement of being necessary in a democratic society.

In practice, it appears that tenants do not enjoy any additional protection from eviction as a result of *Article 1* of the *First Protocol*. In *Gavin Kay and others v (1) London Borough of Lambeth (2) London & Quadrant Housing Trust [2004] 3 WLR 1396*, the Court of Appeal held that as long as the tenancy was lawfully terminated (aside from any considerations under ECHR), the tenant had no additional rights arising under *Article 1*. The court re-iterated that *Article 1* does not confer a right of property as such nor does it guarantee the content of any rights in property.

Principles of construction

10.18 There are essentially three principles that should be taken into account when interpreting human rights. They are set out in **10.19** to **10.25** below.

A teleological approach

10.19 This means that a purposive approach must be taken. The *ECHR* is a 'living instrument which ... must be interpreted in the light of present day conditions'. This also means that the older a decision of the European Court or Commission is, the less reliable a guide it is likely to be to the proper interpretation of Convention rights.

Autonomous concepts

10.20 Human rights should be considered as autonomous concepts. A government cannot attempt to opt out of its human rights obligations by reclassifying them in domestic law. For example, parking offences are civil in nature within the German legal system but are regarded as criminal under Convention law.

The margin of appreciation

10.21 This doctrine has been developed by the European Court of Human Rights and is an acknowledgment by the court that in relation to some issues, the domestic authorities are in a better position than it is to reach a decision in certain cases. The following guidelines are usually applied.

10.22 On issues such as national security, morals, planning policy, tax and social and economic policy, a fairly wide margin of appreciation is allowed.

10.23 The particular importance attached to some rights dictates a narrow margin of appreciation. In free speech cases concerning political debate or matters of public interest, the need for a restriction must be 'convincingly established' because where such issues are in play 'there is little scope ... for restrictions'.

10.24 Where there is a general consensus in Europe about how particular issues are to be dealt with or the right in issue has an 'objective character', only a narrow margin of appreciation will be permitted on the basis that there is less scope for subtle national differences.

10.25 The margin of appreciation is not applicable in domestic law. Domestic courts do not have the same role as the European Court in the determination of cases under *HRA 1998*. The European Court supervises the domestic system for protecting human rights, but courts and tribunals are part of that system and cannot therefore apply a margin of appreciation to their own decision making. That said, there is nothing in the Convention to preclude domestic courts and tribunals from affording some discretion to decision-making bodies when reviewing their actions. The extent will depend on the circumstances of the case and relevant factors will probably include:

- the importance of the right at stake;

- the seriousness of the interference with that right;

- the relative specialist knowledge or experience of the body under review on the one hand and the court or tribunal on the other;

- whether the body under review is elected or is otherwise accountable to the electorate;

- whether the aim of the measure under review is to promote other human rights, including social and economic rights;

- whether heightened scrutiny is needed because the applicants are particularly vulnerable or unpopular;

- whether the context is one in which there are fairly constant standards throughout democratic societies, especially in the states which are parties to the Convention.

See further:

Starmer K, *European Human Rights Law*, (Legal Action Group).

Singh R, Hunt M and Demetriou M, *Is there a role for the margin of appreciation in national law after the Human Rights Act?* [1999] EHRLR 14.

Pannick D, *Principles of interpretation of Convention rights under the Human Rights Act and the discretionary area of judgement* [1998] PL 545.

Compatibility with current legislation

10.26 *HRA 1998, s 4* provides that:
'4(1) Subsection (2) applies in any proceedings in which a court determines whether provision of primary legislation is compatible with a Convention right.
(2) If the court is satisfied that the provision is incompatible with a Convention right, it may make a declaration of incompatibility.

(3)   Subsection (4) applies in any proceedings in which a court deter-
       mines whether a provision of subordinate legislation, made in the
       exercise of a power conferred by primary legislation, is compatible
       with a Convention right.

(4)   If the court is satisfied –
       (a) that the provision is incompatible with a Convention right, and
       (b) that (disregarding any possibility of revocation) the primary
            legislation concerned prevents the removal of the incompatibil-
            ity it may make a declaration of that incompatibility.'

10.27   Courts are defined in *HRA 1998, s 4(5)*. They are:

(a)   the House of Lords;

(b)   the Judicial Committee of the Privy Council;

(c)   the Courts-Martial Appeal Court;

(d)   in Scotland, the High Court of Justiciary sitting otherwise than as a trial
       court or the Court of Session;

(e)   in England and Wales or Northern Ireland, the High Court or the
       Court of Appeal.

These courts can make a finding of incompatibility. Lower courts and
tribunals are under a duty to try to interpret primary legislation in such a
way that it complies with the Convention.

Where a higher court makes such a declaration of incompatibility, this does
not affect the validity, continuing operation or enforcement of the provision
in respect of which it is made, nor does it bind the parties to the proceedings
in which it was made.

10.28   In the White Paper which introduced *HRA 1998*, the government
said that a declaration of incompatibility will 'almost certainly' prompt a
change in legislation. *HRA 1998* provides a fast-track procedure for amending
the law so as to bring it into conformity with the Convention.

10.29   If a court is considering whether to make a declaration of incompatibility, the Crown has a right to be notified [*HRA 1998, s 5*]. A minister or a
person nominated by a minister may then be joined in the litigation as a party
and, in criminal proceedings, may appeal to the House of Lords against any
declaration of incompatibility.

HRA 1998, s 19 provides that a minister must make a statement before the
second reading of a Bill to the effect that the provisions of the Bill are
compatible with the Convention rights. The minister may make a statement

to the effect that the House wishes to proceed with the Bill despite the ability to make a statement of compatibility.

Public authority

10.30 This is not defined in *HRA 1998*. *HRA 1998, s 6(3)* states that it includes:

(a)   courts and tribunals;

(b)   any person certain of whose functions are functions of a public nature.

This will include:

(i)   housing authorities;

(ii)   RSLs providing social housing (see *Donoghue v Poplar Housing [2002] QB 48);*

(iii)   benefits authorities.

Both Houses of Parliament are expressly excluded as is any person exercising functions in connection with proceedings in Parliament.

HRA dedicated housing issues

Article 1 of the First Protocol

10.31 This protects the right of property, ie any interest in a property whether it be that of a landlord, tenant or licensee.

Article 6(1)

10.32 This will apply particularly where there is a landlord and tenant dispute, as this affects civil rights and obligations, resulting in procedural guarantees of a right to a fair trial.

Section 3(1)

10.33 The court will have to decide whether the grounds for possession are compatible with Convention rights.

Article 8

10.34 This protects the rights of individuals to respect for their family life, private life, home and correspondence.

Home is defined as premises or shelter used as a home by an individual whether occupied lawfully or unlawfully, or unoccupied in which an individual holds a legal interest. A home includes the situation where there is continuous residence or where there is clear intention to reside with no intention to establish a home elsewhere. The House of Lords considered the meaning of 'home' in *LB of Harrow v Qazi [2004] 1 AC 983*. The House of Lords unanimously held that accommodation occupied by a former tenant whose tenancy had ended by operation of law was that person's home within the meaning of *Article 8*. The concept of home is an autonomous one, depending on the factual circumstances, namely the existence of sufficient and continuous links with the property.

10.35 Under the rights in **10.31** to **10.32** protection for an individual would include access, occupation and peaceful enjoyment.

In *Buckley v UK (1996) 23 EHRR 101,* an applicant living in her caravan on her own land was found to have protection under *HRA 1998, Art 8(1)* where the local authority had issued an enforcement order requiring the caravan (for which there was no planning permission) to be removed.

In *Turner v UK (1997) 23 EHRR CD 181*, an enforcement notice was issued against an applicant who lived in a caravan on a plot of land. This case demonstrated that the issue regarding ownership of the land need not be established for a breach to occur. The breach of *HRA 1998* here was that of interference with the right of respect for the applicant's home.

In *LB of Harrow v Qazi [2004] 1 AC 983*, the local housing authority was entitled to possession of Mr Qazi's home as a result of a notice given to the local authority by Mrs Qazi. It was accepted that the notice had the effect of bringing the tenancy to an end. The House of Lords had two principal issues before them. Firstly, whether the accommodation where Mr Qazi resided was his home within the meaning of *Article 8*, notwithstanding the fact that he had no legal entitlement to remain in possession. Secondly, whether the possession action commenced by the local authority, or indeed the possession order granted by the court, infringed his right to respect for his home. The first question was answered unanimously in the affirmative – the premises were Mr Qazi's home. By majority of 3:2, the House answered the second question in the negative. The majority held that the contractual and proprietary rights to possession cannot be defeated by a defence based on *Article 8*. It appears that after *Qazi*, a local authority or a private tenant cannot pray in aid of an *Article 8* defence to possession proceedings properly instituted by the landlord or a possession order made in accordance with domestic legislation (namely legislation other than *HRA 1998*).

10.36 *HRA 1998, Art 8(1)* may be restricted by a public authority where:

(a) the grounds for interference are in accordance with the law, for example, in accordance with the relevant Housing Act;

(b) a legitimate aim is pursued, for example, protection of public health, protection of rights of others, etc; and

(c) it is necessary and legitimate, for example, relevant and sufficient reasons can be demonstrated for action taken, rights of all interested parties have been properly taken into account and safeguards exist to prevent or check any abuse of power (there needs to be a fair balance between the protection of the individual's rights and those of the community at large).

10.37 It was previously thought that all actions relating to eviction orders were potential breaches of *Article 8* and therefore that a justification under *HRA 1998, Art 8(2)* may have to be demonstrated in every case (see *Sheffield City Council v Smart [2002] HLR 34, R (McLellan) v Bracknell Forest Borough Council [2002] QB 1129*. The judgment in *Qazi* has altered the landscape on this issue: the majority held that once it has been established that premises constitute a person's home, an order for possession does not automatically constitute an interference with (a *prima facie* infringement of) the right to respect for home under *Article 8*. If the court finds, as a matter of domestic law that a landlord is justified under domestic law, there is no need to further investigate whether the possession is justified under *Article 8(2)*.

10.38 *HRA 1998, Art 8(2)* provides that *Article 8* rights will be compatible with the Convention only if aimed at protecting one of the following interests:

• national security;

• public safety;

• economic well-being of the country;

• prevention of disorder or crime;

• protection of health or morals;

• protection of the rights and freedom of others, for example, the right of the landlord to have his property back – being in the public interest to protect the well-being of others.

Additionally, the interest protected should be:

(i)   *in accordance with law* – ie it has some domestic basis in law and is sanctioned by legal rules which are reasonably clear and accessible to potential victims. In basic terms, an action brought under the grounds prescribed in *HA 1985, 1988* or *1996* will generally be in accordance with the law. (Any notice of intention to seek possession must be correctly issued at the correct time in accordance with *HRA 1998, Art 6(1)*.)

(ii) *necessary in a democratic society* – ie there is a social need for restriction and the restriction in question is proportionate to that need. This will most certainly be met where a local authority or RSL provides social housing.

10.39   In a case concerning discretionary grounds for possession in cases of rent arrears or anti-social behaviour, the courts must make a decision as to whether it is reasonable to grant possession. If the arrears are low or the breaches are unimportant it is unlikely that an order for possession will be granted.

10.40   Cases of serious rent arrears (mandatory ground 8 – see **6.35** above), however, are a different matter. If the court is satisfied that the conditions under the mandatory ground are met, possession must be ordered. Once the court hears evidence, it has no power to suspend or adjourn. If the arrears are in consequence of delays in the assessment of and/or award of Housing Benefit, the best tactic would be to seek an adjournment before evidence is heard and consider issuing a witness summons to the appropriate official. Notwithstanding the fact that the arrears may be caused by delays on behalf of the local authority, *Article 8* and *Article 1* of the *First Protocol* will not furnish the tenant with a defence to automatic possession.

10.41   Where the tenancy agreement prevents the property from being shared with others, this may infringe upon the applicant's right of respect contained in *HRA 1998, Art 8(1)*. Therefore, if a tenancy agreement states that there can be no lodgers, or no overnight stays are permitted, the landlord will have to justify this restriction if he wishes to avoid possible actions being brought.

10.42   The landlord should check:

•   the terms of tenancy agreements in use;

•   in cases where possession is sought on grounds of non-payment of rent, whether that is caused by a delay in the assessment and/or payment of Housing Benefit;

- in cases of non-payment of rent, whether there are any means by which a resolution might be achieved without having to resort to the court.

The court

10.43 The court will have to decide whether the grounds for possession are compatible with *ECHR [HRA 1998, s 3(1)]*. (See *Donoghue v Poplar Housing [2002] QB 48* where the Court of Appeal declined to make a declaration of incompatibility. See further, the criticism of the reasoning, though not the result of *Poplar* in *Qazi*.

If the tenant is seeking to challenge the statutory grounds for possession, or the issue of notices or proceedings, the county court hearing the case does not have the power to make declarations of incompatibility, therefore the court may:

- make an order for possession to be stayed pending a claim under *HRA 1998* being determined in the High Court; or

- dismiss the application and make an award of damages for breaches of *HRA 1998*.

In *Southwark LBC v St Brice [2001] 1 WLR 1537*, it was argued that the issue of a warrant for possession which did not require a formal hearing and no formal notice was required to be given to the occupier infringed his *Article 6* and *Article 8* rights. The Court of Appeal held that there was no breach of the occupiers' rights under *ECHR*. As the issue of a warrant is simply a step in enforcing an order that was subject to a hearing compliant with *Article 6*, there was no need to have a separate hearing. The issue of a warrant did not alter the legal status of the occupier. Further, the court held that the procedure was clearly justified under *HRA 1998, Art 8(2)*.

County court procedures must also comply with *HRA 1998, Art 6* and other aspects of *HRA 1998* because it is also a public authority.

Article 1 of the First Protocol

10.44 *Article 1* of the *First Protocol* provides entitlement to peaceful enjoyment of possessions. No one shall be deprived of possessions except where it is in the public interest and subject to the conditions of law. Therefore there is the power to deprive individuals of their possessions and to control the use of property.

Article 1 of the *First Protocol* takes into account the interests of landlords, tenants and licensees.

Once the right to occupy under a tenancy comes to an end, issues under *Article 1* of the *First Protocol* will not arise.

10.45   In *Spadea and Scalabrino v Italy (1995) 21 EHRR 482* where eviction orders were suspended, rents were frozen and leases were extended to ease a housing crisis, the court found that there was no breach of *Article 1* of the *First Protocol* as the aim was legitimate to prevent people becoming homeless and housing being re-let at much higher rents, and as such the action taken was a means of control rather than deprivation of property.

In *Stretch v UK, The Times, 3 July 2003*, the European Court of Human Rights held that an applicant who had been wrongly deprived of the benefit of a renewal option on a lease granted to him by a local authority (because it transpired at the time of renewal that the local authority had no power in law to grant him the option) suffered a disproportionate interference with the peaceful enjoyment of his possessions, in violation of *Article 1* of the *First Protocol*. When considering the proportionality of the interference, the court was influenced by the fact that it could not be shown that any public or even third party interest would have been adversely affected by the renewal. Thus, the court found that there had been a disproportionate interference with the applicant's peaceful enjoyment of his possessions.

HRA – checklist for possession

Does Article 1 of the First Protocol apply?

10.46   Has the tenant's right to occupy the property under the terms of the tenancy agreement come to an end?

- *Yes* – it does not apply to the tenant.

- *No* – it does apply to the tenant.

Does Article 8(1) apply?

10.47   Has the tenant's right to occupy the property under the terms of the tenancy agreement come to an end?

- *Yes* – it does not apply.

- *No* – it does apply: you must now consider *HRA 1998, Art 8(2)*.

Consideration of Article 8(2)

10.48 Are you taking action aimed at protecting any of the interests set out in **10.38** above?

- Yes – then is that interest in accordance with the law, ie:
  - – in accordance with grounds prescribed under the relevant Housing Act under which the tenancy was granted; and
  - – have those grounds been made reasonably clear and accessible to the tenant and does the tenant understand them?

- Yes – then is the action that you are taking necessary in a democratic society ie:
  - – is there a social need for restriction; and
  - – is the restriction in question proportionate to the aim of responding to that need?

- Are you satisfied that grounds are compatible with Convention rights?

If you have answered yes to all three requirements of *HRA 1998, Art 8(2)* there will be no breach of *HRA 1998*.

If you have answered no to all or any of the three requirements of *HRA 1998, Art 8(2)* the court may have to consider whether the application is in breach of *HRA 1998*, which may result in the possession order being stayed or dismissed.

Are you satisfied that you have applied the correct grounds for possession in accordance with HRA 1998, s 6(1), 6(2)?

10.49 Do you have a choice of bringing proceedings under discretionary grounds?

- Yes – You will need to justify any decision that you have made in relation to bringing an action under mandatory grounds (where an order must be granted) rather than discretionary grounds (where an order may be granted).

- No – You will need to confirm that there were no discretionary grounds on which you may have considered your application.

Are you now applying for a warrant for possession?

10.50 Consider issuing notice to the tenant of your intention to apply for a warrant for possession to save potential action being brought for a breach of Convention rights. The need to alert the tenant is greater where the warrant is sought a long time after the order for possession was granted.

Property rights

10.51 *Article 1* of the *First Protocol* protects the right of possession, thereby protecting any interest in a property, be it that of a landlord, tenant or licensee. This will apply in cases of repair, the right to occupy, the right to recover a property, etc. There is, however, the power to deprive individuals of their possessions and to control the use of property.

Control and use of the property justified under *Article 1* of the *First Protocol* must have a legitimate aim (for example, protection of the environment, protection from abuse, violence or harassment). 'Legitimate aim' means not being manifestly without reasonable foundation.

10.52 The right to property under *Article 1* of the *First Protocol* provides the right to peaceful enjoyment of possessions and property.

Property includes the tenant's home and any benefit to which he is entitled. However, this does not mean that a person cannot be evicted from a property where there are legal grounds for possession, nor does it mean that a person must be awarded benefit if he applies for it.

10.53 The withdrawal of someone's tenancy or benefit will not be in breach of *HRA 1998* provided that the tenant has been provided with a means by which any dispute may be resolved prior to the withdrawal (there must be documentary evidence of this) and there is a legal basis on which removal can be sanctioned by a court [*HRA 1998, Art 8*]. Therefore, regard must be had for peaceful enjoyment, for example in dealing with a neighbour nuisance or entering a tenant's home without being invited.

10.54 Action may be taken against an authority for failure to deal with neighbour nuisance, as this could infringe on others' entitlement to peaceful enjoyment of their individual tenancies.

Action can be taken under *HRA 1998* against a public authority or a body whose functions are of a public nature (so this does include RSLs).

10.55 In *S v UK [1986] 47 DR 274*, it was demonstrated that, provided evictions are carried out in accordance with the law, they are capable of being justified under *HRA 1998, Art 8* as a measure to protect the right of others, in particular the right of the landlord to have property back at the end of a tenancy agreement. This principle has been re-affirmed in *Qazi* where the

House of Lords held that *Article 8* cannot be a defence to possession proceedings where the landlord demonstrates that he is lawfully entitled to possession.

Housing and anti-social behaviour

10.56   *HRA 1998, Art 8* provides that everyone has the right to respect for his private and family life, his home and his correspondence.

Therefore, regard must be had for this, for example, in dealing with a neighbour nuisance, harassment, verbal abuse, physical assaults, damage to property, etc.

10.57   The European Court has imposed positive obligations on public authorities to ensure effective protection for individuals' Convention rights.

This obligation was the subject of *Whiteside v UK (1994) 76-A DR 80* where an unsuccessful application was made by an applicant who complained that she was inadequately protected from the violent actions of her former husband.

10.58   Action may be taken against the authority for failure to deal with the likes of neighbour nuisance, as this could infringe on other tenants' Convention rights.

In all cases of potential nuisance and anti-social behaviour, the public authority should always:

- ensure that it responds to every complaint made by a potential victim;

- establish whether it is a legitimate complaint and make a decision as to the outcome, including providing reasons for the decision;

- keep records of events, complaints, responses, etc;

- be clear as to the evidence relied upon and make available this evidence to all affected parties to any action;

- ensure that all intended action is correct and proportionate;

- keep records of all decisions and the reasons for them.

Right to privacy

10.59   *HRA 1998, Art 8* provides that everyone has the right to respect for his private and family life, his home and his correspondence.

The landlord/public authority must have regard for this, for example, by not contacting relatives without the tenant's consent or not entering a tenant's home without being invited.

Disclosing information about a tenant that has been provided to in connection with an application for housing, or disclosing information in relation to an application for Housing Benefit without the applicant's written consent.

This sharing of information even between departments of the same authority may constitute a breach of *HRA 1998*. (Of course this is in addition to a breach of the *Data Protection Act 1998* and in the case of the Housing Benefit department, a breach of the *Social Security (Administration) (Fraud) Act 1997, s 4*.)

Planning and the environment

10.60   Under *Article 1* of the *First Protocol* the public authority must have a legitimate aim in any control of planning (protection of the environment is a legitimate aim).

Planning restrictions amount to control of the use of a property, therefore the fair trial requirements of *HRA 1998, Art 6(1)* will be applicable to planning disputes *(Bryan v UK 1995 21 EHRR 342)*.

10.61   In *Lopez-Ostra v Spain (1994) 20 EHRR 277*, where the applicant complained about pollution from a waste treatment plant near her home, the court found that although the Spanish authorities did not own the plant, they had granted planning permission for it and when doing so they had not taken measures necessary for protecting the applicant's right to respect for her home and family life under *HRA 1998, Art 8*. Furthermore, they opposed the applicant's application to close the plant and were held responsible for her prolonged exposure to pollution. The applicant was awarded £16,000 for distress and anxiety and the inconvenience of moving.

In *Guerra v Italy 1998 26 EHRR 357*, where applicants lived near a 'high risk' chemical factory, the authority became aware of information relating to dangers inherent in running the factory and delayed passing that information on to the applicants for several years. This resulted in the applicants not being able to make an earlier risk assessment of their continuing to live near the factory. Each applicant was awarded £3,000 in damages.

In *Hatton and others v UK (2003) 37 EHHR 28*, where the applicants lived near Heathrow Airport and complained that the aircraft noise infringed their *Article 8* rights, the court found that the night flight scheme adopted by the UK government was justified, taking into account the economic interests of the operators of airlines and the economic interests of the country as a whole. The was no breach of the applicants' *Article 8* rights.

These cases demonstrate that issues relating to planning applications will need to be carefully considered in the decision-making process.

Implications for allocations and waiting lists

Article 3: the right to freedom from torture and inhuman or degrading treatment or punishment

10.62 The degrading treatment relates to both mental and physical suffering.

Whether ill-treatment qualifies as degrading treatment will depend on factors such as its duration, severity and the vulnerability of the victim; the nature and context of the treatment, its physical and mental effects, and in some instances the sex, age and state of health of the victim.

Therefore, *HRA 1998, Art 3* must be considered when interviewing and/or questioning an applicant and may be breached where:

- the manner in interviewing or questioning the applicant is rude, abrupt or unnecessary;

- the applicant is not allowed the opportunity to have the interview conducted in private;

- unnecessary information and/or evidence is demanded of the applicant that may be difficult or unaffordable to the applicant to supply;

- the applicant is asked unreasonable questions or information or evidence is demanded that is not reasonably required for the purpose of making the decision.

Article 6: the right to a fair and public trial within a reasonable time.

10.63 This affects cases heard by tribunals and some internal hearings or regulatory procedures. *HRA 1998, Art 6* will affect every decision-making procedure of a public authority. What is required depends upon the nature of the case.

If the conditions of *Article 6* are met by the original decision, it is not necessary to provide for an appeal. The right of access to a court or tribunal is not absolute, but restrictions on it must not impair the essence of the right and they must be for a legitimate purpose and proportionate. The system must not be set up in such a way so as in practice to prevent access, for example, by creating inadequate time limits, or not providing for the giving of notice of decisions.

10.64 The right to a fair hearing:

- There should be a reasonable opportunity to present a case and, in certain cases, to examine witnesses. This means that every person affected should be given all the information the authority has relied on in reaching a decision. It is not until all affected persons have all the information that they will be deemed to have had a reasonable opportunity to present their case.

- There should be equality of arms, i e one party should not be placed at a procedural disadvantage compared with the other.

10.65 The right to a public hearing:

Authorities should make provisions for a public oral hearing, particularly where the applicant does not have any further right of appeal to a public body or a court (for instance in cases where the application is an appeal in a possession case in respect of an introductory tenancy).

The right for the hearing to be public does not necessarily mean that the hearing must be open to the public, as any party to the hearing can decline this right. However, decisions at hearings should be kept in a register which can, where required, be made available to the public on request.

When reviewing applications of this nature, the applicant should be given the choice of having his review conducted on the merits of the paper evidence or at an oral hearing in order that he can present his case verbally.

Authorities should prepare for such review procedures by making available staff and resources to hear cases within a reasonable time.

In *Begum (Runa) v London Borough of Tower Hamlets [2003] 1 All ER 731*, the House of Lords examined the procedure of internal review and appeal limited to a point of law (*ss 202* and *204* of the *Housing Act 1996*) in light of the requirements of *Article 6*. The House ruled that the scheme was *Article 6* compliant because there are procedures in place to safeguard the fairness of the proceedings and the internal review decision is subject to ultimate judicial control by a court with jurisdiction to deal with the case as its nature required.

Article 14: the prohibition of discrimination in the enjoyment of Convention rights

10.66   *HRA 1998, Art 14* provides for people to enjoy the Convention rights without discrimination on any ground such as sex, race, colour, language, religion, political or other opinion, national or social origin, association with a national minority, property, birth or other status.

The phrase 'or other status' has been interpreted by the European Court for Human Rights to include, among other things, sexual orientation, marital status, illegitimacy, status as a trade union, military status and conscientious objection.

The application of *HRA 1998, Art 14* involves more than simply deciding whether a person has been discriminated against in the enjoyment of a Convention right, and if so whether he comes within one of the listed categories (including 'other status'). The European Court of Human Rights would also consider whether there was an objective and reasonable justification for treating different categories of people in a different way, and whether any such differential treatment was proportionate to the aim pursued.

It is not possible to pursue a case on *HRA 1998, Art 14* grounds alone: there must be another Convention right at issue to which a claim of discrimination can be attached. Where another Convention right does arise, however, it is possible to find a breach of *Article 14* even if there is no breach of the other Convention right. For example, if an authority, in its allocations, policy were to state that a single person can only be considered for one-bedroom flats, then this might be discriminatory and if the person had special reasons for being considered for some other type of property, ie because he has his children to stay overnight, then the *Article 14* breach could be applied in conjunction with the *Article 8* right: the right of respect to family life.

Proportionality

10.67   This is a crucial concept. Any interference with a Convention right must be proportionate to the intended objective. This means that even if a particular policy or action which interferes with a Convention right is aimed at pursuing a legitimate aim (for example, the prevention of crime) this will not justify the interference if the means used to achieve the aim are excessive in the circumstances. Any interference with a Convention right should be carefully designed to meet the objective in question and must not be arbitrary or unfair. Even taking all these considerations into account, in a particular case an interference may still not be justified because the impact on the individual or group is too severe. In some cases, the court may conclude that there are insufficient reasons to support the decision, policy or law. However, in others it may be willing to accept the opinion of expert decision-makers, such as a government department, health authority or Parliament.

Article I of the First Protocol

10.68 *Article I* of the *First Protocol* aims to ensure that a person's (including a company's) possessions are not unfairly interfered with.

Article I is made up of three rules concerning:

- the principle of the peaceful enjoyment of possessions;

- the deprivation of possessions;

- the right of the State to control the use of property in the general interest or to secure the payment of taxes or other contributions or penalties.

An interference with property must also satisfy the requirements of legal certainty, in other words, there must be a law which permits the interference and that law must be sufficiently certain and accessible. There must also be procedural safeguards against arbitrary State decisions. The procedural requirements of HRA 1998, Art 6 may be relevant.

Allocation

10.69 There is, as yet, no directly enforceable right to housing protected by *HRA 1998* (but see Nicol, *A Right to Housing* [1998] July LEGAL ACTION 8).

Thus ' ... the Commission does not consider that *Article 8* can be interpreted in such a way as to extend a positive obligation to provide alternative accommodation of an applicant's choosing' – *Burton v UK (1996) 22 EHRR CD 135*.

However, if a public housing authority were to fail to make provision of any accommodation at all (or inordinately delay provision of accommodation) so that a person had no option other than to live 'on the streets' that may amount to inhuman or degrading treatment [*HRA 1998, Art 3*] or a failure to respect private or family life [*HRA 1998, Art 8*].

Such challenges are likely to be made in the light of the Court of Appeal's recent reaffirmation that the sick, elderly and other vulnerable people are not to be left destitute on the streets (and are instead to be dealt with by Social Service authorities) – *O v Wandsworth LBC* and *Bhikha v Leicester CC [2000] 22 June, CA.*

10.70   However, some early challenges can be expected to housing alloca-tion and nomination regimes operated under *HA 1996, Part VI* (or 'independ-ently' by RSLs) on procedural grounds. For example:

(a)   Disputes about admission to – or exclusion from – the housing register are presently dealt with by the local authority's own review procedures with no further appeal to the courts [*HA 1996, s 164*]. The absence of an independent determination mechanism may well be in breach of *HRA 1998, Art 6* (and not saved simply by the availability of judicial review – *W v UK (1988) 10 EHRR 29*).

(b)   Some housing authorities restrict allocations to certain types of applicant on the basis of their private or family life (eg only considering married or engaged heterosexual couples for family-sized homes) or give such applicants preference. This may be in breach of *HRA 1998, Art 8* read with *HRA 1998, Art 14*.

(c)   Some authorities will only grant joint tenancies to certain types of household – this may be a failure to respect the private lives of some other applicants.

(d)   Other authorities exclude numerous classes of applicant from eligibility and the statute itself excludes certain applicants by reference to immigration status [*HA 1996, s 161*]; see *Exclusions from the Housing Register* (NCHA) May 2000. Those excluded are likely to assert that exclusion is disproportionate (eg if they are being denied access to a home because of a minor debt).

There may also be human rights-driven disputes about the size of accommo-dation allocated (eg from a parent who wants accommodation so that his children can have 'staying contact') on the basis that providing insufficient accommodation may amount to failure to respect family life.

What sort of tenancy?

10.71   Even in the social sector not all new tenants will enjoy security of tenure. There are numerous exceptions to secure and assured tenure set out in the Housing Acts and at least two widespread schemes for avoiding security of tenure (the introductory tenancy and the assured shorthold).

Succession

10.72   Where a tenant dies leaving a family member in residence there may well be disputes about succession to the tenancy that take a human rights flavour.

Both assured and secure tenancy regimes prescribe the categories of 'family member' who may succeed by right.

Both enable succession by a partner in a heterosexual relationship, but what about succession between gay partners? Although the gay succession case of *Harrogate BC v Simpson (1984) 17 HLR 205* was subsequently held 'inadmissible' by the European Commission (*S v UK [1986] 47 DR 274*) the same result might not follow today. The government is committed to extend the benefits of *Fitzpatrick v Sterling Housing Association* (a Rent Act tenancy case) to the public sector at the first legislative opportunity.

In *Mendoza v Ghaidan [2002] 4 All ER 1162* the Court of Appeal held, in the context of the *Rent Act 1977*, that the difference in treatment based on sexual orientation is an impermissible ground of discrimination which could not be justified by deference to Parliament. Thus the words in the statute '*as his wife or husband*' had to be read to mean '*as if they were his wife or husband*' otherwise the survivor of a same-sex relationship and a survivor of a heterosexual relationship would be treated differently. It is suggested that it is only a matter of time before the same decision is reached in the context of the *1985 Act*.

It might be expected that non-eligible successors (e g the children of assured tenants or of secure joint tenants) will resist possession proceedings contending that eviction in their cases would breach *HRA 1998, Art 8*.

Actions of a public authority

10.73   *HRA 1998, s 6* defines a public authority and makes it unlawful for a public authority to act in a way which is incompatible with a Convention right unless it is required to do so by primary legislation or incompatible secondary legislation. 'Act' also includes failure to act.

However an 'act' is not unlawful if:

- the authority could not have acted differently because of primary legislation; or

- the authority has acted in accordance with a statutory provision that could not be interpreted in a way compatible with the *ECHR*. (This will not apply where legislation is open to interpretation and the authority has exercised its discretion in the wrong way.)

If, however, the authority reaches a decision or acts in a way that is required by virtue of primary legislation, then its defence in such cases will be that it was prohibited by primary legislation from acting in any other way, ie the primary legislation did not provide for the application of any discretion on the part of the deciding authority.

Rights of individuals

10.74 An individual who is having his civil rights or obligations determined is entitled to the following rights.

(a) *The right of access to a court or tribunal* – This does not prevent the creation of a system whereby a decision is first taken by an administrative authority, (like a decision to award Housing Benefit) provided that the decision can be reviewed by a court or tribunal/ appeal committee. In some cases the review may be limited to points of law, but in most cases, the review may need to be in the form of an appeal on both facts and law.

(b) *The right to a fair hearing* – There should be a reasonable opportunity to present a case and to examine witnesses. There should be equality of arms and one party should not be placed at a disadvantage compared with the other. There is a general right to a reasoned decision. There is also a right to be physically present at the hearing unless an individual waives this right. Rules of evidence may also affect the possibility of a fair trial, as may the refusal to disclose evidence or to refuse further evidence that may be submitted.

(c) *The right to a public hearing* – It is possible to exclude the public where it can be justified on one of the grounds set out in *HRA 1998, Art 6*, such as the protection of morals, national security, public order, the interests of juveniles or matters of a confidential nature such as the income of a claimant. A public hearing may be dispensed with if there is an appeal to a court sitting in public. Decisions must be given in public or otherwise be made available to the public.

(d) *The right to a hearing within a reasonable time* – A breach may arise where a state fails to organise its system so as to avoid delays, for example, by providing inadequate staff and resources to hear cases within a reasonable time. In calculating whether or not there has been a hearing within a reasonable time, the European Court not only takes account of the period up to the substantive hearing but the total time required to resolve the matter, including time taken up in appeals.

(e)   *The right to an independent and impartial tribunal* – One element in securing this right is the procedures and rules on the appointment and terms of office of members of the tribunal and members of an appeal committee. Members must be free from outside pressures, and should be independent of the executive and of the parties. The appeal committee or tribunal must not be biased. The appeal committee/tribunal must be established by law.

(f)   *The right to legal aid and representation* – Presently this is not available for claimants attending most appeal committee hearings or Social Security tribunals. This right will most certainly give rise to claimants being represented at hearings far more frequently than has previously been the case.

Housing Benefit entitlements

10.75 Not all of the rights contained in the Convention have been incorporated into *HRA 1998*. However, those which have been incorporated and are most likely to be of relevance to Housing Benefit entitlements are as set out in **10.76** to **10.92** below.

The Convention

ARTICLE 3: PROHIBITION OF TORTURE AND INHUMAN OR DEGRADING TREATMENT

10.76 It is not suggested that a claimant may be subjected to torture in the process of claiming or appealing against a benefit award. Claimants may feel that they are subject to degrading treatment in undergoing medical examinations, investigations and/or questioning by benefit officers or members of the appeal tribunal for the purposes of benefit claims. It is believed that such treatment is likely to fall short of the requirement of *HRA 1998, Art 3*.

Where treatment or questioning is necessary to establish qualifying grounds of entitlement to benefit it is unlikely to amount to a breach of the Convention. However, questioning or behaviour which is genuinely degrading and unnecessary is likely to breach *HRA 1998, Art 3*.

VERIFICATION FRAMEWORK COMPLIANCE IN HOUSING BENEFIT

10.77 VF is not legislation, therefore not enforceable on a point of law. (This does not imply that requesting compliance with VF is in any way illegal, but that certain areas are not legally enforceable.)

10.78 *SI 1987 No 1971, Reg 73* provides for the authority to request any documents, information or evidence that is reasonably required for the purpose of assessing benefit entitlement (this means that the benefit department can ask for information that they 'reasonably need' to assess entitlement to Housing Benefit).

Proof of the following are accommodated by *SI 1987 No 1971, Reg 73*:

- residence;
- income;
- capital;
- members of the household;
- rent;
- National Insurance number.

This information relates to what the benefit office *must* have in order to process a claim for Housing Benefit. Original documents are not legally required nor is evidence of identity. Examples are original bank statements (where the photocopy of a bank statement was of good quality, ie there was no reason to believe that a copy had been tampered with), evidence of identity by way of birth certificate, driving licence, etc as evidence of identity is satisfied by production of the National Insurance number, which is lawfully required.

10.79 Therefore withholding or suspending benefit entitlement where required proof is supplied (but not original documents or evidence of identity) is unlawful and subject to challenge by way of judicial review and a possible claim under *HRA 1998, Art 6 (1), Art 8 (1), Article 1* of the *First Protocol*.

This is because where the benefit authority has 'satisfactory' proof which will allow for a claim to be processed then withholding/suspending benefit could not be deemed to be 'proportionate' and necessary in a democratic society, nor is there a requirement in law for such restrictions to be applied (this is because there is no legislation, primary or subordinate, to support the requirement of the production of original documents or evidence of identity other than a National Insurance number).

ARTICLE 6: THE RIGHT TO A FAIR TRIAL

10.80 *HRA 1998, Art 6* is clearly relevant to decisions of an authority that are subject to a review or appeal of any nature, and since it applies to 'civil rights' it covers all benefits.

Article 6 says that 'everyone is entitled to a fair and public hearing within a reasonable time by an independent and impartial tribunal established by law'.

10.81 A 'fair' hearing means that all parties to the appeal should have the opportunity to prepare and present their case on an equal basis. Where the claimant's case is very complex it must be recognised that the claimant's rights cannot be complied with in the absence of the claimant having a suitably qualified representative, and it is believed that for the first time some appellants to tribunals might be granted legal aid in such cases.

10.82 The claimant has a right to a public hearing. However, if the claimant elects to have a paper hearing then he can be taken to have waived his right to a public hearing.

Oral hearings should be held in a place to which the public have access. *HRA 1998, Art 6* qualifies this by stating that 'the press and public may be excluded from all or part of the trial in the interests of morals, public order or national security in a democratic society, where the interests of juveniles or the protection of the private life of the parties so require, or to the extent strictly necessary in the opinion of the court in special circumstances where publicity would prejudice the interests of justice'.

10.83 What constitutes 'a reasonable time' depends on the circumstances of the case. If a case is listed too quickly in order to achieve a hearing within a reasonable time the claimant may be denied sufficient time to obtain advice or further evidence. A balance will have to be struck, as it is now.

10.84 'Impartiality' means lack of bias, and is a confirmation of the rules of natural justice, ie that no man should be a judge in his own cause and should decide the outcome in accordance with the evidence and not prejudice.

10.85 The Article goes on to provide that 'judgment shall be pronounced publicly' which, on the face of it, would prevent the body hearing an appeal from deciding not to give the decision on the day. However, there are decisions of the European Court of Human Rights which suggest that this part of the Article will be satisfied provided there is a reading of the judgment in open court, a copy of the judgment is sent to the parties, and there is a register of judgments which is open to inspection.

ARTICLE 8: THE RIGHT TO RESPECT FOR PRIVATE AND FAMILY LIFE

10.86 If the appellant specifically requests a private hearing, he will be deemed to have waived his right to a public one, and an insistence on a public hearing could breach his right to privacy under *HRA 1998, Art 8*.

10.87 It may also be alleged that the obtaining of evidence, such as video evidence, breaches the right to privacy provided by *Article 8*. However, the right is not absolute, and public authorities are given the power to interfere with the right in certain specified circumstances, for example, where it is necessary in a democratic society in the interest of the economic well-being of the country or for the protection of the rights and freedoms of others. Therefore the use of video evidence in cases where benefit fraud is alleged may be permitted without the risk of breach.

ARTICLE 1 OF THE FIRST PROTOCOL: PROTECTION OF POSSESSIONS

10.88 All benefits to which the claimant is legally entitled provided he satisfies the necessary qualifying conditions, ie all benefits except purely discretionary payments such as discretionary financial assistance awards, are likely to be regarded as possessions and therefore covered by *Article 1* of the *First Protocol.*

However, the right is qualified as the Article states that no one shall be deprived of his possessions 'except in the public interest'; and subject to the conditions provided for by law and the right of the Secretary of State to enforce such laws as it deems necessary to control the use of property in accordance with the general interest.

SECTION 6

10.89 *HRA 1998, s 6* provides that it is unlawful for a public authority (which includes a court or tribunal) to act in a way which is incompatible with a Convention right unless it is not possible to do otherwise because the breach is contained in primary legislation (ie an Act of Parliament).

In other words, if a section in an Act of Parliament appears to breach the Convention right, the tribunal must try if possible to construe the section in a way which is compatible with the Convention, but if it cannot, then it must apply the section even though the result is that a Convention right is then breached.

The Commissioners must do the same. Even the High Court, the Court of Appeal and the House of Lords must, unless they can construe the statute compatibly, apply it. However, they are given the additional power to make what is called a 'declaration of incompatibility'. The understanding is that if such a declaration is made, then Parliament will immediately change the statute. See *Brown v Procurator Fiscal, The Times, 14 February 2000,* for a good illustration of how a court reads a statute to be compatible with *HRA 1998.*

10.90 If, on the other hand, the breach is contained in secondary legislation (ie regulations), the public authority has the power not to apply it if satisfied that the regulation is not compatible with the Convention, unless primary legislation prevents removal of the incompatibility (which would be very unusual). In most cases, therefore, a social security appeal tribunal can ignore the offending part of the regulation and decide the appeal as if it did not exist.

10.91 As indicated above, anyone who considers that his human rights have been breached is entitled to bring an action in the UK courts for a declaration and appropriate compensation. Such actions may well be brought, but in the benefit context these arguments are most likely to arise once a claim has been refused and the claimant has lodged an appeal.

Provided the decision appealed against, or the action complained of, was after 2 October 2000, the body considering the appeal would then have to deal with the human rights argument and decide whether or not it is justified.

In deciding any question in connection with a Convention right, *HRA 1998, s 2(1)* requires the public authority to take into account any Convention jurisprudence, ie decisions of the European Court of Human Rights or the European Commission or the Committee of Ministers. (The Commission has now ceased to exist and the Committee no longer makes judicial decisions, so all future case law will emanate from the Court – past pronouncements of the Commission and Committee are, however, still valid.)

If, after argument, a public body does find that a Convention right has been breached, and that benefit is therefore payable, or an overpayment is not recoverable, it can only make such orders as are within its existing powers. It cannot, for example, award compensation. It can only make the same decisions which it could make prior to 2 October 2000. If a claimant wants compensation, he will have to apply to the court. Legislation may direct that such claims be brought before a specified tribunal.

Duty to provide information on HRA 1998

10.92 There is no direct duty on a public authority to provide information on *HRA 1998*. However, all procedures and statutory obligations in relation to making information available (for example, how to avoid homelessness under *HA 1996 s 179(1)*) will require consideration of *HRA 1998, Art 6* compliance when advising of the right to review or appeal.

10.93 The duty to provide information will be looked at in the context of *HRA 1998, Art 6*. The authority must consider whether it has an existing duty to provide information. For example, *HA 1996, ss 179–180* impose a duty to ensure that information is available on how to avoid homelessness and related matters. Where such a duty exists, leaflets, notices, signs and forms must be considered: are they clear, accessible, in appropriate languages; and clear as to specific matters relating to the procedure for making a claim.

10.94 The courts will be looking to protect the rights of the most vulnerable in particular under *HRA 1998*. Thus, in this context an authority may also wish to examine any procedures for enabling people to appoint someone else to act for them if, for example, they are mentally incapacitated.

10.95 Where there is not a specific duty to provide information, obligations will depend on:

- whether you are making a decision on someone's civil rights and obligations – if so you must comply with *HRA 1998, Art 6;*

- whether another right under *HRA 1998* is relevant to contact with the public – if so, has all relevant information been disclosed?

10.96 Disclosure of information is relevant in the following ways:

- in the determination of civil rights and obligations, the procedural safeguards in *HRA 1998, Art 6* will bite;

- if a challenge under *HRA 1998, Art 8* is made and the authority argues there is no breach because of *HRA 1998, Art 8(2)*, the court will look at procedural safeguards, including the provision of information, in deciding whether what is effectively a defence in *HRA 1998, Art 8(2)* can be relied upon (See *W v UK and McMichael v UK*);

- proportionality – the greater the discretionary nature of the authority's power, the keener the court will be to see that it has built-in procedural safeguards and has complied with them.

Bringing and defending a claim under HRA 1998

10.97 If a person considers that his human rights have been breached, he may bring a claim in the courts in one of two ways:

(a) a free-standing claim under *HRA 1998;* or

(b) by relying on Convention rights in any legal proceedings [*HRA 1998, s 7(1)*].

The steps which must be satisfied are:

(i) the complainant must be a 'victim' of the unlawful act;

(ii) the complaint can only be made against a 'public authority';

(iii) the claim must be brought within one year of the date on which the act complained of took place unless there is a shorter time limit in the proceedings, for example, for judicial review the time limit is three months;

(iv) the claim must be brought in a court which has the necessary jurisdiction.

Victim

10.98 For the purpose of *HRA 1998, s 7* a person is a victim of an unlawful act only if he would be a victim for the purposes of *ECHR, Art 34* if proceedings were brought in the European Court.

A person is a victim under *ECHR, Art 34* if he can show that he is the victim of a violation by a contracting state of a Convention right. This means he is directly affected by the impugned provision.

10.99 The case law of the Commission and European Court establishes that individuals are not permitted to 'complain against the law *in abstracto* simply because they feel that it contravenes the Convention'. In *Klass v Germany (1979–80) 2 EHRR 214,* the court held that all users or potential users of the postal and telecommunication services were 'directly affected' by legislation which provided for secret surveillance and would therefore qualify as victims. The applicants in the case were held not to be deprived of their victim status merely because the government made a retrospective statement to the effect that they had not been subject to surveillance.

If an individual runs the risk of being directly affected, that will suffice: in *Open Door Counselling and Dublin Well Woman v Ireland* two women were accepted as victims by the court on the basis that they belonged to a class of women of child-bearing age which might be adversely affected by an injunction imposed on the dissemination of information by an abortion centre.

10.100 The test for judicial review actions is 'sufficient interest', which has been held to include representative groups such as trades unions, Child Poverty Action Group, Joint Council for the Welfare of Immigrants, Greenpeace, the World Development Movement and the Equal Opportunities Commission. These groups would not be able to bring themselves within the definition of victim under *HRA 1998*. Public interest groups may be able to give assistance and provide representation for victims or amicus briefs.

10.101 Companies can be victims. Shareholders cannot be the victims of breaches of the Convention rights of the company. Trades unions cannot be victims on the ground that they represent the interests of members, but the union qua union may be the victim of a breach of its own rights under the Convention.

CHAPTER 11

Common Problems

Introduction

11.1 This chapter contains some examples of common problems and solutions in various different areas of Housing and Housing Benefit law.

Housing applications

Example 1

11.2   Q. My boyfriend and I made an application for housing with the council. We were living with my parents in their two bedroom home. I have one baby and am expecting another. Our application was accepted because we were overcrowded, but things just went from bad to worse with my parents so we've moved in with my boyfriend's parents. The house is the same size, so we are still overcrowded. Will we have to tell the council about this?

A. Yes, you must tell the housing department about this change, even though you are still overcrowded – honesty is always the best policy. You will already have agreed to tell the housing authority of any changes in your circumstances, and your failure to do so could result in your application for housing being withdrawn. Furthermore, because your housing conditions are overcrowded, you should make an appointment with the housing advice team at the local council because they will explore all of your housing options with you. They may be able to offer practical assistance such as help with a deposit so you can start looking for accommodation in the private rented sector. You might also consider making applications to housing associations in the area. The council should be able to give you a list of the ones that work in your locality. There are no restrictions at all on the number of applications for housing that you make. You must also advise the housing authority as soon as your baby is born; this is a change of circumstances which may affect your priority for housing, so it may well be very much in your interest to do so.

Example 2

11.3 Q. Our tenant was allocated a three bedroom property as she presented herself as a single parent with three children. In her application for housing she said that her children were to live with her, but we have since found out that the children did not move in with her at all as the children's grandparents have a residence order and are their legal guardians. At the time of making the application for housing the children did live with their mother, but the grandparents had already made the application for residence. At the time of the allocation of the property the children were no longer living with their mother, but we were not advised of this. Is there anything that we can do?

A. Unfortunately in this situation, unless you have specifically advised the tenant that she must notify you of any changes in her circumstances following her application for housing, or unless the tenant made a false statement when making her application for housing or on accepting the tenancy, there really is nothing that you can do. A policy on such declarations and checking that prospective tenants' circumstances have not changed when offering a tenancy should be incorporated into your housing policy in the future. In so doing, you may then rely on Ground 17 of *HA 1996* (see **6.46**) when considering action to recover the property.

Homelessness

Example 3

11.4 Q. I am a homeowner, but because of changes in interest rates and a change in my income I can no longer afford to pay my mortgage as well as all my other debts. I am in arrears and my mortgage lender is threatening to take me to court. I have been told that if this happens the council will have to give me a house because I have children. Is this correct?

A. First of all the council is not under any obligation to give you housing. The authority will look at why you are at risk of losing your home and whether this is your fault. If they find that it is your circumstances that have brought about this problem, rather than your neglect, then they may have a duty to provide you with housing under the homelessness legislation, but you must not assume this will be the case. The best advice you can be given now is to approach the housing advice centre in your town, or go to the Citizens Advice Bureau. They will be able to tell you exactly what your rights are, and could prevent you from becoming homeless. They can, for example, negotiate with your lender on your behalf, and could even represent you in court.

Example 4

11.5 Q. We are a housing authority and have an applicant who is a single person with shared care of his two children, who stay with him two to three nights per week. We have advised the applicant that we can only accommodate his housing needs as a single person because the children do not live with him. We are now presented with a letter from his solicitors saying that his human rights have been breached. Is this right and does it mean that we have to consider him for larger accommodation?

A. The solicitor's letter is most likely referring to your applicant's right to 'family life' under Article 8 of the European Convention on Human Rights (*HRA 1998, Art 8(1)*). Article 8 challenges, which seek to impose a housing duty on a state or local authority, rarely succeed but it is advisable to ensure that the decision-making process is open and above board and that all factors have been considered. It is therefore advisable for you, as a public authority, at least to consider the applicant for a larger property. You must also have regard for *Article 8(2)* of *HRA 1998* which provides circumstances where *Article 8(1)* rights may be restricted where there is a very good reason (eg needing to keep available family property for those who have children living with them) (see **CHAPTER 10 HUMAN RIGHTS IN HOUSING**). You should therefore establish exactly why you cannot consider this applicant for larger accommodation, and if possible ensure that any accommodation that is offered is suitable for children to visit to stay overnight, eg a bedsit may not be a suitable offer, whereas a one bedroom flat may be more suitable.

Tenancies

Example 5

11.6 Q. I have lived in my council house for many years. At first I was a joint tenant with my husband, who has since died. My disabled son, who is aged 35, lives with me and I am the sole tenant now. If anything happens to me will my son be able to take over the tenancy?

A. Because there has been one succession already in this tenancy, which occurred when you changed from a joint tenant with your husband to the sole tenant, it is unlikely that there would be any further right to succession. The only alternative available to you is to consider talking to your landlord about perhaps becoming a joint tenant with your son now (where you will be liable for 50% of the rent and your son will be liable for 50% of the rent). Alternatively, you may be able to obtain some assurance from your landlord that it will allow succession to your son on your death, but you must bear in mind that there is no automatic right to this and the further succession can only be granted at the discretion of your landlord.

Example 6

11.7 Q. Our tenant Susan, a lone parent, has died. She had three children under the age of ten. The eldest child (aged eight years) has been given the tenancy of his deceased mother's council property under *section 89* of *HA 1988* which sets out the grounds on which family members can succeed to tenancies on the death of tenants. Presently the rent account for this property is £1,560 in arrears and no rent is being paid.

Susan's sister, Gail is living at the former home of the deceased with her daughter, who is aged 18 and is expecting a baby. Prior to living in this property Gail gave up her tenancy on her council flat. Gail helps her mother Jane look after the children.

Jane (the children's grandmother) is the legal guardian of Susan's children until their 18th birthday (unless different guardians are appointed), and, in the case of the child with the tenancy, his trustee for the purposes of the tenancy and the obligations which fall under it. Jane also receives Child Benefit and Guardian's Allowance for the children.

Who is responsible for paying the rent on this property? What problems might we encounter if we look to recover this property because of rent arrears, in particular because the tenant is only aged eight?

A. First of all, the tenant is the person responsible for paying the rent. However in this case, because the tenant is a minor, this responsibility rests with his trustee, so all notices in respect of the rent liability and arrears must be served on the trustee. Secondly, it appears that the tenant is living with his grandparents and not in the property of which he is a tenant. Subject of course to the terms of the tenancy, which I presume will require the tenant to live in the property as his sole or main residence, there would appear to be a breach of the tenancy agreement here, therefore notice may be served on the trustee in respect of this breach.

Rent arrears enforcement

Example 7

11.8   Q. Our housing association tenant is 12 weeks in arrears with his rent. He is on Income Support and says that he claimed Housing Benefit when he moved into the property. We have tried to contact the Housing Benefit department about this. They will not disclose any information to us, but they confirm that they have a ten-week backlog. The tenant has not paid any rent at all since moving in. Should we delay enforcement of rent arrears until Housing Benefit is sorted out?

A. It would be good practice to obtain a signed authority from the tenant to obtain information from the Housing Benefit department in relation to the claim (see **APPENDIX A** (Letter 4)) and, if you have not already done this, asking for any Housing Benefit to be paid to the housing association on the grounds that your tenant has rent arrears of more than eight weeks. On doing so, you may be able to establish whether the Housing Benefit claimed will actually accommodate the due rent when processed. You should also point out to the Housing Benefit section that it has a duty to make a payment of rent allowance within 14 days of receiving the claim and all necessary information (or as soon as reasonably practicable thereafter). If the local authority is unable to do this, *regulation 91(1)* of the *Housing Benefit (General) Regulations 1987 (SI 1987 No 1971)* requires it to make a payment on account, provided that the delay is not because the claimant has not supplied information or documents which the local authority has reasonably requested from him. Additionally and/or alternatively, with rent arrears due exceeding eight weeks, there is nothing to prevent you from issuing a NSP now. This of course will not expire for 12 months and may be relied on if full rent due is not forthcoming. It is always important to remember that when a tenant signs a tenancy agreement, he signs to say that he will pay the full due rent (regardless of whether or not he has access to Housing Benefit).

Example 8

11.9   Q. Our tenant has no previous record of rent arrears as she has been getting full benefit for her rent for many years. She started work four months ago and says that she is on a low income, is receiving Tax Credits and that she has applied for Housing

Benefit. She has not paid any rent now for four months. We have issued a NSP and are looking to issue possession proceedings. She has telephoned us to say that she can only pay £10 per week. Will we have any problems if we commence possession proceedings?

A. You may wish to obtain an authority from the tenant to obtain information from the Housing Benefit department about the benefit status (see **APPENDIX A** (Letter 4)) and, if you have not already done this, asking for any Housing Benefit to be paid to the housing association on the grounds that your tenant has rent arrears of more than eight weeks. You may find that, because the tenant is working and in receipt of Tax Credits, she will not qualify for full Housing Benefit. Therefore it is essential to commence the recovery of rents due as quickly as possible, otherwise the rent arrears will continue to accrue. It would be considered to be good practice to establish the tenant's means in order to give full consideration to her ability to pay her actual rent, plus an amount off the arrears. This really should be done prior to any court hearing.

Possession proceedings

Example 9

11.10 Q. Our tenant's children, aged nine and eleven, have a history of creating problems for the next door neighbour. There have been numerous complaints about the children of the family calling the neighbour names, swearing at the neighbour and generally making offensive racial comments aimed at the neighbour. We have written to the tenant a number of times, asking her to come into the office and we have issued a NSP. We now intend to proceed to possession under Ground 14 of *HA 1996* (see 6.42). Is there anything further that we need to do?

A. You must at least interview (or at least attempt to interview) the tenant who is the subject of the complaint. Your investigation into this matter will not be complete until this is done. You need to try to establish that the tenant knows of his obligations to control the residents of his property under the terms of the tenancy agreement; you also need to try to establish whether the complaint is legitimate. If this form of enquiry is not performed then the tenant may well have a defence, in addition to a possible human rights issue and claim. The tenant may also be successful in defending any claim for costs made by you in the possession proceedings.

Defending possession

Example 10

11.11   Q. I have been issued with a summons for possession. My rent arrears are £1,059 and I cannot afford to pay this. I have offered my landlord £15 per week off my arrears plus my rent, but the landlord has said that the minimum offer that he can accept is my rent plus £50 per week. I am trying to work and support my family and if I lose my home I will probably lose my job. Do I have to attend the court hearing and will I get help with re-housing?

A. You do not necessarily have to attend the court hearing, but it may well be in your interest to do so. The summons issued to you will have invited you to make comments in your defence (whether you have one or not). You should respond to the summons within 14 days, stating that you have made an offer to pay the rent plus £15 per week off the arrears. The court will look to ensure that this is a reasonable offer of repayment and in doing so they will need to assess your means. This means that you will have to provide details of all your income and expenditure. The court will look at what you have coming in, what you have to pay out (including current rent liability) and how much you have left at the end of the week. If this is not an amount substantially exceeding the £15 offer, the court may well make an order for possession, but suspend that order on the condition that you pay the due rent plus the agreed £15 off the arrears. If you have substantially more than £15 excess income the court may suspend the order on condition that you pay a greater sum off your arrears each week. As long as you continue to pay your rent, plus the agreed amount off your arrears you will not lose your home. If you ignore the summons, the court will make an order for possession. If you become homeless in consequence of rent arrears this may affect your future housing prospects, as you may be considered to be intentionally homeless. You must seek advice immediately. Go to the local housing advice centre or approach the Citizens Advice Bureau. They will be able to negotiate with your landlord on your behalf and may well be able to attend court with you and help you put your case (see **CHAPTER 7 DEFENDING POSSESSION**).

If the amount that you have offered towards your arrears is deemed to be a reasonable offer, there might also be a case for consideration of *HRA 1998, Article 1* of the *First Protocol*, in so far that possession has been sought without such action being necessary for the recovery of rent. This might frequently be the case where a housing authority uses the courts for the purpose of making arrangements for rent repayment, rather than recovering their property. Such arrangements should be considered prior to court action; and court action should be reserved only as a last resort.

Housing Benefit

Example 11

11.12 Q. I was in receipt of full Housing Benefit and Income Support. I have been working part time and did not tell the local authority or the Department for Work and Pensions. This resulted in my being overpaid Housing Benefit and Income Support. My Housing Benefit has now stopped and I have not paid any rent because I am worse off now than when I was on benefit, but I have now applied for Tax Credits. I have been issued with a NSP for the rent arrears. The overpayment of Housing Benefit on my rent account has also been mentioned for consideration. Is there anything that I can do?

A. You should immediately apply for Housing Benefit again, as you may still be entitled to some help. You must also provide all the information and evidence of your income when you were working (for the period of the Housing Benefit overpayment). If you do this the Housing Benefit department can calculate how much benefit you would have been entitled to if you had given that information at the correct time. The department may then offset the amount of benefit that you would have been entitled to against the amount that you have been overpaid. You should do this as quickly as possible (see **APPENDIX A** (Letter 15)).

Example 12

11.13 Q. We are a housing association and have recently been advised that our tenant has been overpaid Housing Benefit of £3,000 because she was found to be working. We did not know that the tenant was working, and her rent from Housing Benefit was paid directly to us. The Housing Benefit department has said that we have to repay this sum regardless of whether we were aware that the tenant was working or not. The department always recovers all overpayments from our account, which they say they can do because we signed an agreement to repay overpayments as a condition of receiving direct benefit payments. However, such large overpayments do have an impact on our organisation which may result in increasing tenants' rents generally. Is there anything that we can do in this situation?

A. You can appeal against the council's decision to recover the overpayment from you. When deciding to recover an overpayment of Housing Benefit, the council has discretion as to whom the overpayment can be recovered from.

In using its discretion, the council must consider each case on its individual merit. Therefore the council cannot simply have a policy to recover the rent from you.

Your right of appeal is limited. You can appeal on the grounds that there has not been an overpayment, or that the amount of the overpayment has been wrongly calculated. However, you can only appeal against the decision about whom the overpayment should be recovered from on limited grounds.

For an appeal to succeed there has to be evidence which would be admitted in a judicial review case, i e evidence of bad faith, or evidence that both parties have not been heard, or evidence that the decision is totally unreasonable. The tribunal has no power to reconsider the way in which the local authority has exercised its discretion in deciding whom to recover from.

Letter 14 in **APPENDIX A** sets out some of the possible grounds for challenge if it is decided to pursue this course.

Housing and human rights

Example 13

11.14   Q. I have an introductory tenancy and have been issued with a NSP. I understand that if possession is sought then the court must grant the order. Does this breach my human rights?

A. No. At the time the NSP was issued, you would have been given the right of appeal against the decision. You can appeal to the authority and a senior officer who was not involved in the decision to serve the NSP will consider your appeal. You will be able to challenge the decision in this manner and will be given the opportunity to state your case either in person or in writing. The fact that the authority that made the decision is the same authority that is considering your appeal will not necessarily breach *Article 6* of *HRA 1998*, because the housing authority is only able to act as the rules allow them to (ie *HA 1996*). Even if your NSP gave a time limit for making the application for review or appeal against the NSP and that time limit has expired, you should still request late consideration of your application for appeal. You may be able to get assistance with this from your local housing advice office, Citizens Advice Bureau, law centre or solicitor. In making your application for review or appeal, you should ensure that you tell the housing authority why you think the decision is wrong, or if there has been any breach of the tenancy, why that occurred and what action you are going to take to ensure that this problem does not recur.

Example 14

11.15   Q. The new summons asks that we identify *HRA 1998* cases in possession – when will this apply? Also, we rely on the courts for suspended possession orders as we find this policy to be very effective in the recovery of rents. How will *HRA 1998* affect this? Finally, we often get to court (in cases where the tenant alleges Housing Benefit as being a problem) and the judge automatically adjourns the case and orders that we sort out the Housing Benefit problem, regardless of the fact that we have no control over Housing Benefit. Is this right?

A. In possession cases you are looking to recover a tenant's property (*HRA 1998, Art 1* of the *First Protocol*) and/or you are taking action which will affect the tenant's private and family life and his home. So generally the answer to this question is yes, there is a *HRA 1998* issue in virtually every case.

When you apply to the court for possession of a tenant's home, you are asking the court to return the property to you. The decision as to whether to suspend that order is entirely at the discretion of the court. (There is no such provision as a request for a suspended order.) This means that when you apply to the court you must have a clear intention to recover your property. Regardless of previously having relied on the courts to reach an arrangement to control your rent accounts, the *HRA 1998* implications mean that you must look at whether your action in resorting to the court to recover the property is necessary in the control of your rent arrears. This means that you may well have to demonstrate that you have done all that you can reasonably do to resolve the problem prior to resorting to the court (see **CHAPTER 10 HUMAN RIGHTS IN HOUSING**). Therefore, you should ensure that you have at least attempted to establish the tenant's means and ability to come to a realistic, sustainable arrangement prior to commencing court action (see **CHAPTER 4 ENFORCEMENT OF RENT ARREARS**).

With regard to problems with Housing Benefit, both you and the tenant have equal rights in the court. You need to ensure that you have clearly identified the problem relating to Housing Benefit and have tried to resolve this problem. However, the court must give consideration to the fact that the claim for Housing Benefit is the responsibility of the tenant and not you. If you have tried to obtain an authority from the tenant to obtain information from the Housing Benefit department about the claim, but the tenant has refused this consent, you must point this out to the court. If the Housing Benefit department has not processed a claim you might ask an officer from the department to attend the hearing to explain why this is the case. Most importantly, you must point out to the judge that you have no authority to obtain information about Housing Benefit without the tenant's consent (unless you are receiving direct payments of Housing Benefit, in which case you are entitled to certain limited information about the claim). As long as you can show the court that you have done everything that you reasonably can do to assist the tenant in resolving the Housing Benefit issue, the court cannot make unreasonable demands of you. If the court does make such unreasonable demands of you, this could constitute a breach of *Article 6* of *HRA 1998* as you are equally an affected party at the hearing.

APPENDIX A

Standard Letters

Letter 1: Request for a review of an offer of housing

To [Housing officer]

From [*Housing applicant*]

Date

Dear Sirs,

I am writing to request that you review your decision in respect of my application for housing, as I do not consider the accommodation to be suitable for my needs or the needs of my family.

My reason for this is because the accommodation offered [see *example reasons below*].

[Examples:

- is not in any of the areas that I selected on my housing application form.

- is a long way from my children's schools and living there would cause great difficulty in accommodating my children's educational needs, which may result in them suffering unduly in their education and social integration.

- is a long way from any family and friends on whom I (or a member of my family) rely on for support, which is essential to me.

- is in an area near to a person/persons from whom I feel my family would be placed at risk because ...

- the property is very damp and would affect my health or the health of a member of my family.

- the property is not suitable and cannot accommodate my disabled needs.]

In consideration of this information I request that you review your decision in relation to whether the accommodation offered is suitable.

Yours sincerely

Signed [...] (claimant)   Signed [...] (partner)

Letter 2: Tenant giving notice to end his tenancy

To [Landlord]

From [*Tenant*]

Date

Dear Sirs,

I am writing to advise you that I wish to give four weeks' notice of my intention to end my tenancy in respect of the above address.

I intend to move out of this property on [*date*].

I will return my keys to you on [*date*].

My forwarding address is [...]

I understand that I am responsible for the payment of my rent until the date of expiry of this notice.

Yours sincerely

Signed [...] (claimant)   Signed [...] (partner)

Letter 3: Letter to register a Housing Benefit claim

To Housing Benefit Department

Date

Dear Sirs,

I/We [*name of tenant/s*]

Of [*Address*]

NI number [...] (Claimant) NI number [...] (Partner)

wish to register a claim for Housing Benefit and Council Tax Benefit. We understand that we must provide a completed claim form for Housing/ Council Tax Benefit to your office within four weeks of the date that the form was issued to us.

We understand that if we do this that you will treat the date of your receipt of this letter to be the effective date of claim for my/our claim for Housing

Benefit and Council Tax Benefit in accordance with Regulation 72 of the Housing Benefit (General) Regulations 1987 and Regulation 62 of the Council Tax Benefit (General) Regulations 1992.

[*To be completed by new tenants*]

My/our tenancy commenced on [*date*].

I/we moved into this property on [*date*].

My/our previous address was [...]

Yours sincerely

Signed ... (claimant)   Signed ... (partner)
Housing officer contact name [...]
Telephone number [...]
Standard Housing Benefit form
issued to tenant   YES   NO

Letter 4: Housing Benefit letter of authority

To Housing Benefit Department

Date

Dear Sirs,

I/We [*name of tenant/s*]

Of [*address*]

NI number [...] (claimant) NI number [...] (partner)

hereby authorise my landlord [*housing association name/council housing services*] to make enquiries and to obtain information from you in relation to:

My/our application for benefit.

My/our application for review of benefit entitlement.

My/our backdated request for Housing Benefit.

My/our appeal against the benefit officer's decision in relation to my/our claim for benefit.

Yours sincerely

Signed [...] (claimant)   Signed [...] (partner)

Letter 5: Authority to obtain information relating to tenancy conduct

Date

[*Tenant name*] date of birth [...]

[*Partner name*] date of birth [...]

Address [...]

I/we the above named authorise our landlord [...] to obtain information and/or evidence from any relevant third party, including the police, Social Services, Housing Benefit department, probation that may be reasonably required by them in enquiries related to the conduct of our tenancy.

Signed:

Tenant [...]   Partner [...]

Letter 6: Two weeks' rent arrears

Date

Dear [*tenant*]

Rent and/or water charges arrears

Unless a payment crosses with this letter, there is a sum of £ [...] outstanding on your rent account as at today's date, which may be an oversight on your part.

I must remind you of the terms of the tenancy agreement 'Tenant Obligations', that you as the tenant of the above property are required:

'To pay rent and other charges as specified on the rent card weekly in advance in accordance with your tenancy agreement'.

Please pay your current rent and the arrears by return of post.

If there are any special difficulties with payment that you would like to discuss, please contact me on the above telephone number. If you wish to pay your rent on a monthly basis, this must be made in advance and not in arrears. It is usually possible to reach an agreement to pay an acceptable amount each week, fortnight or month to reduce any arrears.

If you are struggling with bills and debts you should contact your local housing advice centre or the Citizens Advice Bureau immediately. They will be able to help you work out what you can afford to pay and who you should pay first. The enclosed leaflet gives details of the offices in your area. If you are on a relatively low income, you may qualify for Housing Benefit. You can obtain an application form by telephoning the council offices or by visiting the offices in person.

Yours sincerely

Signed [...] (claimant)   Signed [...] (partner)

Letter 7: No arrangement made for rent arrears

Date

Dear [tenant]

At the close of business on the previous working day your account was £ [...] in arrears.

Will you please either clear the account in full or return the enclosed financial statement and undertaking within seven days from the date of this letter, explaining the reason for your arrears and detailing your future payment plan.

In the absence of any communication from you within seven days, we will have no alternative but to serve a notice seeking possession. This could lead to legal action being taken to recover possession of the property in the [...] County Court and costs in the region of £130 being added to your debt.

If you wish to discuss the matter further, or if you disagree with my records, please contact me immediately. An interview can be arranged, either at our offices or in the comfort of your own home and, if necessary, a Housing Benefit form can be completed at the same time.

If full payment has crossed with this letter and future payments are made when due, no further action will be taken.

Yours sincerely

I/We [...]

tenant(s) of [...] admit that, as at Friday [...] I/we am/are in arrears with my/our rent and other charges in the sum of £ [...].

I/We hereby undertake to clear my/our arrears by the payment of £ [...] per week *in addition to my/our current rent.*

I/We understand that if I/we breach my/our undertaking I/we may be served with a NOTICE SEEKING POSSESSION FOLLOWED BY COURT ACTION.

Signed: ...

Signed (if joint tenancy): ...

Date: ...

Telephone No: ...

Note: The payment undertaken must not be less than £ [...] per week off the total arrears.

Please state below the reasons, if any, why your rent is in arrears.

....

....

....

....

Please complete the attached financial statement

FINANCIAL STATEMENT

(Delete as necessary) **Weekly/monthly net income** £ p	**Weekly/monthly expenditure** £ p
Wages – tenant	Rent
Wages – partner	Council Tax
Tax Credit payments	Electricity
Income Support	Gas
Jobseeker's Allowance	Telephone
State Pension	Catalogue
Widow's/Bereavement Pension	Life insurance
Private pension	Contents insurance
Child Benefit	TV rental and licence
Incapacity Benefit	Maintenance
Sickness Benefit	Travelling expenses
Industrial Injuries Benefit	Clothing
War pensions	Housekeeping
Maintenance	Cigarettes/alcohol
Income from children	School meals, etc
Income from lodgers	Childminding fees
Disability benefits	Court orders
Other income	Others
Other income	Others
Total £ _____	**Total** £ _____
Under/overspend	£_____

Who can help me?

If you find, after completing the statement, that you do have problems (however large or small), contact your housing officer. Telephone number [...]

If you prefer, you can make an appointment with your local Citizens Advice Bureau, who will be able to assist you with completing this form.

In order to reach an agreement to reduce your rent arrears, you need to complete all the details above, which will help us in negotiating a payment arrangement to clear your arrears without putting your home at risk of being repossessed. Once you have completed this form your housing officer will then contact you to discuss the arrangements for payment.

Letter 8: Notice seeking possession

Date

Dear [...]

Notice seeking possession

The enclosed notice seeking possession has been served on you due to the outstanding balance on your rent account. Please read the notice carefully and note, in particular, your rights as detailed on the reverse.

Your account must be paid in full by expiry of the notice or an agreement made and adhered to. Failure to comply will leave us no alternative but to make an application to [...] County Court to obtain an order for possession of your home. If this action is taken, court costs in the region of £130 will be charged and added to your rent account.

If on hand delivery of this notice you were unable to discuss the matter, please contact me immediately so that we may reach a mutually agreed payment plan.

Should you be experiencing financial difficulties, you may wish to contact your local Citizens Advice Bureau who are qualified to assist in such matters.

Yours sincerely

HOUSING ACT 1985, SECTION 83

THIS NOTICE IS THE FIRST STEP TOWARDS REQUIRING YOU TO GIVE UP POSSESSION OF YOUR DWELLING. YOU SHOULD READ IT AND ALL THE NOTES VERY CAREFULLY.

1. To: [tenant]

[name of landlord council] intends to apply to the court for an order requiring you to give up possession of: [...]

2. Possession will be sought on Ground 1 of Schedule 2 to the Housing Act 1985 which reads:

'Rent lawfully due from the tenant has not been paid or an obligation of the tenancy has been broken or not performed.'

As at the [...] day of [...] 2005 your rent account showed an arrears of £ [...]

3. The reason for taking this action is non-payment of rent and/or other charges as specified in the terms of your tenancy agreement.

4. The court proceedings will not be begun until after [...] this being after four weeks from the service of this notice.

Dated this [...]

Housing Services Manager, Agent to and on behalf of [...] Council, the Landlord and duly authorised by the said council to sign this notice.

NB: This notice is given without prejudice to the right of the council to recover any rent that may be due to it on the expiration of the tenancy. If you wish to discuss this notice, you should get in touch with [...] (See notes attached).

FOR OFFICE USE ONLY: The original of this Notice was served by me this [...] day of

[...] on [...]

Signed: ...

Notes

Grounds for possession

1. If you have a secure tenancy under the Housing Act 1985, you can only be required to leave your dwelling following an order of the court on one or more of the grounds set out in the Act. Paragraph 2 of this notice tells you on what grounds an order is sought against you and paragraph 3 gives the landlord's reasons for believing those grounds apply. If you do not agree that they apply, you will be able to argue your case at a hearing in court.

Does the court have to grant the landlord possession?

2. Before the court grants an order on any of the Grounds 1 to 8 or 12 to 16 it must be satisfied that it is reasonable to require you to leave. This means that, if one of these grounds is set out in paragraph 2 of this notice, you will be able to argue to the court that it is not reasonable that you should have to leave, even if you accept the grounds.

Suitable alternative accommodation

3. Before the court grants an order on any of the Grounds 9 to 16 it must be satisfied that there will be suitable alternative accommodation for you when you have to leave. This means that the court will have to decide that, in their opinion, there will be other accommodation which is reasonably suitable for the needs of you and your family, taking into particular account various factors such as nearness of your place of work and the sort of housing that other people with similar needs are offered. Your new home will have to be let to you on another secure tenancy or a private tenancy under the Rent Act of a kind that will give you similar security. There is no requirement for suitable alternative accommodation where Grounds 1 to 8 apply.

One of the requirements of Ground 10A is that the landlord must have approval for the redevelopment scheme from the Secretary of State (or, in the case of a housing association landlord, the housing corporation). The landlord must have consulted all secure tenants affected by the proposed redevelopment scheme.

4. Whatever grounds for possession are set out in paragraph 2 of this notice, the court may allow any of the other grounds to be added at a later stage. If this is done, you will be told about it so you can argue about the new grounds if you want to.

Time limits

5. Court proceedings cannot be begun until after the date given in paragraph 4 of this notice. This date cannot be earlier than the date when your tenancy or licence could have been brought to an end. This means that if you have a weekly or fortnightly tenancy, there should be at least four weeks between the date this notice is given and the date in paragraph 4.

6. After the date in paragraph 4, court proceedings may be begun at once or at any time during the following 12 months. Once the 12 months is up the notice will lapse and it will be necessary for a new notice to be served before possession can be sought.

Leaving without a court order

7. If you are willing to give up possession without a court order, you should notify the person who signed the notice as soon as possible and say when you would leave.

Further advice

8. If you need advice about this notice and what you should do about it, take it as quickly as possible to a Citizens Advice Bureau, a housing aid centre, or a law centre, or to a solicitor. You may be able to receive legal services financial assistance/legal aid but this will depend on your personal circumstances.

Letter 9: Possession proceedings

Date

Dear [...]

PLEASE READ THIS LETTER CAREFULLY. It concerns the security of your tenancy and possibly your right to remain in your home.

Due to your escalating arrears, a court application has now been made and you will shortly receive a summons from [...] County Court. As at [date] the amount outstanding was £ [...].

The summons means that you will be required to attend the county court on [...]. The District Judge will consider your case and decide which order for possession to make. It is usual, when the tenant attends court, for the possession order to be suspended, provided you pay the current rent due and the amount set by the court.

Court costs are awarded to us and are added to the rent account. These costs are charged by the court for the preparation and issue of the summons.

You are strongly advised to discuss the matter with this office before the hearing date. In addition, independent advice can be sought from the Citizens Advice Bureau, your local law centre or from a solicitor.

Yours sincerely

Letter 10: Court outcome

Date

Dear [...]

At the county court hearing on [...] a suspended possession order was granted to [*name of landlord*] in respect of your home. It was suspended on the basis that you pay your weekly rent £ [...] plus £ [...] per week off the arrears as from [date]. The court will send you written confirmation of this.

If you miss one payment or fail to make it on time, you will automatically lose your security as a tenant. This means that you will no longer have the following rights:

(a)   to exchange or transfer your home;

(b)   for a member of your family to succeed to your tenancy;

(c)   to buy your home at a discount (council tenants).

The loss of these and other rights as a secure tenant is automatic and not discretionary to the landlord.

Any payments made by you or a person paying on your behalf after your security has been lost will be accepted as mesne profits. Mesne profits are payments made by someone who has ceased to be a tenant.

In addition, once you have lost your security as a tenant, we [landlord] may apply to the court to obtain an order to evict you from your home. There is no automatic right to obtain an order to evict you from your home. The council does not have an automatic right to re-house you under homelessness legislation. Each case is considered and a decision is reached based on the relevant facts, which include whether your actions have contributed to your homelessness.

Please do not ignore this letter. If you do not understand it or require further information, please contact me or seek independent advice from the Citizens Advice Bureau, local law centre or solicitor.

Yours sincerely

Letter 11: Court order default – intention to apply for a warrant

Date

Dear [...]

You have failed to make the necessary payments as ordered by the [...] County Court on [...].

You have now lost your rights as a secure tenant. Any future payments made by you, or a person acting on your behalf will be by someone who has ceased to be a tenant.

You were ordered by the court to pay the current rent of £ […] plus £ […] per week towards your arrears. Your current account balance is £ […]. This is in breach of your court order by £ […].

Due to the severity of the arrears, I have no option but to apply for an eviction. However, before taking action I am offering you a final opportunity to explain your situation and would therefore request that you contact me immediately upon receipt of this letter to arrange a mutually convenient appointment.

If you fail to respond to this letter within 14 days, I shall have no option but to proceed with the bailiff application.

Please do not ignore this letter – if you do not understand it or require further help or information, please contact me or seek independent advice from the Citizens Advice Bureau.

Yours sincerely

Letter 12: Challenge to Housing Benefit department's discretion to refer to rent officer

To [Housing Benefit Department]

From [Registered Social Landlord]

Date

Dear Sirs,

Housing Benefit Reference number [...] Tenant' s name [...] Tenant's address [...]

We understand that you are considering referring/have referred the above named tenant's rent to the rent officer under your discretionary powers because you consider the tenant's property to be larger than they reasonably need.

However, we feel that you have not fully considered the circumstances of the tenancy so as to make a decision based on individual merit as is required in the administration of your discretionary powers.

We would therefore bring to your attention the reasons for our letting this larger property to this tenant, being that [see examples below].

[Examples:

- this property is hard to let and the tenant was referred to us by the homeless welfare department of the council.

- the tenant is a disabled person and needs extra accommodation for the purpose of accommodating a carer.

- the tenant is expecting a baby and would need to be re-housed following the birth of the child.

- the tenant has additional family considerations and was allocated this larger property in consideration of Article 8(1) of the Human Rights Act.]

As you have not made further enquiries of the reasons for our letting this property to the tenant, we feel that your decision to refer this rent to the rent officer has been made in ignorance of a material fact as outlined above. We therefore request that you review your decision to refer this rent to the rent officer.

Yours sincerely

Letter 13: Backdating application

To [*Housing Benefit Department*]

From [*Claimant*]

Date

Dear Sirs,

Housing Benefit Reference number [...]
Tenant' s name [...] Tenant's address [...]

Dear Sirs,

I am writing to request that you consider backdating my application for Housing and Council Tax Benefit to [*date*].

My reasons for not having made this claim at an earlier date are that [*see examples below*].

[Examples:

- I am disabled, suffering from [...] and was not able to complete my claim form earlier because I could not obtain the assistance that I needed to complete the claim.

- I suffer from a severe mental impairment and because of this I was unable to realise that the claim form needed to be completed.

- at the time when I should have completed my claim form I had special circumstances which prevented me from being able to complete the form or gaining assistance to do so, and my special circumstances were [...].

- I had previously completed a claim form and I was wrongly advised by my solicitor that I did not need to complete another. When I found out that this was wrong, I immediately completed and sent in my claim.

- I was awaiting an award of disability living allowance. Until I was awarded disability living allowance I did not qualify for Housing Benefit because of my other circumstances. I claimed as soon as possible after I was awarded disability living allowance.]

From the date that I should have claimed Housing and Council Tax Benefit up to the date that I did register my claim, my reasons for not claiming as outlined above were continuous.

I therefore request that you consider my application for backdated benefit in accordance with Regulation 72(15) of the Housing Benefit (General) Regulations 1987 and Regulation 62(16) of the Council Tax Benefit (General) Regulations 1992.

Yours sincerely

Signed [...] (claimant)

Letter 14: Challenge to a decision to recover overpayment from the landlord

To [*Housing Benefit Department*]

From [*Landlord*]

Date

Dear Sirs,

Housing Benefit Reference number [...] Tenant's name [...] Tenant's address [...]

Further to your decision of [*date*] to recover the overpayment of Housing Benefit in respect of our tenant, the above named, directly from us, we request that you revise your decision to recover this benefit from us.

We understand that Regulation 101 of the Housing Benefit (General) Regulations 1987 provides the authority with the discretion to recover overpaid benefit from either the claimant or the landlord. However, in using its discretion we believe that the authority has a statutory duty to decide each case on its individual merit, having due consideration to each party from whom recovery may be sought.

We consider you to have failed in your application of this discretionary power by not having made sufficient enquiries of us as to the effect that such recovery might have.

We consider it to be unreasonable to recover this overpayment from us because [*see examples below*]

[Examples:

● by continuously recovering overpayments of Housing Benefit from our rent accounts, the impact of such debts result in many other tenants suffering a rent increase to accommodate our shortfall in income.

236

- the tenant has abandoned the property and we have no means by which to trace him, leaving arrears on our rent accounts. This is not acceptable to us as we are a charitable, non-profit-making organisation. However, we believe that the tenant has made a further claim for Housing Benefit therefore the authority is sufficiently able to contact him and enact recovery directly from him either by way of a payment arrangement or by deductions from other benefit entitlement. This form of recovery is not available to us.

- the tenant's only rent arrears are those of claw back of Housing Benefit payments, which do not constitute rent that is legally due. Therefore we are unable to recover this debt by way of possession proceedings. However, we understand that you are able to recover from the tenant by way of deductions from ongoing benefit entitlement of a number of different sources.

We therefore request that you revise your decision to recover our tenant's overpayment of housing benefit directly from us.

Yours sincerely

Letter 15: Challenge to a decision in relation to overpayment

To [*Housing Benefit Department*]

From [*Claimant/landlord*]

Date

Dear Sirs,

Housing Benefit Reference number [...] Tenant's name [...] Tenant's address [...]

I am writing to request that you revise your decision of [*date*] in respect of the amount of overpayment that you are going to recover.

I consider your decision in respect of the amount of overpayment is wrong because [*see examples below*]

[Examples:

- although I did not tell you about my change of circumstances immediately, I did tell you about them on [*date*]. However, you did not deal with my change of circumstances claim until [*date*] which resulted in my overpayment being more than it would have been had you dealt with

237

my claim earlier. I understand that Regulation 99 of the Housing Benefit (General) Regulations 1987 provides that in these circumstances such overpayments should not be recovered from me unless it was reasonable for me to know at the time of the overpayment that I was being overpaid. It was not reasonable for me to know that I was being overpaid at that time because [...].

- I have provided you with details of all of my income for the period that you say I was overpaid, but you have not recalculated how much benefit I would have been entitled to had you known this information earlier. I understand that Regulation 104 of the Housing Benefit (General) Regulations 1987 provides that you should offset against the overpayment the amount of benefit that I would have been entitled to in these circumstances. Furthermore I did not provide this information earlier because you did not ask for it.]

In consideration of the above information I request that you revise your decision in respect of the amount of overpayment of benefit that I am to repay.

Yours sincerely

Letter 16: Late application for review (made outside of one month)

To [*Housing Benefit Department*]

From [*Claimant/landlord*]

Date

Dear Sirs,

Housing Benefit Reference number [...] Tenant's name [...] Tenant's address [...]

I am writing to request that you revise your decision of the [date] 'out of time'.

My reasons for not making this application earlier are that I had special circumstances, which resulted in my not being able to make this application earlier.

My special circumstances were [*see examples below*]

[Examples:

238

- I am disabled, suffering from [...] and could not obtain the assistance I needed to request a revision earlier.

- I am mentally impaired and in consequence of this I did not know that there was anything that I could do to challenge your decision until it was pointed out to me by someone else.

- at the relevant time I was under exceptional pressure because [...] which resulted in it not being practicable for me to be able to request a revision at the appropriate time.

I have made this application as soon as possible following my special circumstances and I believe that if you allow this late application it will result in my award of benefit being increased. I would therefore request that you allow this late application for revision.

Yours sincerely

Letter 17: Request for review of suspended benefit

To [*Housing Benefit Department*]

From [*Claimant*]

Date

Dear Sirs,

Housing Benefit Reference number [...]

Tenant's name [...] Tenant's address [...]

I am writing to request that you revise your decision to suspend my award of Housing Benefit. My reasons for this request are that [...].

This suspension of my benefit is causing me severe financial hardship and may result in my losing my home.

As I have provided you with all the information that you have said that you require to assess my benefit entitlement I consider your continued suspension of my benefit to be unreasonable and may amount to a breach of Article 1 of the First Protocol of the Human Rights Act 1998.

I understand that you have further enquiries that you need to make and that this is taking time. However your suspending my benefit could result in my losing my home, this being a far greater risk than the possibility of an overpayment occurring, which you will be able to recover if the suspension of my benefit was lifted.

I would therefore request your immediate consideration of this request for revision in respect of your decision to suspend my benefit.

Yours sincerely

Housing Benefit calculation sheet

Note – if claimant or their partner is over 60, the applicable amount will consist of their appropriate minimum guarantee plus any additional amounts. If either is over 65, the maximum amount of savings credit is also added to the applicable amount.

Applicable amount	£	Income	£
Adult personal allowance		Claimant's net earned income	
Child addition – age		Partner's net earned income	
Child addition – age		Total	
Child addition – age		*Less* earnings disregard	
Child addition – age		*Less* childcare costs	
Child addition – age		*Less* 30-hour disregard	
Family premium		Assessed net income	
Disabled child premium		Child Benefit	
Disability premium		Child Tax Credit	
Severe disability premium		Working Tax Credit	
Enhanced disability premium		Other benefit income	
Carer premium		Other income	
Bereavement premium		Maintenance	
		Less disregard	
		Maintenance (less disregard)	
		Tariff income from capital	
Total applicable amount		**Total assessed income**	

Total assessed income

£

Less total applicable amount

£

= Difference (income less applicable amount)

£

Difference (income less applicable amount)

£

x 65% = Excess income

£

Eligible rent

£

Less excess income

£

= Housing Benefit

£

Less non-dependant deductions

£

= Housing Benefit payable

£

If the claimant's applicable amount is the same as or greater than the total assessed income, then Housing Benefit will be 100% of the eligible rent, less any non-dependant deduction.

APPENDIX B

Court Forms

N5 Claim form for possession of property

Claim form for possession of property	In the
	Claim No.

Click here to clear all fields   Click here to print form

Claimant
(name(s) and address(es))

SEAL

Defendant(s)
(name(s) and address(es))

The claimant is claiming possession of :

which (includes) (does not include) residential property. Full particulars of the claim are attached.
(The claimant is also making a claim for money).

This claim will be heard on: 20   at   am/pm

at

At the hearing
• The court will consider whether or not you must leave the property and, if so, when.
• It will take into account information the claimant provides and any you provide.

What you should do
• Get help and advice immediately from a solicitor or an advice agency.
• Help yourself and the court by **filling in the defence form** and **coming to the hearing** to make sure the court knows all the facts.

Defendant's name and address for service		Court fee	£
		Solicitor's costs	£
		Total amount	£
		Issue date	

Claim No.

Grounds for possession

The claim for possession is made on the following ground(s):

☐ rent arrears

☐ other breach of tenancy

☐ forfeiture of the lease

☐ mortgage arrears

☐ other breach of the mortgage

☐ trespass

☐ other *(please specify)* _____

Is the claimant claiming demotion of tenancy?　　　　☐ Yes　☐ No

See full details in the attached particulars of claim

Does, or will, the claim include any issues under the Human Rights Act 1998?　☐ Yes　☐ No

Anti-social behaviour

The claimant is alleging:

☐ actual or threatened anti-social behaviour

☐ actual or threatened use of the property for unlawful purposes

---

Statement of Truth

*(I believe)(The claimant believes) that the facts stated in this claim form are true.
* I am duly authorised by the claimant to sign this statement.

signed _____ date _____

*(Claimant)(Litigation friend *(where the claimant is a child or a patient)*)(Claimant's solicitor)
delete as appropriate

Full name _____

Name of claimant's solicitor's firm _____

position or office held _____
　　　　　　　(if signing on behalf of firm or company)

Claimant's or claimant's solicitor's address to which documents or payments should be sent if different from overleaf.

Postcode

if applicable

Ref. no.	
fax no.	
DX no.	
e-mail	
Tel. no.	

Click here to print form

N5B Claim form for possession of property (accelerated procedure) (assured shorthold tenancy)

**Claim form for
possession of property**
(accelerated procedure)
(assured shorthold tenancy)

In the	
Claim No.	

Click here to print form | Click here to clear all fields

Claimant
(name(s) and address(es))

SEAL

Defendant(s)
(name(s) and address(es))

The claimant is claiming possession of:

for the reasons given in the following pages.
[The claimant is also asking for an order that you pay the costs of the claim.]

IMPORTANT - TO THE DEFENDANT(S)

This claim means that the court will decide whether or not you have to leave the premises and, if so, when. There will not normally be a court hearing. You must act immediately.

Get help and advice from an advice agency or a solicitor.
Read all the pages of this form and the papers delivered with it.
Fill in the defence form and return it **within 14 days** of receiving this form.

The notes on the last page of this form tell you more about what you can do.

Defendant's
name and
address for
service

Court fee	£
Solicitor's costs	£
Total amount	£

Issue date	

N5B Claim form for property (accelerated procedure)(assured shorthold tenancy) (06.04)   *Printed on behalf of The Court Service*

Claim No.	

<table>
<tr>
<td>If you are a registered social landlord claiming possession of premises let under a demoted assured shorthold tenancy, you should complete only sections 1, 2, and 7 to 11. Please see Notes for the claimant in Form N5C.</td>
<td>If you are not claiming possession of premises let under a demoted tenancy do not complete section 2 but complete all other sections as appropriate. Please see Notes for the claimant in Form N5C.</td>
</tr>
</table>

1. The claimant seeks an order that the defendant(s) give possession of

   ("the premises") which is a dwelling house [part of a dwellinghouse].

2. On the   20   , the   County Court
   made a demotion order. A copy of the most recent (assured) (secure) tenancy agreement marked 'A' and
   a copy of the demotion order marked 'B' is attached to this claim form. The defendant was previously
   (an assured) (a secure) tenant.

3. On   , the claimant entered into a written tenancy agreement with the defendant(s).
   A copy of it, marked 'A' is attached to this claim form. The tenancy did not immediately follow an assured
   tenancy which was not an assured shorthold tenancy.
   [One or more subsequent written tenancy agreements have been entered into. A copy of the most recent
   one, made on   , marked 'A1', is also attached to this claim form.]

4. Both the [first] tenancy and the agreement for it were made on or after 28th February 1997.

   a) No notice was served on the defendant stating that the tenancy would not be, or continue to
      be, an assured shorthold tenancy.

   b) There is no provision in the tenancy agreement which states that it is not an assured shorthold tenancy.

   c) The "agricultural worker condition" defined in Schedule 3 to the Housing Act 1988 is not fulfilled
      with respect to the property.

(or)

5. Both the [first] tenancy and the agreement for it were made on or after 15 January 1989.

   a) The [first] tenancy agreement was for a fixed term of not less than six months.

   b) There was no power for the landlord to end the tenancy earlier than six months after it began.

   c) On the   19   (before the tenancy began) a notice in writing, stating that the tenancy
      was to be an assured shorthold tenancy, was served on the defendant(s). It was served by:

   d) Attached to this claim form is a copy of that notice marked 'B' [and proof of service marked 'B1'].

6. Whenever a new tenancy agreement has replaced the first tenancy agreement or has replaced a replacement
   tenancy agreement,

   a) it has been of the same, or substantially the same, premises, and

   b) the landlord and tenant were the same people at the start of the replacement tenancy as the landlord
      and tenant at the end of the tenancy which it replaced.

Claim No.	

7. On the   20   , a notice in writing, saying that possession of the premises was required, was served upon the defendant(s). It was served by:

The notice expired on the   20   .
Attached to this claim form is a copy of that notice marked 'C' [and proof of service marked 'C1'].

8. *(any further information, continue on separate sheet if necessary)*

9. If the defendant(s) seek(s) postponement of possession on the grounds of exceptional hardship, the claimant is content that the request be considered without a hearing.

10. The claimant asks the court

to order that the defendant(s) deliver up possession of the property.

[to order the defendant(s) to pay the costs of this claim.]

11. Statement of Truth

*(I believe)(The claimant believes) that the facts stated in this claim form (and any attached sheets) are true.
* I am duly authorised by the claimant to sign this statement.

signed _____ date _____

(Claimant)(Litigation friend(where claimant is a child or a patient)*)(Claimant's solicitor)
delete as appropriate

Full name _____

Name of claimant's solicitor's firm _____

position or office held _____
                   (if signing on behalf of firm or company)

Claimant's or claimant's solicitor's address to which documents should be sent if different from that on the front page.

Postcode

	if applicable
Ref. no.	
fax no.	
DX no.	
e-mail	
Tel. no.	

Notes for the defendant

The claimant has used the accelerated procedure because it is said you have an assured shorthold tenancy or demoted assured shorthold tenancy. If so, the court is not allowed to consider whether it is reasonable or fair to make the order for possession. Therefore, if what is written in the claim form and in the defence form make it clear that the claimant is entitled to possession, the court will make the order without fixing a hearing.

If you think there are reasons why the court should not make a possession order, you should consider getting advice from a solicitor or an advice agency immediately. If you dispute the claim, fill in the defence form and return it to the court office within 14 days of receiving the claim form. If you cannot give exact dates in your defence form, give them as nearly as you can. Make it clear that the dates you give are approximate. The judge can only take account of legally valid reasons.

You may qualify for assistance from Community Legal Service Fund (CLSF) to meet some or all of your legal costs. Ask about the CLSF at any county court office or any information or help point which displays this logo.

Community Legal Service

Court staff can only help you complete the defence form and tell you about court procedures. **They cannot give legal advice.**

If the court makes a possession order without a hearing, you will be entitled to apply, within 14 days of receiving the order, for it to be reconsidered. The application would have to show some good legal reason for varying or revoking the order.

Normally, if the court makes a possession order, it will tell you to leave the premises within 14 days. The judge can allow up to 42 days but only if satisfied that leaving within 14 days would cause you hardship which is exceptional (that is, worse than would usually be suffered by someone having to leave within 14 days). If you believe there are exceptional circumstances in your case, fill in section 9 of the defence form and return it to the court office. Usually, an order for possession in 14 days will still be made but a hearing will be fixed within the 14 day period. The judge will decide at the hearing whether or not to extend the period.

If the court orders you to pay the claimant's costs, normally the order requires payment within 14 days. If you would be unable to pay in that time, fill in section 10 of the defence form and give details of your means.

If you use the defence form, you **must** sign the Statement of Truth. Proceedings for contempt of court may be brought against a person who signs a Statement of Truth without an honest belief in its truth.

CERTIFICATE OF SERVICE

(completed on court copy only)

I certify that the claim form of which this is a true copy was served by me on

_____

by posting it to the defendant(s) on

_____

at the address stated on the first page of the claim form.

OR

The claim form has not been served for the following reasons:

Officer of the Court

Send documents for the court to the court office at

Telephone:
Fax:

Please address all correspondence to "The Court Manager".

NII Defence form

Defence form

Click here to clear all fields

In the

Claim No.

Claimant

Defendant(s)

I dispute the claimant's claim because:-

Statement of Truth

*(I believe)(The defendant(s) believe(s)) that the facts stated in this defence form (and any continuation sheets) are true.

* I am duly authorised by the defendant(s) to sign this reply form.

signed _____   date _____

(Defendant(s))(Litigation friend(where the defendant is a child or a patient)*)(Defendant's solicitor)
*delete as appropriate

Full name _____

Name of defendant's solicitor's firm _____

position or office held _____
(if signing on behalf of firm or company)

Defendant's or defendant's solicitor's address to which documents should be sent.		if applicable	
		Ref. no.	
		fax no.	
		DX no.	
		e-mail	
	Postcode	Tel. no.	

N11 Defence form (10.01)

Printed on behalf The Court Service

251

N11B Defence form (accelerated possession procedure) (assured shorthold tenancy)

Defence form
(accelerated possession procedure)
(assured shorthold tenancy)

Click here to print form   Click here to clear all fields

Name of court	Claim No.
Name of Claimant	
Name of Defendant(s)	

To the Defendant

Please read the notes on the back page of the claim form before completing this form.

Some of the questions in this form refer to numbered sections in the claim form. You will find it helpful to have that open as you answer them.

Please note that if section 2 of the claim form has been completed because you are a tenant of premises let under a demoted assured shorthold tenancy, you need only answer questions 1 and 6 to 10.

In all cases you **must** complete and sign the statement of truth.

Please write clearly and in black ink. If there is not enough room for an answer, continue on the last page.

1 Are you the tenant(s) named in the tenancy agreement, marked 'A' (or 'A1'), attached to the claim form?   ☐ Yes   ☐ No

Does that tenancy agreement (or do both) set out the present terms of your tenancy (except for any changes in the rent or the length of the tenancy)?   ☐ Yes   ☐ No

If not, say what terms have changed and what the changes are:

2 Do you agree the date, in section 3 of the claim form, when the claimant says the tenancy began?   ☐ Yes   ☐ No

If not, on what date did it begin?   on _____

3 If the claimant has completed section 4 of the claim form, do you agree with what is said there?   ☐ Yes   ☐ No

If not, what do you disagree with and why?

4 If the claimant has completed section 5 of the claim form, did you receive the notice (a copy of which is attached to the claim form and marked 'B') and, if so, when?

☐ Yes   ☐ No

If Yes, give date _____

Do you agree with the rest of what is said in section 5? If not, what do you disagree with and why?

☐ Yes   ☐ No

5 If the claimant has not deleted section 6 of the claim form, do you agree that what is said there is correct?

☐ Yes   ☐ No

If not, what do you disagree with and why?

6 Did you receive the notice referred to in section 7 of the claim form, (a copy of which is attached to the claim form and marked 'C') and, if so, when?

☐ Yes   ☐ No

If Yes, give date _____

7 If the claimant has put any additional information in section 8 of the claim form, do you agree that what is said there is correct?

☐ Yes   ☐ No

If not, what do you disagree with and why?

8 If there is some other reason, not covered above, why you say the claimant is not entitled to recover possession of the property, please explain it here.

Postponement of possession

| 9 | Are you asking the court, if it makes a possession order, to allow you longer than 14 days to leave the premises because you would suffer exceptional hardship? | ☐ Yes | ☐ No |

If so, explain why the hardship you would suffer would be exceptional.

Say how long you wish to be allowed to remain in the premises. (The court cannot allow more than 42 days after the order is made.)

up to _____ 20 ___

Payment of costs

| 10 | If the court orders you to pay the claimant's costs, do you ask it to allow you more than 14 days to pay? | ☐ Yes | ☐ No |

If so, give details of your means
(continue onto last page if necessary)

Statement of Truth

*(I believe)(The defendant(s) believe(s)) that the facts stated in this defence form (and any attached sheets) are true.

* I am duly authorised by the defendant(s) to sign this statement.

signed _____ date _____

(Defendant)(Litigation friend(where defendant is a child or a patient)*)(Defendant's solicitor)
*delete as appropriate

Full name _____

Name of defendant's solicitor's firm _____

position or office held _____
(if signing on behalf of firm or company)

Defendant's or defendant's solicitor's address to which documents should be sent.			*if applicable*
		Ref. no.	
		fax no.	
		DX no.	
		e-mail	
	Postcode	Tel. no.	

Claim No.

Additional Information
(Include the number of the section which is being continued or to which the information relates)

Signed .... Date ....

(Continue on a separate sheet if necessary, remembering to sign and date it and heading it with the Claim Number)

Click here to print form

N119 Particulars of claim for possession (rented residential premises)

**Particulars of claim
for possession**
(rented residential premises)

Click here to print form

Click here to clear all fields

Name of court	Claim No.
Name of Claimant	
Name of Defendant	

1. The claimant has a right to possession of:

2. To the best of the claimant's knowledge the following persons are in possession of the property:

About the tenancy

3. (a) The premises are let to the defendant(s) under a(n)   tenancy
which began on

(b) The current rent is £   and is payable each (week) (fortnight) (month).
(*other*   )

(c) Any unpaid rent or charge for use and occupation should be calculated at £   per day.

4. The reason the claimant is asking for possession is:
(a) because the defendant has not paid the rent due under the terms of the tenancy agreement.
(Details are set out below)(Details are shown on the attached rent statement)

(b) because the defendant has failed to comply with other terms of the tenancy.
Details are set out below.

(c) because: (including any (other) statutory grounds)

N119 Particulars of claim for possession (rented residential premises) (06.04)   *Printed on behalf of The Court Service*

5. The following steps have already been taken to recover any arrears:

6. The appropriate (notice to quit) (notice of breach of lease) (notice seeking possession) (notice seeking a demotion order) (*other* _____) was served on the defendant on   20   .

About the defendant

7. The following information is known about the defendant's circumstances:

About the claimant

8. The claimant is asking the court to take the following financial or other information into account when making its decision whether or not to grant an order for possession:

Forfeiture

9. (a) There is no underlessee or mortgagee entitled to claim relief against forfeiture.

or (b)   of

is entitled to claim relief against forfeiture as underlessee or mortgagee.

What the court is being asked to do:

10. The claimant asks the court to order that the defendant(s):

    (a) give the claimant possession of the premises;

    (b) pay the unpaid rent and any charge for use and occupation up to the date an order is made;

    (c) pay rent and any charge for use and occupation from the date of the order until the claimant recovers possession of the property;

    (d) pay the claimant's costs of making this claim.

11. In the alternative to possession, is the claimant asking the court to make a demotion order?

    ☐ Yes   ☐ No

Demotion claim
This section must be completed if the claim includes a claim for demotion of tenancy in the alternative to possession

12. The demotion claim is made under:

    ☐ section 82A(2) of the Housing Act 1985

    ☐ section 6A(2) of the Housing Act 1988

13. The claimant is a:

    ☐ local authority   ☐ housing action trust   ☐ registered social landlord

14. Has the claimant served on the tenant a statement of express terms of the tenancy which are to apply to the demoted tenancy?

    ☐ Yes   ☐ No

    If Yes, please give details:

APPENDIX C
Appeal Tribunal Documents

Example decision notice

Housing Benefit Appeal Tribunal		**Held on:**	20 May 2003
Tribunal Reg No:	U/70/103/2003/0001		
Appellant:	Smith J (Ms)	**NI No:**	AA 00 11 22 G

Unanimous/*majority decision of the tribunal

The LA decision of 17 March is confirmed.

Ms Smith is not entitled to Housing Benefit from 10/2/03 to 9/3/03.

Ms Smith was unable to show good cause for not having made a claim for Housing Benefit in accordance with Regulation 72(15) of the Housing Benefit (General) Regulations 1987.

Signed Chairman:	K Jenkins	**Date:**	20 May 2003

*Delete as appropriate

For clerk's use only

Decision notice issued to:	**Appellant on:**	20 May 2003
	Respondent on:	20 May 2003

TAS/DN/HB

Example statement of reasons for decision

This statement is to be read together with the decision notice issued by the tribunal.

Appeal Tribunal held at Westhoughton on 20 May 2003

Tribunal Reg No:	U/70/103/2003/0001		
Appellant:	Smith J (Ms)	**NI No:**	AA 00 11 22 G

The issue before the tribunal was whether Ms Smith has continuous good cause for not having renewed her claim for Housing Benefit following the expiry of her previous award, in accordance with Regulation 72(15) of the Housing Benefit (General) Regulations 1987.

The tribunal considered all the schedule of evidence and heard oral evidence from the appellant and submissions from the Presenting Officer.

The tribunal did not consider that Ms Smith satisfied the condition of showing continuous good cause throughout the period that the backdated benefit award was sought.

In addition, the tribunal noted that the local authority issued a renewal claim form to Ms Smith on 11 December 2002 and a further reminder on 27 January 2003.

Ms Smith said that she did not receive any of these, but she could not recall having problems with receiving any other post at that time.

Ms Smith further stated that she was under a lot of stress because it is difficult being a single parent with three young children; she further confirmed that she had not sought any medical or support assistance in relation to this stress.

The tribunal sympathises with Ms Smith's situation, but did not accept that this situation was one that would amount to her demonstrating continuous good cause for not having renewed her claim for Housing Benefit.

The above is a statement of the reasons for the tribunal's decision.

Signed   K Jenkins   **Date:**   12 June 2003
Chairman:

For clerk's use only
*Decision Notice/Statement   Typed by KMT
Issue to appellant on [...]
Statement requested   *Yes/No

(*delete as appropriate)

TAS/SR

APPENDIX D

Housing Benefit Rates 2004/2005

Personal allowances

	£
Single person under 25	44.50
Single person 25 or over	56.20
Lone parent under 18	44.50
Lone parent 18 or over	56.20
Couple – one or both 18 or over	88.15
Couple – both under 18	67.15
Child/young person	43.88
Pensioner aged 60 or over not on Income Support or income-based JSA:	
Single under 65	109.45
Single 65 or over	125.90
Couple both under 65	167.05
Couple one or both 65 or over	188.60

Premiums

Family	16.10
Family – one (or more) children aged under one year	26.60
Family (lone parent protected rate)	22.20
Family (lone parent protected rate) – one (or more) children aged under one year	32.70
Disabled child	43.89
Disability	
Single person	23.95
Couple	34.20
Severe Disability	
Single person	45.50
Couple – one qualifies	45.50
Couple – both qualify	91.00
Enhanced Disability	
Couple	16.90
Single person/lone parent	11.70
Child	17.71
Pensioner aged 60 or more on Income Support or income-based JSA	
Single person	53.25
Couple	78.90

Carer premium	25.80
Bereavement premium	25.85

Housing costs – non-dependant deductions

Aged 18 or over and in remunerative work	
Gross income £322 or more per week	47.75
Gross income £258–£321.99 per week	43.50
Gross income £194–£257.99 per week	38.20
Gross income £150–£193.99 per week	23.35
Gross income £101–£149.99 per week	17.00
Gross income less than £101 per week	7.40
Aged 18 or over and not in remunerative work	7.40
Aged 25 or over and on income support or income-based JSA	7.40

Earnings disregards

Single person	5.00
Couple	10.00
Lone parent	25.00
Disabled or carer	20.00
30-hour working	14.50
Disregarded childminding fees	
One child	175.00
Two or more children	300.00

Other income disregards

Child/young person maintenance disregard	15.00
War pension and war widow/widower	10.00
Voluntary and charitable payments	20.00
Student loans	10.00
Income from boarders	20.00
plus 50% of balance of charge	
Income from childminding	Two thirds

Capital disregarded

£3,000 then tariff income of £1 per £250 up to maximum capital of £16,000 (if aged 60 or over, £6,000 disregard, then £1 per £500).

Fuel and meal deductions

Heating	10.55
Hot water	1.25
Lighting	0.85
Cooking	1.25
All fuel	13.90
One room (heating and any hot water and/or lighting)	6.32
One room (cooking)	1.25
3 meals	
Each adult	20.05
Each child under 16	10.15
Less than 3 meals	
Each adult	13.35
Each child under 16	6.70
Breakfast only	
Each person	2.45

Applicable amounts for hospital patients after 52 weeks in hospital

Single claimant	20.50
Couple (both in hospital)	41.00
Couple (only one in hospital) applicable amount reduced by	16.40

Index

References are to division and paragraph numbers.

A

Almshouse
secure tenancy, licence not being,
3.3

Anti-social behaviour
Act 2003, 5.7
complaints–
common causes of, 5.9–5.16
drugs and drink, 5.13
making, 5.7
noise, 5.9
pets, 5.15
racial harassment, 5.16
rubbish and litter, 5.14
unruly children, 5.11
verbal abuse, 5.10
violence, 5.12
filmed evidence of, 5.22
Home Office Unit, 5.7
human rights issues, 10.56–10.58
injunctions, 5.20
mutual exchange rights, suspension
of, 3.45
orders, 5.19
possession proceedings, 5.23
remedies–
acceptable behaviour contracts,
5.20
early intervention, 5.17
eviction, 5.21
injunctions, 5.20
mediation, 5.18
orders, 5.19

Anti-social behaviour – *contd*
social landlords, power of, 5.7, 5.8
TOGETHER campaign, 5.7

Appeal
homelessness decisions, of, 2.13
housing benefit decision, against,
8.61, 8.80–87.109. *See also*
HOUSING BENEFIT APPEALS

Assignment
premium paid for, 6.13
tenancy, of–
assured shorthold, 3.39
assured, 3.39
deed, by, 3.34
introductory, 3.36
meaning, 3.34
protected shorthold, 3.38
regulated, 3.37
rent arrears, liability for, 3.40
right of, 3.33
secure, 3.35

Assured shorthold tenancy
assignment, 3.39
changes to, 3.26
housing association, 3.24, 3.26
meaning, 3.26
possession, court order for, 3.27
setting-up procedure, 3.26

Assured tenancy
assignment, 3.39
changes to, 3.26
meaning, 3.26
possession–
accelerated procedure, 3.31
court order for, 3.27
discretionary grounds for, 3.30